WITHDRAWAL

READ, RESEARCH AND WRITE

READ, RESEARCH AND WRITE

Academic Skills for ESL Students in Higher Education

Caroline Brandt

Los Angeles • London • New Delhi • Singapore • Washington DC

First published 2009

SAGE Publications Ltd
1 Oliver's Yard
55 City Road
London EC1Y 1SP

SAGE Publications Inc.
2455 Teller Road
Thousand Oaks, California 91320

SAGE Publications India Pvt Ltd
B 1/I 1 Mohan Cooperative Industrial Area
Mathura Road
New Delhi 110 044

SAGE Publications Asia-Pacific Pte Ltd
33 Pekin Street #02-01
Far East Square
Singapore 048763

Library of Congress Control Number: 2008922550

British Library Cataloguing in Publication data

A catalogue record for this book is available from the British Library

ISBN 978-1-4129-4736-7
ISBN 978-1-4129-4737-4 (pbk)

Typeset by C&M Digitals Pvt Ltd, Chennai, India
Printed in Great Britain by the Cromwell Press, Trowbridge, Wiltshire
Printed on paper from sustainable resources

Contents

Writing has laws of perspective, of light and shade just as painting does, or music. If you are born knowing them, fine. If not, learn them.

Truman Capote, *Writers at Work*

To Tutors

This book is based upon research into the needs of pre-sessional and in-sessional ESL students who are studying in a range of academic institutions around the world. These institutions have one feature in common – English is the language of instruction, while their students come from a different language background or backgrounds.

The research addressed the issue of content on courses aimed at preparing ESL students for academic study in English-medium contexts. It was found that courses either adopt a discipline-specific approach or a general-interest approach to content selection, or a combination of the two. However, outcomes identified several problems with these approaches, and an alternative approach is suggested in response to these: the use of content about English for Academic Purposes (EAP), on the grounds that for the duration of their studies, at least, EAP is a subject that all ESL students are involved in, whether directly, through taking EAP courses, or indirectly, by studying another subject through the medium of English. The research outcomes suggested that the field of EAP itself can provide examples of academic writing that are at once relevant to students in terms of content and appropriate in terms of level of English language proficiency required of the reader.

This book therefore takes an innovative approach to the development of academic skill for ESL students in higher education. As its content, 10 articles about aspects of EAP are provided. These have been selected (and abridged and edited in some cases) for the relevance of their content and the appropriacy of the language for pre-sessional and early in-sessional EAP students. Both the content and the language of these articles are systematically explored through a range of tasks provided at the end of each article.

The book has a number of other features that may be unexpected in a book aimed at developing students' skills in the area of EAP. Firstly, no space is provided for students to record their answers. Instead, students should be encouraged to take their own notes throughout. Research outcomes indicated that textbooks which provide space for 'answers' encourage a 'complete the gap' approach and remove the opportunity for students to develop the skills they need to make comprehensive and personally meaningful notes. The outcomes suggested that the process of taking such notes enhances learning, and that the product is much more useful to students at a later stage, for example, for revision purposes.

Secondly, as EAP tutors are expected to be experienced teachers of students of English as a second or foreign language, few suggestions are provided for teaching from this book, and there is no teacher's book. It is understood instead that tutors have at their disposal a range of techniques and approaches that can be applied throughout. Likewise, no indication is provided of the amount of time that a tutor should spend on each section. Instead, it is recognized that tutors want to be able to respond to their students' needs by paying greater attention to some areas than to others, and that this may be accomplished through the identification of the most useful tasks and activities for a particular group of students in their context.

Thirdly, much of the material in this book relies upon student response and pair or group interaction and discussion. In such cases, there is no one right answer to be found. It is expected instead that 'answers' will be negotiated, a skill identified in the research as essential for students to develop. For this reason, the answers provided in the key (available on the companion website) www.sagepub.co.uk/brandt are largely limited to the comparatively few cases where it is possible to identify 'one right answer' with a degree of certainty.

Fourthly, all chapters have been piloted with classes of students drawn from the target population of this book. These students had a number of features in common. During the pilot phase, they were:

- attending pre-sessional or first-year credit-bearing courses towards their majors
- taking different majors at an English-medium tertiary level institution
- learning English as a second or additional language.

Examples of students' work gathered during the piloting phase have been included throughout this book. A few quotes from the feedback received on each chapter have also been included. Students were also largely responsible for the answer key, and they also wrote the following section 'To students'. In taking this approach, it is hoped that the involvement of students throughout this book may be experienced by the reader.

Finally, there is a companion website which provides a scheme for annotating students' writing, a collection of links to articles that relate to the content of the 10 chapters of this book, as well as an answer key for several of the tasks and activities. If a key is provided, the symbol " ANSWERS " appears next to the text.

To Students

We strongly recommend this book if you are in tertiary education. This book provides you with appropriate strategies in dealing with texts, new words and how to organize your thoughts, as well as many other academic issues that are discussed in detail within the covers of the book. It is particularly helpful for students in various majors because you will be learning new skills and applying them to your own context in every chapter, which gives you the opportunity to learn the theoretical and linguistic aspects of the topic as well as giving you opportunities to practise in your field. We believe that the best use of this book is accomplished in a university foundation programme or if you are a freshman/first-year student; however, we think it would be useful for all university levels as well. Since many academic institutions use English as the language of instruction worldwide, whether it is as a lingua franca or it is the mother language, this book will widen students' access to tertiary level.

> 'As a petroleum geosciences student, I need to have outstanding skills in reading, language, writing, research and study because I need to read a lot of materials, write reports, communicate with my professors and do research.'
>
> Saif Ali Mohamed Saeed Al Mesaabi (first-year student)

What makes this book different from other books is that it can be approached in several ways, as described in the map in the first chapter. We recommend that you make sure you have a careful look at the map, decide in which way you will benefit most, and then go directly to the material you need. In this way you do not have to follow the same order as the material is presented in the book. Each chapter contains six focus points: reading, learning language, writing, researching, studying, and applying to your own subject. The transitions between these points are smooth and they are coherently related to the article in the chapter.

Don't be discouraged if you have to read a paragraph more than once in order to understand it. You might encounter a little difficulty when reading the articles in each chapter but this should not be discouraging because 'life is a journey of learning which never stops'. You should have pencil and paper at hand and make the best use of the tables provided in the book such as the vocabulary record and the related words record. For example, the article in Chapter 3 is quite long – but it is very readable. Try to read ahead and prepare for your next class, and, especially, consider reading the articles before coming to class. This will allow you to save your class time for discussion with your instructor. We think that this book provides interesting articles with just the right level of challenge. The articles are neither very difficult nor they are too easy to handle.

'I really like the idea of the book. It contains articles which are about different topics and themes in EAP. I think that such areas are interesting to any ESL student whatever his/her major is. I see that a university student has to be prepared for academic reading, writing and researching. From that point of view, I believe that the book is going to be very helpful for ESL students.'

Yasmine Guefrachi
(first-year student)

Another remarkable feature of the book is that there are recommended websites to be used in order to improve and expand readers' vocabulary knowledge. For example, there is a website to familiarize the reader with many academic words: the 'Academic word list'. There are also websites to translate from English to many other languages and a website to check collocations entitled 'just the word'. There are many such helpful websites suggested in this book.

Finally, the book is provided with priceless information that captured our attention; these are the 'strategies for success' which appear throughout the chapters. These strategies provide you with powerful methods to ease the very many academic tasks required of a typical university student. There is also a companion website with many additional links and resources to help you – www.sagepub.co. uk/brandt

We wish you 'good luck' with your studies.

Moutaz Bassam Falih Saleh
Saoud Ali Abdulla Fadhel Al Maamari
(first-year students at the Petroleum Institute, Abu Dhabi, United Arab Emirates)
July 2007

Acknowledgements

The research for, and development of, this book was undertaken with the support of a grant awarded by the Research and Graduate Studies Committee of the Petroleum Institute, Abu Dhabi, United Arab Emirates, 2007.

I would like to thank in particular my colleagues at the Petroleum Institute: Robert Craig, Roger Nunn and Matthew J. Webb for their support and contributions.

Many students volunteered to pilot the material. I would like to thank the following in particular for their participation and feedback: Ibrahim Ali Al Kodssi; Karam Abdollmnem Khatib; Marwan Mohsin Al Haj Atalla Hasan Abu Aasi; Mohamed Saeed Mohamed S. M. Al Khanbooli Al Shehhi; Moutaz Bassam Falih Saleh; Saif Ali Mohamed Saeed Al Mesaabi; Saoud Ali Abdulla Fadhel Al Maamari; Tariq Ibrahim Abdul Rahim Al Jallad; Fatima Al Zaabi; Sara Ali Al Abadi; Khawla Abdulla Al Manthari; Yasmine Guefrachi; Tuka Al Hanai; Reem Mohammed Nasser; Basma Ali Abdulkareem Ahmed; Meera Al Marzouqi, Mariam Tareq Ahmed Khalil and Emina Taher Helja.

The following articles have been reprinted and in some cases abridged with permission:

Chapter 2
Gillett, A. (1996, updated 2007, personal communication). 'What is EAP?'
Reprinted with permission of the author.

Chapter 3
Beder, S. (1997). 'Addressing the issues of social and academic integration for first-year students: a discussion paper'.
Reprinted with permission of the author.

Chapter 4
Coxhead, A. (2005). Reviewed work: Upton, T. A. 'Reading Skills for Success: A Guide to Academic Texts' (2004).
Reprinted with permission of the Assistant Editor of *Reading in a Foreign Language*, published by the University of Hawaii.

Chapter 5
Spack, R. (1998). 'Initiating ESL students into the Academic Discourse Community: how far should we go?' by Spack, R. and Zamel, V.
Reproduced by permission of Taylor and Francis Group LLC., a division of Informa plc.

Chapter 6
Sutherland-Smith, W. (2005). 'Pandora's box: academic perceptions of student plagiarism in writing.'

Reprinted with kind permission of Elsevier.

Chapter 7
Brandt, C. (2007). 'Material matters: the case for EAP as subject matter of EAP courses.' Reprinted with permission of David Palfreyman, Editor of *Learning and Teaching in Higher Education: Gulf Perspectives*. Vol. 5, Issue 1, January 2008.

Chapter 8
Nunn, R. (2007). 'Making reasonable claims.'
Reprinted with permission of the author.

Chapter 9
Thompson, C. (1999). 'Critical thinking: what is it and how do we teach it in English for Academic Purposes (EAP) programs?'
Reprinted with permission of the Manager, Administration, Higher Education Research and Development Society of Australasia.

Chapter 10
Cioffi, F. L. (2005). *The Imaginative Argument*. Princeton University Press. Reprinted by permission of Princeton University Press.

Introducing *Read, Research and Write*

In this chapter, you can read the **introduction** to *Read, Research and Write: Academic skills for ESL students in higher education*.
You can develop your skills in these areas:

Focus A: Reading

A.1 Looking ahead
A.2 The purpose of introductions
A.3 Understanding and responding

Focus B: Learning language

B.1 Dealing with unfamiliar words

Focus C: Writing

C.1 Feedback on written work
C.2 Autobiography: writing about yourself
C.3 Different types of academic writing
C.4 Knowing your audience

Focus D: Researching

D.1 Using a library
D.2 Building an annotated bibliography

Focus E: Studying

E.1 Good study habits
E.2 Keeping a portfolio
E.3 Understanding rationale

Focus F: Applying to your own subject

F.1 Assessing the quality and usefulness of an article
F.2 Applying quality criteria
F.3 Finding new words and inferring meaning from context

▌ FOCUS A: READING

A.1 Looking ahead

---

introduction *n.* [C]
A written or spoken explanation at the beginning of a book, speech, etc. *In the introduction, he explains why he wrote the book.*

'What I liked about this chapter is that it asks the students to relate the assignments to their majors – this is what makes it most enjoyable.'

Ibrahim Ali Al Kodssi
(first-year student)

Below, you can read the **introduction** to this book. It performs the same function as other introductions to books that you will read in the course of your studies.

➢ Before you read, think about and/or discuss your answer to these questions:

1 What kind of information do you expect to read about in the introduction to an academic book?
2 Do you always read the introductions to books? Why/why not?

➢ Make a note of your ideas, then read the introduction to this book – Article 1.

◗ ARTICLE 1: INTRODUCING READ, RESEARCH AND WRITE

Who is this book for?

This book is for students who:

- speak English as a second (or third, or fourth …) language (these students are sometimes known as ESL students, or English as a Second Language students)
- will be attending an institution where English is the medium of instruction, or the dominant language   5
- have achieved a standard of English that may be called 'high intermediate' or sometimes 'modest user', meaning that they have partial command of the language and can cope with overall meaning in most situations. They are able to handle basic communication in their own subject area, although they may make   10 frequent errors
- are about to begin a course of study or have already begun undergraduate studies (these students are sometimes known as pre-sessional or in-sessional respectively)
- will be studying or are studying within any discipline (an area or a branch of   15 knowledge or teaching, such as science) or academic subject (that is, one where an emphasis is placed on reading, researching and writing), at college or university
- want to study in order to improve their ability to read, research and write as part of their own personal development
- are required to take a course to help them to improve their ability to read,   20 research and write as part of the admission requirements of the college or university.

Students who will benefit from this book may be studying, or intending to study, any subject within arts, humanities or sciences, including, for example: psychology, medicine, linguistics, chemistry, environmental studies, literature or geography.   25

Whatever your subject, this book will help you to improve the reading, language, writing, research and study skills you need in order to perform well in your chosen field.

Why has this book been designed in the way it has?

This book is based upon the results of an international research project which inves-   30 tigated university lecturers' expectations of their students, in terms of their ability to read, research and write.

The research questions that were asked included:

'What skills do lecturers in various subjects expect first-year students to have?'

'What skills do English for Academic Purposes (EAP) tutors teach?'   35

Tutors who took part in the research were required to have taught in at least two different international contexts. They were asked to reflect upon their experiences of teaching EAP, and to consider the needs of those students who had achieved, or were considered to be capable of achieving, an International English Language
40   Testing System (IELTS) score of 5 or above, or its equivalent.

The research outcomes indicated that students needed to develop their abilities and understandings in several areas of EAP, including:

- making cautious claims
- becoming more aware of their university culture and expectations
45   • understanding and describing data presented graphically
- thinking critically and reflectively
- responding to ideas in articles
- documenting skills, that is, how to refer to others' writing, and why it is important to avoid plagiarizing another's writing, as can happen when someone else's writing
50   is used without proper reference or acknowledgment.

Such topics are within the scope of 'English for Academic Purposes' or 'EAP'. EAP may be seen as an academic subject in its own right, and all of the topics above are addressed in this book.

People who study EAP are interested in questions such as:

55   • What language and skills do students need to operate effectively in an academic context?
- How can EAP tutors help students to develop the language and skills they need?
- How do EAP students learn the language and skills they need, and then apply
60   this knowledge to their contexts?

Being an academic subject in its own right, then, EAP has its own body of literature which includes:

- newsletter articles
- journal articles
65   • textbooks
- chapters in edited collections
- reviews
- reports
- monographs
70   • conference proceedings
- abstracts
- bibliographies.

Sample articles drawn from this literature form the heart of each of the ten chapters of this book. Using articles about EAP alone as the basis for the study is a new approach to developing the skills needed by EAP students. In Chapter 7, you can read more about the research on which this book is based.

Each article is followed by a number of questions and tasks (indicated by the symbol ➤) designed to help you to practise and develop your skills in these areas:

- *reading* (for example, you will consider such issues as: Who was the article written for? How has the author organized his or her ideas? How are the ideas presented in the article linked to one another? How does the author develop his or her argument?)
- *language* (for example: What vocabulary does the author use when reporting the results of research? How does the author express a claim (a belief that something is true) cautiously? What tense does the author use to describe a project, or to report results?)
- *writing* (for example: how do you write an introduction or a conclusion? What's the difference between a conclusion and a summary? What differences are there between academic writing and non-academic writing?)
- *research* (for example, you will learn how to use the structure of a text to guide your research, and about the purpose of an abstract)
- *study* (for example, you can learn how to make the best use of an English–English dictionary).

However, the research outcomes on which this book is based also suggested that students benefit from applying such knowledge and skills in their own subject areas. These research results indicated that ultimately, in reading a book such as this, you will be doing so in order to apply what you have learned to your own personal context, to enable you to be a more effective student of psychology, for example, or engineering, or physics, or whatever subject you have chosen to study. For this reason, the last part of each chapter encourages you to apply what you have learned to your own field.

In working through this book, therefore, you will:

- *read* a variety of academic articles written for different audiences and purposes and learn about aspects of the subject of EAP that are of particular relevance to you (including, for example, what is meant by 'academic culture', and how you can adapt to it and survive; and why it can be important to express any claims you make cautiously, and so forth)
- study the specific *language* used in different types of academic articles
- practise useful skills and language in your own *writing*
- develop your *research* and *study* skills
- *apply* the skills and language you have studied to your own subject.

To summarize, by:

- studying the examples of academic writing about EAP (and so learning not only
  115   about EAP but also reading good examples of academic articles)
- working through the associated questions and tasks that focus on the development of reading, language, writing, research and study skills; and
- applying these skills to your own subject area

… you will find that the personal benefits are multiplied.

120 ## How can I make the best use of *Read, Research and Write*?

The ten articles, and the accompanying focus on reading, language, writing, research and study skills, are described in greater detail in the map of the book below.

    The book has been written to give you freedom in how you approach it. Here are some of your choices. Perhaps you:

125 ☐ plan to study at college or university in your home town or country; or
    ☐ plan to study in a foreign country

☐ are studying the book as part of a course of instruction; or
☐ plan to use the book to support you while following a course of instruction, where you have other materials to help you

130 ☐ would find it useful to work through each article, in the order in which they are presented; or
☐ want to work through all of the articles, but follow a different order to the one in which they are presented; or
☐ prefer to select only those articles that you feel would help you most

135 ☐ want to read the articles and do the questions and tasks that follow; or
    ☐ just read the articles only

☐ want to develop in all areas (reading, language, writing, research and study skills); or
☐ want to develop a particular area, such as your research skills, or your language
140   skills

☐ have not yet decided what you want to study; or
☐ have chosen, but not yet begun to study, your university or college subject; or
☐ are in your first or second year of studying your university or college subject.

    In deciding how to make the best use of the book, think about the options avail-
145 able to you above and check (✓) those that relate to your particular context. Then, if you wish, you can use the map on the next two pages to help you make your decisions.

The last section of every chapter asks you to apply what you have learned to your own subject area. In doing this, you can build up a bank of your own articles, ones you have selected because you find them interesting and relevant. You can keep   150
these for study while you are following this book, and also for future reference. See the section below, entitled 'Organizing your work' for a suggestion to help you manage these articles.

To help you make the most of this book, it is strongly recommended that you purchase an English–English learner's dictionary. There are several good ones   155
available – ask your tutor to recommend one. The *Longman Dictionary of Contemporary English* (2003) is a good example. Except where otherwise stated, all of the definitions provided in this book are taken from this dictionary.

If you find that, having completed a particular article, you would like more practice (or perhaps you are simply interested in the topic), you can refer to the   160
 companion website, www. sagepub.co.uk/brandt, where you will find a collection of articles from a variety of different sources related to the topics in each of the book's ten articles.

Throughout this book, you will find many highlighted 'strategies for success'. These are for you to read, enjoy, and reflect upon. You will also find helpful   165
explanations of key words used in the text (Written in bold). In these explanations, a number of abbreviations are used. They are: v = verb; n = noun; adj = adjective; [T] = **transitive**; [I] intransitive; [C] = countable; [U] = uncountable; BrE = British English; AmE = American English.

The map on the next four pages provides an overview of the book and what it offers.

> **transitive** *adj technical*
> A transitive verb must have an   170
> object, for example, the verb
> 'break' in the sentence 'I broke
> the cup'.

▶ MAP OF READ, RESEARCH AND WRITE

Focus / Article and type	A. Reading	B. Learning language	C. Writing	D. Researching	E. Studying	F. Applying to your subject
1. Introducing 'Read, Research and Write': Introductory chapter to book	A.1 Looking ahead A.2. The purpose of introductions A.3 Understanding and responding	B.1 Dealing with unfamiliar words	C.1 Feedback on written work C.2. Autobiography: writing about yourself C.3 Different types of academic writing C.4 Knowing your audience	D.1 Using a library D.2 Building an annotated bibliography	E.1 Good study habits E.2 Keeping a portfolio E.3 Understanding rationale	F.1 Assessing the quality and usefulness of an article F.2 Applying quality criteria F.3 Finding new words and inferring meaning from context
2. Understanding EAP: Newsletter article	A.1 Looking ahead A.2 Note-taking A.3 Understanding and responding A.4 Text structure	B.1 Word analysis B.2 Enquiring about meaning	C.1 Writing definitions C.2 Writing about another person	D.1 Using text structure as a guide	E.1 Using an English–English dictionary E.2 Recording new words E.3 Annotating E.4 Note-taking	F.1 Locating subject-related newsletter articles F.2 Applying word analysis to a subject-related article F.3 Finding and recording new subject-related words
3. Entering Higher Education: Discussion paper	A.1 Looking ahead A.2 Understanding gist A.3 Understanding and responding	B.1 Discourse markers B.2 Academic vocabulary: related words	C.1 Using discourse markers. C.2 Writing introductions	D.1 Understanding the purpose of abstracts D.2 Identifying sources of information	E.1 Expectations and norms of behaviour in higher education institutions E.2 Recording related words	F.1 Identifying various sources of subject-related information F.2 Locating and reading abstracts and introductions F.3 Recording related words in subject related articles

Focus Article and type	A. Reading	B. Learning language	C. Writing	D. Researching	E. Studying	F. Applying to your subject
4. Reading in Higher Education: Book review	A.1 Looking ahead A.2 Understanding and responding A.3 Reading with a purpose A.4 Features of informal writing	B.1 Concrete and abstract meanings B.2 Collocations	C.1 The purpose of the paragraph C.2 The purpose of conclusions	D.1 Identifying genre D.2 Thinking critically about sources of information	E.1 Reading efficiently and effectively E.2 Recording collocations	F.1 Locating and reading reviews of subject-related books F.2 Identifying collocations in subject-related articles F.3 Identifying concrete and abstract language in subject-related articles
5. Writing in Higher Education: Book chapter	A.1 Looking ahead A.2 Understanding and responding A.3 Identifying arguments	B.1 Presenting sides of an argument B.2 Reference words B.3 Synonyms, superordinates and hyponyms	C.1 Writing summaries C.2 Critiquing peer writing	D.1 The research cycle D.2 The purpose of literature reviews	E.1 Preparing an outline for an assignment	F.1 Locating, reading and summarizing a subject-related book chapter F.2 Locating, reading and note-taking from a subject-related literature review F.3 Identifying subject-related issues

(Continued)

(Continued)

Focus — Article and type	A. Reading	B. Learning language	C. Writing	D. Researching	E. Studying	F. Applying to your subject
6. Documenting skills: Journal article	A.1 Looking ahead A.2 Understanding and responding	B.1 Identifying citations B.2 Paraphrasing B.3 Introducing short quotes B.4 Introducing long quotes	C.1 Citations C.2 Writing a list of references C.3 Using sources in your own writing C.4 Critiquing peer writing	D.1 Different citation systems D.2 Identifying your discipline's citation system	E.1 Recording sources	F.1 Identifying citations in subject-related article
7. Researching skills: Research report	A.1 Looking ahead A.2 Understanding and responding A.3 Identifying steps in a process A.4 Alternatives in data presentation	B.1 Words commonly used in descriptions of research B.2 First person, singular and plural B.3 Using the passive voice B.4 Referring to data presented graphically	C.1 Summarizing a research process C.2 Paraphrasing and synthesizing ideas	D.1 Understanding qualitative and quantitative research	E.1 The 'prepare, draft, evaluate, proofread, improve, reflect' cycle	F.1 Presenting subject-related data F.2 Summarizing a subject-related research process
8. Making reasonable claims: Journal article	A.1 Looking ahead A.2 Understanding and responding	B.1 Different ways of expressing modality B.2 Identifying examples of modality	C.1 Adding appropriate degrees of caution to peer writing C.2 Writing a newsletter article	D.1 Using primary, secondary and tertiary sources	E.1 Recording cautious language	F.1 Identifying modality in subject-related articles F.2. Redrafting with appropriate caution

Focus / Article and type	A. Reading	B. Learning language	C. Writing	D. Researching	E. Studying	F. Applying to your subject
9. Thinking critically: Conference proceedings	A.1 Looking ahead A.2 Key skills for thinking critically A.2 Understanding and responding A.4 Text structure	B.1 Language of evaluation B.2 Key words for thinking critically	C.1 Critiquing in writing C.2 Critiquing peer writing	D.1 Asking good questions D.2 Evaluating internet sources	E.1 Analysing term papers and examination questions E.2 Responding to tutor feedback on the content of written work	F.1 Thinking critically about a subject-related article F.2 Thinking critically about subject-related term papers and examination questions
10. Finding your voice: Book chapter	A.1 Looking ahead A.2 Understanding and responding	B.1 Language of logic B.2 Transitions	C.1 Writing logically C.2 Logical fallacies to avoid C.3 Redrafting peer writing C.4 Fifteen steps to writing a good academic argument	D.1 Developing, supporting, and presenting an argument	E.1 Reflecting upon the effectiveness of learning	F.1 Identifying and summarizing a subject-related argument

Organizing your work: keeping a portfolio

175   This book has been designed intentionally without space for answers or notes. Instead, you are encouraged to get into the good study habits of making your own notes and keeping your work organized in a portfolio. This portfolio should include the articles you collect and study that are related to your subject.

To store and organize your portfolio, you will need:

180   • an A4 ring binder and some lined paper
   • a set of A4 dividers.

These items will enable you to organize your portfolio according to each focus in the 'map' above:

1 Reading
185   2 Language
3 Writing
4 Research
5 Study
6 Applying to your subject.

190   Organizing your work in this way will reinforce your learning and provide you with a useful resource bank for future reference.

A.2 The purpose of introductions

Before reading the introduction above, you were asked to look ahead and consider two questions.

➢ Revisit the notes you made in answer to the two questions in Section A.1 at the beginning of this chapter. In relation to Question 1, did you find the information you expected to find? Was anything not included which you expected to find? Was anything included which you did not expect to find? Discuss your ideas with another student.
➢ What is the most useful part of the introduction for you? Describe the reasons for your choice to another student.
➢ Discuss the following statement:

'Students who understand the purpose of introductions and take the time to read them are likely to learn more efficiently and effectively.'

On what grounds do you think the writer is making this statement? Do you agree with this? Find out your tutor's opinion.

> **Strategy for Success #1:**
> **Consider the writer's reasons for writing**
>
> Always question a writer's basis – or reason – for making a statement.

A.3 Understanding and responding   `ANSWERS`

Read Article 1 ('Introducing *Read, Research and Write*') again and use the information to help you to answer the following questions. In each case, make a note of where in the article you found your answer. This will help you to justify your answer later.

Use the line numbers in the article provided for this purpose.

Record your answers in your portfolio.

1   What level of English are readers of this book expected to have? What terms do you know that are used to describe people who have learned English as a second language? What terms are common in the community in which you are studying?

2   Studying this book will help you to develop in five broad areas. What are they? Which of these areas do you think you will find most helpful?

3   What was the most significant influence upon the design of this book?

4   What particular condition was placed upon the tutors who participated in the research? Why do you think this was made a condition of participation?

5   What forms the core – or the heart – of each of the ten chapters of this book? How does this make the book unique? Can you think of alternative approaches to the content, or subject matter, of a book designed to develop ESL students' academic skills?

6   Where can you read more about the project that influenced the design of this book? Would you be interested in doing so? Why (not)?

7   In the last part of each chapter in this book, you are asked to apply what you have been studying to your own subject. Why do you think this might be a good idea?

8   Why is it suggested that the 'personal benefits are multiplied'? (line 119)

9   According to the map of the book, if you completed all the chapters in this book, how many different types of academic article would you have studied? What other types of academic article do you know of?

10   There is no space for answers or notes in this book. Name two ways in which this feature may help you.

> **Strategy for Success #2:**
> **Be able to explain yourself**
>
> It's fine to disagree with what is said or written, but make sure you are able to explain why you disagree.

➢   Compare your answers to Questions 1–10 above with those of another student. Justify your answers, where appropriate, by referring to the line or lines in the article that helped you to answer the question.

▶ FOCUS B: LEARNING LANGUAGE

B.1 Dealing with unfamiliar words

Words or phrases may be new to you for a number of reasons:

1   You have never seen the word or phrase before.
2   You have seen the word or phrase before but have forgotten what it means.
3   You have seen the word or phrase before and thought you knew what it meant, but clearly it is being used with a different meaning in this context.

➢   Scan Article 1 (that is, read it through quickly with the task in mind), making a note of words that, for you, fall into each category above. Compare your words with those of another student.

context *n.* [C, U]
The words that come just before and after a word or sentence and that help you to understand its meaning. *The meaning of 'mad' depends upon its context.*

There are a number of strategies which can help you when you find a word or phrase that is unfamiliar to you. One useful strategy is to study the **context** in which the word or phrase appears, and look for clues provided by that context. Research (Laufer, 1989) has shown that this can be successful if you understand at least 95% of the text you are reading.

By studying the context of the word, you might find that:

- the definition is provided, or suggested, by the writer
- words with a similar meaning are used in the same sentence or nearby sentences and can be used as a guide
- you understand the context fully and can use it to help you make a good guess at the meaning of the unfamiliar word.

➢   For example, take a look at the context in which the words 'pre-sessional' and 'in-sessional' are used in Article 1:

'To improve my language, I'm always trying first to guess, and then to look up, any new or hard vocabulary words that are not familiar to me, to make sure of their meaning. This has helped me to build up a powerful vocabulary base.'

Tariq Ibrahim Abdul Rahim Al Jallad (first-year student)

This book is for students who [...] are about to begin a course of study or have already begun undergraduate studies (these students are sometimes known as pre-sessional or in-sessional respectively). (lines 12–14)

Explanations are provided of the terms 'pre-sessional' (about to begin a course of study) and 'in-sessional' (having already begun undergraduate studies). The use of the word **respectively** also helps the reader to understand the terms.

You might therefore say something like:

'I think that "pre-sessional" must mean "about to begin a course of study" because the writer uses this word to describe students who are about to begin their studies.'

In making such statements, you are **inferring** the meaning of an unfamiliar word from its context. Another way of saying this would be that you are making an informed guess; 'informed' by the context of the word.

You have also inferred its word class – you have decided that the word describes students, so it must be an adjective.

You might want to confirm your inferences at some later stage. You can do this by using an English – English dictionary (see Chapter 2) or by checking your ideas with a friend or tutor. Doing this little bit of extra work will help to reinforce your learning of the words.

> **respectively** *adv.*
> In the same order as the things you have just mentioned. *The cups and saucers cost £5 and £3 respectively.*

> **infer** *v.* [T] *formal*
> To form an opinion that something is probably true based on the information that you have. *From the evidence, we can infer that the victim knew her killer.*

➤ Infer from their context the meaning of the following words in the introduction:

- discipline (line 15)
- plagiarizing (line 49)
- literature (line 61)
- argument (line 83)
- claim (line 85)
- outcomes (line 95)

When thinking about their 'word class', the most likely word classes (and their abbreviations) that you will need are:

- noun (n.)
- verb (v.)
- adjective (adj.)
- adverb (adv.)

➤ Scan the article and find three examples of each of the above. Make a note of the words you find along with the abbreviation for their word class. This is a good habit to get into.
➤ Find three more words of your own and infer their meanings from their contexts. (Ignore a word if you are not able to infer its meaning – simply move on to another one. It is not always possible.) Think about the likely meaning of the word and its word class. Make notes.
➤ Describe your words to a partner or your tutor, if you can, and confirm your guesses. Remember that you can use language like this:

'I think that … must mean … because … '

'I think that … is probably a/an $\begin{Bmatrix} \text{noun} \\ \text{adjective} \\ \text{verb} \\ \text{adverb} \end{Bmatrix}$ because …'

▶ FOCUS C: WRITING

C.1 Feedback on written work

As a student of reading, researching and writing skills, you are likely to want and need feedback on the language and content of the writing you do while studying this book. It is possible for your tutor to provide you with feedback by *correcting*, *marking* and/or *grading* your work.

➢ Discuss the difference between correction, marking and grading with another student and your tutor.

A benefit in having your work marked but not corrected is that you can take steps to make the correction yourself. It may be that this is a more effective strategy for learning.

> **annotate** *v.* [T usually passive]
> To add short notes to a book or piece of writing to explain parts of it: *an annotated edition of 'Othello'.*

A commercially available computer programme called 'Markin' (see Holmes, 2007 and www.cict.co.uk/software/markin/features.htm) allows tutors to mark written work by **annotating** it to indicate weaknesses or strengths in the writing. The software is useful for two reasons in particular:

a) it may be customized to suit your needs and purposes by your tutor
b) the annotations may be inserted manually – you and your tutor do not need to have a computer to use the system. Instead, your tutor can use a code for each annotation which can be handwritten into your writing.

➢ Turn to Chapter 2, Section C.2, to see an example of text marked using 'Markin'.

> **authentic** *adj.*
> A painting, document, book, etc. that is authentic has been proved to be by a particular person = genuine: *an authentic work by Picasso.*

➢ A set of coded, customized, annotations is provided in the companion website, with **authentic** examples drawn from students' writing, showing the annotations as they were inserted by a tutor. Scan these now and discuss any that you do not understand with your tutor, then work with another student to answer the following questions:

1 How do content errors differ from language errors?
2 If you see the annotation 'supply evidence' in your writing, what should you do to improve it?
3 If you see the annotation 'count/non-count' next to a noun in your writing, you may want to look up that noun in your dictionary. What abbreviations will you find next to the noun to help you address your problem?

4   Explain 'parallel construction problem' to another student as you understand it.
5   What's the difference between a verb form error and a verb tense error?
6   What's the difference between a word form error and a word choice error?
7   If you make a slip, is it likely to be serious?
8   What does it mean if your work is 'well signposted'?

➢   Check your answers to questions 1–8 above with your tutor.

➢   Your tutor may not want or need to use all of the possible annotations in marking your work, on every occasion. Before you write, with your tutor, discuss this issue with your tutor. Find out his or her preference and opinion, and, if appropriate, agree upon a subset of annotations from the companion website for him or her to use when marking your work. Keep these annotations in mind as you write. They tell you what your tutor will be looking for as he or she tries to help you improve your writing.

C.2 Autobiography: writing about yourself

➢   Read again the section in the introduction entitled 'How can I make the best use of *Read, Research and Write*?' As you read, reflect upon your own personal circumstances.

➢   Write a short article describing your personal circumstances. Imagine that you are writing for your class or institution newsletter. Give your article a title, and include information about any of the following points that are relevant:

- which institution you have chosen or hope to attend
- why you want to study there
- the subject you are studying or planning to study
- why you want to study this particular subject
- what you hope to do once you graduate
- your strengths in relation to any or all of the following areas in English: reading, language, writing, research, study
- your weaknesses in relation to any or all of the following areas in English: reading, language, writing, research, study
- which parts of this book you feel would help you most, and why
- any other information you would like to include.

➢   Exchange your work with another student, and read his or her work. Try to do this with as many others as you can. When you have finished reading, ask each other questions.

➢   From reading other students' work, try to improve the language in your own article in at least one way. You can do this by changing or adding words or phrases.

➢   Make a copy of your work and give it to your tutor next time you meet. He or she will keep it for his or her records.

> **reflect.** *v.* [T]
> To think carefully about something, or to say something that you have been thinking about: [+on] *He had time to reflect on his successes and failures.*

> Add your work to your portfolio. Put it in your 'writing' section.
> **Reflect.** In this task, you were asked to imagine that you were 'writing for your class newsletter'. This instruction told you something about your audience, or reader. Why do you need to know this information?

Strategy for Success #3:
Know your audience

Always write with a clear picture in your mind of your audience. Is it: Your peers? Your lecturer or lecturers? An examinations committee? A reader of a journal?

C.3 Different types of academic writing

> Discuss. In lines 63–72 of the introduction, various types of academic articles or work were mentioned. Without looking back, which ones can you remember? Make a list.

C.4 Knowing your audience

> Discuss. In what ways would the audiences for a newsletter article and a journal article be different? How might this affect the writing? Make a note of your ideas and then share them with your class or group.

▶ FOCUS D: RESEARCHING

D.1 Using a library

Your library contains articles and texts of the type mentioned in lines 63–72 of the introduction. Such texts are an essential resource for any student, and you need to know where they are located in your library and how you can access them. For example, are they available online? Can they be borrowed, or are they for reference only?

Type of texts	Location	How to access them
Newsletters		
Journals		
Textbooks		
Abstracts		

➢ Visit the library in your institution. Copy this table into your portfolio, and complete it during your visit. Add other texts and resources that you find in your library.

D.2 Building an annotated bibliography

➢ In your library, find one example of each of the following types of books. Work in your subject area and choose books that appeal to you.

- A book written by one author.
- A book written by two authors.
- A book that is a collection of articles or chapters, edited by one person.

In each case, note down the following information:

1. Author's or author's surname(s) and first name initial(s)
2. Editor's surname and initial, if your book is an edited collection
3. Year of publication
4. Title of book
5. Place of publication
6. Name of publisher

However, *do not* write your information in a list like this!

Instead, record it **horizontally**. If you were to do this exercise for this book, you would write:

> **horizontal** *adj.*
> Flat and level: *A horizontal surface.*

Brandt, C. (2009). *Read, Research, Write: Academic Skills for ESL Students in Higher Education.* London, United Kingdom: SAGE Publications.

➢ Make a note of the punctuation you need when you writing a reference like the one above. Pay particular attention to the use of commas, full stops, colons, parentheses, italics and capitalization.

➢ Create a file in Word (or any word-processing program) on your computer. Call it 'bibliography' and add to it the source information, as above, for every work you consult. Arrange this information in alphabetical order according to the first surname. If you do not have easy access to a computer, you can use index cards (see Chapter 6, section E.1) – put the source information for one book on each card so that you can insert others as you progress.

➢ For each book you add to your bibliography, write a comment below the bibliographic information. Adding a comment turns your bibliography into an annotated bibliography. You do not need to write complete sentences here. Brief notes would be fine.

> **Strategy for Success #4:**
> **Carry a notebook with you**
>
> Have a notebook with you at all times, particularly when you visit your library. Don't forget to note down the bibliographic details of that interesting book or article you've found.

Here are some examples of the kind of comment you might write:

Contains an article that looks as if it could be useful for my essay on ...

Looks like a good but basic introduction to the area of ...

A really useful guide to jargon in the field of ...

Covers relevant topics for my essay on ... but may be too advanced.

Here is an example completed by a student, Marwan Mohsin Al Haj Atalla Hasan Abu Aasi:

Therrien, C. and Tummala, M. (2004). *Probability for Electrical and Computer Engineers.* US: CRC.

Covers relevant topics for my essay on Electrical and Computer Engineering but may be at too high a level.

> ➤ From time to time, print out an updated copy of your bibliography to add to your portfolio. You can make use of this bibliography when studying your subject.

▶ FOCUS E: STUDYING

E.1 Good study habits

In the last part of the introduction, in the section called 'Organizing your work: keeping a portfolio', two 'good study habits' were mentioned.

> ➤ What were the 'good study habits'? Make a note of them in your portfolio.
> ➤ Think of other 'good study habits'. Make a list, and compare your list with another student's. Create a new combined list with no duplication.

- ➤ Get together with another pair of students and repeat the process: compare your lists and make a new one.
- ➤ Use this list to design a classroom poster on A3 paper. Add the names of the people who contributed towards it. Make an A4 copy of this poster for your portfolio.

E.2 Keeping a portfolio

One of the 'good study habits' that was mentioned in the introduction was 'organizing your work'.

It is important to organize yourself from the very start of your course. This is true for all your courses, not just this one.

> **Strategy for Success #5:**
> **Keep legible, organized notes**
>
> Well-organized legible notes can make revisiting them – and revising from them – a real pleasure.

- ➤ Organize your A4 portfolio. Label all of your dividers and place the work that you have completed so far into the right section. Make a cover page for your portfolio. Add some or all of this information:

- your name
- student number
- course title and code
- institution
- your email address and/or phone number (so that if you misplace your file, it can be returned to you).

E.3 Understanding rationale

- ➤ Scan the headings in the introduction. In which section would you expect to find information about the **rationale** for this book?
- ➤ The following outline summarizes the rationale for this book. However, there are some words missing, indicated by numbers.

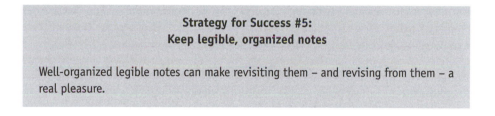

rationale *n.* [C, usually singular]
formal
The reasons for a decision, belief, etc. [+behind/for/of] *The rationale for using this teaching method is to encourage student confidence.*

Work with another student. Note down numbers 1–15 in your files. Then read the outline and, using your own ideas, try to complete the missing words. Where you see a number, there is a missing word. You need only one word in each case.

Do this first without looking at the missing words, which are given in the box below. Cover the box with a sheet of paper.

Summary of the rationale for this book

This book is based upon the results of an international – 1 – project. This project investigated – 2 – expectations of their students, in terms of their ability to – 3 –, research and write. The research – 4 – indicated that students needed to develop their – 5 – and understandings in a number of areas including expressing – 6 – cautiously. Such topics come under the umbrella of 'English for – 7 – Purposes' or 'EAP'. EAP may be thought of as an academic – 8 – in its own right, and all of the topics above are addressed in this book. Being an academic subject in its own right, then, EAP has its own body of – 9 –. Sample – 10 – drawn from this literature form the heart of each of the ten chapters of this book. Using – 11 – about EAP alone as the basis for the study is a novel approach to developing the skills needed by – 12 – of EAP. Each article is followed by a number of – 13 – and – 14 – designed to focus your attention on developing your skills. The outcomes also suggested that students benefit from – 15 – such knowledge and skills in their own subject areas. For this reason, the last part of each chapter encourages you to apply what you have learned to your own field.

➤   Complete the outline again, using the words in the box below. Make another list – put this second one side-by-side with your own. Compare your two lists. Do not cross out your ideas. Your word may fit well!
➤   Share your ideas with your tutor, and find out if they are possible in terms of their grammar and meaning. Only cross them out if they are wrong.

literature	subject	Academic	research
applying	claims	outcomes	abilities
students	articles (×2)	lecturers'	questions
	tasks	read	

➤   Discuss. How important do you think it is for you to understand the rationale for the following:

- A book?
- A website?
- Research?
- A task, exercise, project or assignment set by your lecturer or tutor?
- Keeping a portfolio of your work?
- An examination?

Find out your tutor's opinion for each of the above.

> **Strategy for Success #6:**
> **Be an active learner**
>
> Seek out other people's views and opinions. Include your lecturer as well as your fellow students when you do this.

▶ FOCUS F: APPLYING TO YOUR OWN SUBJECT

F.1 Assessing the quality and usefulness of an article

To help you make a decision about the quality and usefulness of any article or book, you need to ask questions about six areas:

1   The *author*: who is he or she? What are his or her qualifications and/or experience? (Knowing something about the author can help you to decide how important the conclusions in the article are, and it can help you to recognize where his or her interests and biases lie.)

2   The *content*: what is the article about? (The title and introduction will give you a good idea of what the article is about. This will help you to decide how useful the article is for you personally. How relevant is it to your needs? Do you want to continue to read the article, or will you reject it?)

3   The *audience*: who is the intended audience for the article? (Knowing something about the intended audience will tell you if the article was written for someone who knows a great deal about the subject – an expert – or for someone who knows less – a general reader. Which would you find most useful?)

4   The *readability*: how easy is it for you to understand? (There is no point in struggling to read something that is too challenging. There are plenty of books and articles, so select another one.)

5   The *evidence*: what research and/or sources does the author use to support his claims? (The reference list can tell you more about the focus and direction of the author, and this can help to decide if you want to continue to read.)

6   The *age*: when was the article published? (Knowing this can tell you how current the conclusions in the article are. If you are looking at an 'old' article, you might find that the ideas it contains are outdated. But how old is old? Age is not *necessarily* a problem. Find out your tutor's view.)

These are your six quality **criteria** for selecting an article. You can memorize them or make a note of them to add to your portfolio.

> **criterion** *n. plural* Criteria
> A standard that you use to judge
> something or make a decision
> about something: *the criteria we
> use for selecting candidates.*

If you want to memorize them, try making the first letter of each into an **acronym**: Author, Content, Audience, Readability, Evidence and Age gives us: ACAREA.

F.2 Applying quality criteria

The six criteria were applied when selecting the ten articles on which this book is based.

> ➤ Scan the article in Chapter 2, 'Understanding EAP' by Andy Gillett, and answer the six criteria questions. Discuss your ideas with another student and make notes in your portfolio under these headings:

> **acronym** *n.* [C]
> A word made up from the first
> letters of the name of some-
> thing such as an organization.
> For example, NATO is an
> acronym for the North Atlantic
> Treaty Organization.

1 Author
2 Content
3 Audience
4 Readability
5 Evidence
6 Age.

> ➤ Find an article in your library or online with a clear introduction. Choose one that is readable and closely related to your subject and interests. Apply the six criteria. Reject any article if you cannot answer one of the six questions. Make notes under the six headings above.
> ➤ When you are satisfied that your article meets your criteria, make a copy of the whole article for your portfolio. You will revisit it later.
> ➤ Read the introduction to your article. Does it make you want to read more? Tell another student why, or why not.

F.3 Finding new words and inferring their meaning from context

> ➤ Scan your subject-related article and identify five unfamiliar words. Using their context to help you, make a note of what you think they mean and their word class. Write:

'I think that … must mean … because …'

'I think that … is probably a/an $\begin{cases} \text{noun} \\ \text{adjective} \\ \text{verb} \\ \text{adverb} \end{cases}$ because …'

➤ Find a student with similar interests to yours, if you can, and share your words and meanings with him or her. Can you agree on their definitions?

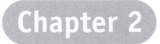

Chapter 2

Understanding EAP

In this chapter, you can read a **newsletter article** about English for Academic Purposes.

You can develop your skills in these areas:

Focus A: Reading

A.1   Looking ahead
A.2   Note-taking
A.3   Understanding and responding
A.4   Text structure

Focus B: Learning language

B.1   Word analysis
B.2   Enquiring about meaning

Focus C: Writing

C.1   Writing definitions
C.2   Writing about another person

Focus D: Researching

D.1   Using text structure as a guide

Focus E: Studying

E.1   Using an English–English dictionary
E.2   Recording new words
E.3   Annotating
E.4   Note-taking

Focus F: Applying to your own subject

F.1   Locating subject-related articles
F.2   Applying word analysis to a subject-related article
F.3   Finding and recording new subject-related words

▶ FOCUS A: READING

A.1 Looking ahead

Below, you can read a **newsletter** article called 'What is EAP?' by Andy Gillett, principal lecturer at the University of Hertfordshire, UK.

➢   Think about or discuss the following questions before you read the article:

1   Can you remember what 'EAP' stands for?
2   In what ways do you think 'EAP' might differ from the kind of English that you learned as a child or teenager at school?

newsletter *n.* [C]
A short written report of news about a club, organization, place, etc. that is sent regularly to people who are interested.
The society publishes a newsletter three times a year.

'Article 2 is very relevant and useful to my context because EAP courses are offered at my institution.'

Moutaz Bassam Falih Saleh
(first-year student)

▶ ARTICLE 2: WHAT IS EAP?

Andy Gillett (1996, updated 2007)
University of Hertfordshire, UK

Introduction

What is EAP? Who are EAP lecturers? What do they do? What are they interested in? I would like to try to answer some of these questions. It is probably true that most EAP lecturers are working in institutes of higher education where English is the medium of
5   instruction. They see many students for whom English is not a first language and who could benefit from English classes. For some students, improving their English is essential – they will fail their courses otherwise. Some think they can get better grades if they learn more English; others study English because they like it. The object of an EAP – English for Academic Purposes – course is to help overseas students overcome
10   some of the linguistic difficulties involved in studying in English. The job of the EAP lecturer is to find out what the students have to do and help them to do it better.

Courses

EAP courses are very often pre-sessional courses. That is, they are taken before the students' main academic courses start. Most universities in the UK offer these pre-
15   sessional courses, which vary in length from one year to two weeks. The EAP courses often take place at the institution where the students intend to take their main academic course, but this need not be the case. These courses are intended to prepare international students coming to study in the UK to study in English. They also allow students to familiarize themselves with the new environment and facilities
20   of the institution before their main courses start. The students need to learn to adopt particular approaches to their study and learn strategies and skills that will enable them to succeed in the UK HE system. The purpose of the pre-sessional EAP course is to bring them up to the level that is necessary to start a course. In this case, EAP tutors need to liaise with admissions tutors to find out what is necessary.
25   EAP courses can also be in-sessional courses. That is, they are taken at the same time as the students' main academic course. In-sessional courses can take one of two forms. They can be seen as language support classes – these are usually free drop-in classes held at lunch-times or Wednesday afternoons and students attend when they are able. Increasingly, it is also becoming possible for international stu-
30   dents to take credit-bearing EAP courses as part of their degree.

EAP/Study Skills

There is often discussion whether these two terms – EAP and study skills – mean the same. I find it useful to make a distinction between general study skills that are not concerned with language and language study skills that will probably form part of an EAP course. There are many study skills books available for native speakers and they usually concentrate on matters like: where to study, when to study, time management, remembering, developing study habits, filing and organizing books, how to spend leisure time and so on, although they do often deal with aspects of study skills that involve language such as planning essays and so on. These general study skills are obviously important to our international students, but they are not usually the main objective of EAP courses. The language study skills will form an essential component of the EAP skills classes.

Academic Writing Classes

For many students, writing is probably the most important skill to develop as it is the way in which most of their work is assessed. The aim of an academic writing class is to prepare students for academic writing tasks. These tasks vary very much from writing short answers in exams to writing dissertations and theses. Of course, accurate grammar, punctuation and language use forms an important component of an EAP writing class, along with specific teaching of the formal language required. This will involve teaching of different text types, linking words, signposting expressions, introductions and conclusions. It is also important to teach UK writing conventions as these can vary very much from those even in neighbouring European countries.

However, EAP lecturers often find they need to concentrate on the process of writing – planning, organizing, presenting, re-writing, proofreading, etc. (Robinson, 1988). In my opinion, the most useful single skill that I can teach most of the students I meet is organizing. If students make little grammatical mistakes, they get a small correction. However, if there is a problem with organizing, they will get a big red question mark. Writing classes are often task-based and project work allows students to work in their own field (see Bloor and St John, 1988). Projects also allow students to become familiar with ways of working in British HE. In particular, they will have the opportunity to develop the right kind of approach to studying in the UK. This involves developing a willingness to accept responsibility for their own learning so that they are able to learn independently using initiative and self-discipline. They will need to develop the ability to think logically and independently, to be reflective and critical, to analyse, to synthesize and to be creative. They will also need to develop the ability to use IT, to mount well-presented arguments, to solve problems and to work as a member of a team.

The following would be typical content:

- Researching, and using the library: finding relevant information, using catalogues, books, periodicals, bibliographies and indexes.
- Using sources: making notes and writing up notes – paraphrasing, organizing, quoting and referring to sources, writing a bibliography.
- Writing descriptions of places, objects, etc.; classifying and organizing; comparing and contrasting; reporting and narrating.

75 • Describing processes and developments: expressing purpose, means and method, degrees of certainty, reasons and explanations/cause and effect; describing developments and changes; describing a sequence of events/time relations.
• Writing instructions.
• Developing an argument: presenting arguments, ideas and opinions; expressing
80 certainty and doubt; supporting an argument: illustrating and exemplifying ideas; refuting arguments, ideas and opinions; drawing conclusions.
• Writing skills: different kinds of writing; organizing – presentation and layout; spelling and punctuation; including graphs, charts and tables; style; revising the essay; proofreading.

85 ## Academic Reading Course

The big difficulty with reading is the amount involved. These classes therefore aim to assist the non-native speaker of English studying in the medium of English at tertiary level to use a wide range of reading strategies in order to receive more benefit from the course. Many students still rely on painstakingly slow word-by-word reading. It soon
90 becomes clear to them, however, that they cannot read every word in the library. General efficient reading strategies such as scanning to find the book or chapter, skimming to get the gist and careful reading of important passages (Wallace, 2004, pp. 9–38) are necessary, as well as vocabulary building exercises in the student's own area. Learning about how texts are structured can help students to read more efficiently.
95 An academic reading course could include:

• Understanding meaning: deducing the meaning of unfamiliar words and word groups; relations within the sentence/complex sentences; implications (information not explicitly stated); conceptual meaning, e.g. comparison, purpose, cause, effect.
• Understanding relationships in the text: text structure; the communicative value
100 of sentences; relations between the parts of a text through lexical and grammatical cohesion devices and indicators in discourse.
• Understanding important points; distinguishing the main ideas from supporting detail; organizing unsupported claims and claims supported by evidence; distinguishing fact from opinion; extracting salient points to summarize; following an
105 argument; reading critically/evaluating the text.
• Reading efficiently: surveying the text, chapter/article, paragraphs, skimming for gist/general impression; scanning to locate specifically required information; reading quickly.
• Note-taking.

110 ## Testing

Most EAP lecturers are involved to some extent in testing international students. This can involve advising admissions tutors on what external English language tests

are available and what the scores mean. On the basis of these scores, students can be accepted or given offers conditional on reaching a particular level of English, or attending a certain length pre-sessional course. The most well-known EAP test is   115
the IELTS (International English Language Testing System) test. This test is jointly managed by the University of Cambridge Local Examinations Syndicate, the British Council and IDP Education Australia. The test tests academic reading, writing, speaking and listening and reports the level of each skill on a band from 1 to 9. Many universities also have their own proficiency tests which are written,   120
administered and updated by EAP lecturers.

Conclusion

EAP is thus an important area of ESP (English for Specific Purposes), accounting for a large amount of the ESP activity worldwide. Most of the work, however, takes place, unknown to much of the English language teaching world, in universities.   125
It is discussed in journals and at conferences such as IATEFL and BALEAP (British Association of Lecturers in English for Academic Purposes). There have been several EAP-related articles in this newsletter, and maybe there would be interest in more.

References

Bloor, M. and St John, M. J. (1988). Project writing: The marriage of process and product. In P. C. Robinson (Ed.), *Academic Writing: Process and product* (ELT Documents 129, pp. 85–94). London: Modern English Publications.

Robinson, P. C. (Ed.) (1988). *Academic Writing: Process and product* (ELT Documents 129). London: Modern English Publications.

Wallace, M. J. (2004). *Study Skills in English* (2nd edn). Cambridge: Cambridge University Press.

Andy Gillett is Principal Lecturer in EAP in the School of Combined Studies at the University of Hertfordshire, Hatfield, UK. He has spent most of the last 30 years teaching ESP in private language schools, state colleges and universities, both in the UK and abroad. He is now mainly involved in organizing, planning and teaching EAP courses to students taking a wide range of courses at the University of Hertfordshire's campuses at Hatfield, north of London, UK.

A.2 Note-taking

Before reading Article 2, you were asked to look ahead and consider two questions. In answer to the first question, you may have remembered that EAP stands for 'English for Academic Purposes'.

> **Strategy for Success #7:**
> **Match your reading approach to your purpose**
>
> Identify your purpose in reading something, and adopt a reading approach to suit that purpose. So:
>
> Scan: with a question in the back of your mind, move your eyes quickly over a text to try to find the answer to it.
>
> Skim: read something quickly to find the main ideas.

➤   The second question asked you to consider ways in which EAP might differ from the kind of English you learned at school. Find any notes you made in answer to this question, and skim the article again. As you read, identify and highlight key points to help you to respond to the question headings below.

Then reorganize your notes under the question headings below, and supplement them with any additional information provided in the article.

Your aim is to arrive at a broad description – in note form – of what EAP is all about.

> **Strategy for Success #8:**
> **Use headings to help you to organize your notes**
>
> When you take notes, always do so under questions or headings. This will help you later, when you want to locate something of particular relevance to your current task.

Use these question headings to organize your notes:

- Why do some students need EAP?
- Where can you study EAP?
- What types of EAP courses are there?
- How does EAP relate to study skills?
    - What skills would you expect to develop on a good EAP course?

comprehensive *adj.*
Including all the necessary facts, details, or problems that need to be dealt with. *A comprehensive study of alcoholism.*

➤   Now describe what you have learned to another student, and listen to another student's description. Had you forgotten anything? If so, update your notes to make them as **comprehensive** as possible.

➤   Discuss the following statement:

EAP is a myth. There's no such thing. It's only English used in a particular context, which is what people always do anyway. All students need is to learn more English.
(Lecturer, University of Bahrain English Language Centre, 2004)

On what grounds do you think the lecturer might have made this statement? Do you agree with her? Discuss with another student and then find out your tutor's opinion.

A.3 Understanding and responding

➢   Read the article again and answer the following questions. Where possible, make a note of where in the article you found your answer. You may need to justify your answers later. Use the line numbers provided for this purpose. ANSWERS

Strategy for Success #9:
See EAP as one of your subjects

As an EAP student, you have two subjects to study: 1) EAP and 2) your own specialization, such as Engineering, or Economics.

Make a note of your answers in your portfolio.

1   What do you understand by the phrase 'where English is the medium of instruction'? (lines 4–5)
2   The author provides three reasons why students study English. What are they?
3   A pre-sessional course in the UK helps to prepare students to study in English. In what other way can it help students?
4   What phrase tells you that in some institutions students can take an EAP course that counts towards their degree?
5   The writer gives one example of what he calls a 'language study skill'. What is it?
6   Why does the author think writing is so important for students?
7   What do you think the phrase 'signposting expressions' means? (line 50)
8   Why does the author believe that 'organizing' is the most important skill for students to acquire? What words does the author use to show you that he knows his **assertion** is not supported by research in the text?

> **assertion** *n.* [C]
> Something that you say or write that you strongly believe. *She makes very general assertions about marriage in the poem.*

9   What is meant by 'British HE' (line 60). (Paragraph 1 – and the title of this book! – could help you here).

10   What do you need to do if you want to have 'the right kind of approach to studying in the UK'? (lines 61–62)

11   What does the writer mean by 'using sources'? (line 71)

12   What major problem with reading does the author identify?

Strategy for Success #10:
Relate the new to the known

Always try to relate what you are studying to your own current personal circumstances, and potential future needs.

➤   Now look again at the answers that you have given to the questions above, and think about your own situation and your own opinion. Write a sentence or sentences in response to each. The questions have been numbered to correspond to those above.

1   Use the phrase 'English is the medium of instruction' in relation to your own experience or current situation.

2   Which of the reasons for studying English apply to you, if any?

3   How important is it for you 'to learn to adopt particular approaches to [your] study and learn strategies and skills that will enable [you] to succeed' (line 20–22) in your own context?

4   Are you taking an EAP course that counts towards your degree? If not, how would you describe the kind of course that you are taking?

5   What other 'language study skills' can you think of? If you find this difficult to answer, you can try looking back at the 'map' of the book in Chapter 1 to help you.

6   What forms of written assessment can you think of? Which of these forms do you have personal experience of?

7   How did you figure out the meaning of the phrase 'signposting expressions'?

8   What steps do you think you could take to help you with the skill of 'organizing' your written work?

9   Describe the HE system in your own country. What choices does it offer students?

10   What are your strengths and weaknesses in relation to 'the right kind of approach to studying in the UK'? (lines 61–62)

11 Give an example of a 'source' in your own field. You do not need to provide full bibliographic details if these are not to hand. The name of an author and text would be sufficient.

12 What strategies will you use if you find that you have too much reading to do?

➤ Explain your answers to questions 1–12 above to another student or group of students.

A.4 Text structure

➤ Without looking back at the text, can you recall some of the headings the author used?

- First, discuss your ideas with another student and make a note of the headings you can recall.
- Then, compare your list with another pair of students. Update your own list if you find you have missed anything.
- Finally, return to the text and see how many headings you remembered. Did you include the title? And the heading for the reference list?

> **generic** *adj.* [usually before noun]
> Relating to a whole group of things rather than one thing.
> *Fine Arts is a generic term for subjects such as painting, music and sculpture.*
>
> **specific** *adj.* [only before noun]
> A specific thing, person, or group is one particular thing, person, or group. *A specific example of alcohol's effect on the body.*

➤ Which of the headings in your list would it be possible to use in another piece of writing on a completely different academic topic?

➤ Study the list of headings below. Some of them could readily be used in other articles (they could possibly be called **generic**) while others could only be used in a particular article about a particular topic (they may be called **specific**). In your notebook, write down those you think are generic. Share your ideas with another student and use an English–English dictionary to help you if you wish.

- Glossary
- Critical thinking
- Plagiarism
- Literature review
- Hedging language

- Appendix
- Bibliography
- Summary
- Abstract
- Background

➤ If you are uncertain about any of the words above, discuss them with your tutor. Make notes.

➤ Take some of the generic headings that you have identified and arrange them into a possible order for an academic article. Compare your idea with that of another student.

➢   Work in a small group with other students and discuss the following
     questions:

1   What is the difference between an introduction and an abstract?
2   What would you do if you were asked to write a literature review?
3   What is the difference between a bibliography and a list of references?
4   What is the purpose of a glossary? Give an example from your field of a word
     you might put in a glossary.
5   What is the difference between a conclusion and a summary?

➢   Work alone and make notes in answer to the five questions above.

Strategy for Success #11:
Engage in dialogue

Talk it through. Discuss any or all of the following with friends or fellow students:

- How to tackle an assignment or essay.
- The answer to a task in this book or other books.
- Any problems you might be experiencing.

▶ FOCUS B: LEARNING LANGUAGE

B.1 Word analysis

When you come across an unfamiliar word, one strategy you can use to help you to
understand it is to study its context (as described in Chapter 1). Another strategy is
to try to identify the *parts* of the word.

For example, the word 'pre-sessional' is composed of three parts:

1   A prefix: 'pre-'
2   A main part: 'session'
3   A suffix: '-al'

You may find that you already know the meaning of each part above, and so this
approach can help you to understand the word as a whole. In this case, the prefix
means 'before'; the main part means 'a period of time used for a particular activity'
(*Longman Dictionary of Contemporary English*, 2003) and the suffix tells you that the
word is an adjective.

As with the strategy of examining the context, the 'word analysis' strategy will not always work. But it is worth considering before you move on to another approach, because it can be very time-efficient.

➤ Work with another student. Identify the parts of the following words (you will meet them all in this book) and discuss what your analysis tells you about their meaning. Make notes. Do not worry about their word class at this stage.

1	In-sessional	11	Forefront
2	Unfamiliar	12	Overshadow
3	International	13	Undergraduate
4	Updated	14	Postgraduate
5	Overseas	15	Geography
6	Comfortable	16	Rewrite
7	Research	17	Thereby
8	Cross-cultural	18	Interactive
9	Monograph	19	Input
10	Framework	20	Subconscious

➤ Discuss your ideas for the above with your tutor and add to your notes any other information that he or she may give you.

B.2 Enquiring about meaning

If someone says something to you that you do not understand, there are a variety of approaches that you can take. You can:

- ignore the word or phrase that you have not understood
- try to guess the meaning of the word or phrase that you have not understood from its context
- ask the speaker to help you.

If you want to ask the speaker to help you, try the following language:

'I'm sorry, but what does "X" mean?'
'Could you explain what you mean by "X", please?'
'I'm sorry, what did you say?'
'I'm sorry, I didn't catch that.'
'Could you say that again, please?'

If you need to write the word down, you may want to ask:

'Could you spell that for me, please?'
'I'm sorry, but could you tell me how to spell that, please?'

Your tutor will have other ideas. Make a note of the language above and any other ideas that your tutor gives you.

> ➤ Ask your tutor about his or her job. Find out as much as you can. Below, you will find a list of points you could ask about.

Read these instructions first:

1 Consider recording the discussion if your institution has the equipment to do this.
2 Choose only those points that you would feel comfortable asking about.
3 Add any other points of your own that come to mind.
4 For each point, make a note of the actual questions that you will ask. For example, Point 1 could translate into any of the following:

   - 'What do you like most about your job?'
   - 'What do you enjoy most about your job?'
   - 'Which aspects of the job provide you with the greatest job satisfaction?'
   - 'Which aspects of the job give you greatest job satisfaction?'
   - 'Which aspects of the job do you find most satisfying?'

5 Think about the *order* in which you would like to ask about the points you have selected. You would probably not want to ask about the points in the order given below.
6 As you listen to your tutor, do not hesitate to ask for help if he or she uses a word or phrase that you do not understand.
7 Make notes of:

   - what your tutor tells you
   - any new words that catch your attention.

8 When you have finished your discussion, think about the meaning of the words you have noted. Work with another student and use the context approach and/or the word analysis approach where possible.
9 Compare your notes with those of another student. Working together, make both sets of notes as comprehensive as possible. You will need them later.

Ask your tutor about:

1 Which aspects of the job provide him or her with the greatest job satisfaction.
2 What aspect of the job he or she likes least.
3 How you become an EAP tutor.
4 Career progression.
5 Why he or she became interested in the field.

6 What he or she does when not teaching.

7 What qualifications are needed.

8 Where he or she sees him/herself in five or 10 years' time.

9 Other places/countries that he or she has worked in, and what they were like.

10 An amusing story from his or her own experience.

11 One or two of his or her career highlights.

12 One or two of his or her values in relation to teaching.

13 If he or she would recommend the job/career to someone else, and why/why not.

▶ FOCUS C: WRITING

C.1 Writing definitions

➤   Read the following statement.

You can't possibly survive in **academia** unless you are able to write good definitions and preferably do so in a number of different ways.
(Tutor, University of Brunei Department of English Language and Applied Linguistics, 2006)

> **academia** *n.* [U]
> The activities and work done at universities and colleges or the teachers and students involved in it.

Why do you think definitions are so important in academic writing? What is their purpose? Discuss these questions with another student and make a note of your ideas.

In Article 2, the author defines 'pre-sessional courses' and 'in-sessional courses' for the reader. He does so like this:

EAP courses are very often pre-sessional courses. *That is, they are* taken before the students' main academic courses start.

EAP courses can also be in-sessional courses. *That is, they are* taken at the same time as the students' main academic course.

This is a good way of writing a definition for your reader.
Here are some other good ways:

Pre-sessional courses *may be defined as* courses that are taken before the students' main academic courses start.

Pre-sessional courses *can be defined as* courses that are taken before the students' main academic courses start.

Pre-sessional courses *are defined as* courses that are taken before the students' main academic courses start.

By pre-sessional courses, *I mean* courses that are taken before the students' main academic courses start.

By pre-sessional courses, *I am referring to* courses that are taken before the students' main academic courses start.

Strategy for Success #12:
Use a language corpus as a resource

A language corpus is a collection of examples of language from many different sources. Try entering 'language corpus' into your search engine. Explore the results, until you find one that you think might be useful. The 'British National Corpus' is a good example.

➤ The examples below have all been drawn from the website 'Just the word' (193.133.140.102/JustTheWord/) as a result of a search for the word 'defined'. This website will search about 80,000,000 words of data to give you examples of words in their contexts, as they were actually used. You will make more use of this website in Chapter 4. As you read, underline the words used to introduce the definition, as has been done above. Include words such as 'loosely', which qualify the strength of the definition.

- Adoption is defined as to: 'take (a person) into a relationship he did not previously occupy especially as one's child'.
- The shoulder angle is simply defined as the angle between the upper arm and the torso when viewed from the front.
- English was defined as including both language and literature and we were to take into account relevant aspects of drama, media studies, information technology and information handling.
- For the study, a fast-food outlet was defined as one with highly systemized operations, normally with counter service, and a high volume of customers.
- Culture may be defined as those ideas, traditions, points of view and modes of behaviour which exist amongst a particular people, and which are transmitted, through learned behaviour, from generation to generation.
- International law can be defined as the framework of legal obligations which states view as being binding upon themselves.
- … then noise is best defined as interference, something which blocks transmission, jams the code, prevents sense being made.
- … it could be loosely defined as the cell-wall material of plants…
- The purpose of an audit should be defined as being 'to provide an independent opinion to those with an interest in a company that they have received from those responsible for its direction and management an adequate account of: the proper conduct of the company's affairs; the company's financial performance and position; future risks attaching to the company'.

➤ Write definitions for the words or phrases listed below. Use different ways to introduce your definitions. Define the word as it would be used in an academic context.

1   academic [adjective]
2   an EAP tutor [noun phrase]
3   study skills [noun phrase]
4   higher education [noun phrase]
5   linguistics [noun]
6   thesis [noun]
7   dissertation [noun]
8   field [noun]
9   discipline [noun]
10   argument [noun]

➢   Scan this book. Find three words or phrases that you would like to define. Write your definitions of them (use your dictionary or ask your tutor if you need to) and then dictate your work to another student. Listen to his or her dictation and write down your partner's definitions too.

➢   Refer to the list of generic headings you made for use in academic articles. In which section or sections would you expect to find the most definitions, and why? Discuss your ideas with another student.

C.2 Writing about another person

A group of students was asked to use the data they had gathered about their tutor in section B.2 above, and write an article about him for their class newsletter. Below, you can read an extract from two students' collaborative work. It has been annotated by a tutor using 'Markin' (Holmes, 2007). The annotations indicate the type of problem in the work.

➢   Read the extract, discuss what each 'mark' means with your tutor. Then work with another student and correct the errors. Check your work when you have finished with your tutor.

When Dr Nunn was young, he used to play sports and music when he is [VTense] not teaching. Nowadays, during his vacations he usually visits countries in Europe, especially Britain and France, as well as doing some writing.

For this job you should have a doctorate in applied linguistics or a master[WForm]. Publications would be a great help to get the person reputation more than his/her qualifications [Awkwardly expressed]. In 5 to 10 years, Dr Roger imagines himself in Ras Al-Khaimah, on the beach. He is planning to take [Art]rest and quit working.[Paragraphing] One of Dr. Roger's career highlights are[S/VAgreement] working as and[Minor slip] editor for the Asian EFL journal. Which involves organizing articles reviews [Fragment]. He doesn't recommend some [WChoice] one to join [WChoice] teaching because in 20 years he thinks there will be too many qualified people for teaching.[???]

Moutaz Bassam Falih Saleh and Ibrahim Ali Al Kodssi, June 2007

Strategy for Success #13:
Read your written work out loud to 'test' it

Read out loud all of your written work before you submit it. Read it to a willing friend or family member, or simply to yourself. Reading out loud can help you to *hear* problems in your work that you may not be able to see.

➤ Using the data you have gathered about your tutor, write an article about him or her for your class or institution newsletter. Before you write, with your tutor, remember to agree upon a subset of annotations from the companion website, which you would like him or her to use when marking your work.

Follow these instructions:

1 Work with another student.
2 Organize and plan your work. Give your work a title and identify the headings you would both like to include. Think carefully. Are you likely to want to use 'literature review' or 'conclusion'? Why/why not?
3 Make notes under each heading.
4 Include at least one definition.
5 Write a first draft on paper.
6 Re-read your work together and make any changes.
7 Read your work out loud to each other. Doing this will help you to *hear* errors or **ambiguities** that you might not be able to *see*.

8 Make any changes as a result of your second re-reading.
9 Write your final draft onto an overhead transparency, or OHT, which your tutor will give you. Your tutor will use this to review your work with the whole class. He or she will make any changes onto the transparency and return your work to you. You can then make two photocopies of it so that you both have a copy in your portfolios.

> **ambiguity** *n.* [C, U]
> The state of being unclear, confusing, or not certain, or things that produce this effect. *There was an element of ambiguity in the president's reply.*

▶ FOCUS D: RESEARCHING

D.1 Using text structure as a guide

In Chapter 1, Focus F.1, it was suggested that you should ask questions about six areas to help you to make a decision about the quality and usefulness of any article or book.

➢ What were the six areas? One – the second one – was 'Content'. Without looking back at Chapter 1, discuss this question with another student and try to recall the other five areas.

> 'The vocabulary boxes are very helpful, because some of the words were difficult to understand in the dictionary.'
>
> Yasmine Hedi Guefrachi
> (first-year student)

When searching for texts to read in relation to a particular assignment, it is important to be able to identify those which offer relevant content and those which may be less relevant. You can skim the structure and headings of an article or book to help you make this judgement.

➢ You have been asked to research this essay topic:

What is a **Monolingual** Learner's Dictionary, and what are the advantages and difficulties for you as a language learner in using one? In answering this question, you should refer to hard-copy dictionaries rather than web-based dictionaries.

> **monolingual** *adj.*
> Speaking or using only one language. *A monolingual dictionary.*

You have found four articles in recent editions of a journal. The headings used in each article are printed below. Look at the headings (let yourself be guided by the title too, of course!). Which article(s) is/are likely to be most relevant and helpful? Number them according to their likely relevance. Use 1 = most relevant to 4 = least relevant. Be prepared to explain and justify your decisions.

Dictionaries are unpredictable	Electronic dictionaries for learners of English
Amritavalli, R. (1999) *ELT Journal*, 53(4), pp. 262–9.	Birgit Winkler (1998) The Centre for English Language Teacher Education, Research Students' Conference Proceedings. UK: University of Warwick.
Some fundamentals	
An episode of dictionary reference	
Some typical problems	Introduction
with explanations	Desk-top computerized dictionaries
with examples	A new medium
with authenticity	Advantages and disadvantages
A live online dictionary	Pedagogical aspects
A telling example	Conclusion
Meaning-making as a mental process	
Expert to expert	
A comparison again	
'Word learning' as an autonomous activity	

(Continued)

(Continued)

Language Learners and Their Use of Dictionaries: The Case of Slovenia	Why Shouldn't Monolingual Dictionaries be as easy to use as Bilingual or Semi-Bilingual ones?
Alenka Vrbinc/Marjeta Vrbinc, EESE 3/2004 Available at www.uni-erfurt.de/eestudies/eese/ artic24/marjeta/3_2004.html	Scholfield , P. (2005) Available at www.etni.org.il/monodict.htm (reprinted from the Longman Language Review, Issue 2)
Abstract Introduction Description of the study Results Identification of parts of speech Recognition of the grammatical properties of words Lexical items and their expected place in a dictionary Selection of the appropriate prepositional complement Understanding polysemous words in context Deciphering the international phonetic alphabet Filling the slot in context Selection of the appropriate word Discussion Conclusion	The learner's choice The monolingual advantage How to 'easify' monolingual dictionary use What really *are* the problems? Where one word corresponds to several different meanings Signposting Conclusion

▌ FOCUS E: STUDYING

E.1 Using an English–English dictionary

➤ What type of information does your English–English dictionary contain? Working as part of a small group of students, copy the table at the top of p. 45 into your notebook. Add as many rows as you need. Do not use your dictionary to help you just yet. Two have been done for you as examples.

➤ When you have completed your table, get together with another group and compare tables. Can you add to yours by studying theirs? Can you help them to supplement theirs?

➤ Turn to your English–English dictionary and search for anything you may have forgotten. Then share your ideas with your tutor, and supplement your table.

My dictionary provides information about...	It provides this information through...
Spelling, including where to hyphenate the written word	The headword, and indicating the syllables with the symbol: •
Pronunciation	The use of phonemic symbols adapted from the International Phonetic Alphabet, or IPA

Strategy for Success #14:
Use an English–English dictionary

An English–English dictionary can help you to:

- learn more about a word than might be possible with other dictionaries
- develop, reinforce, and practise what you already know.

E.2 Recording new words

In completing the table above, you will have seen that there are many aspects to learning a new word. Your list will probably have included the need to learn its:

- spelling
- word class
- definition(s)
- relation to other words in the same family.

You may also like to learn its translation in your own language.

➢ Study the completed example of a personal 'vocabulary record' printed below. You will see that it is arranged to provide you with space to include the information given above, for each new word that you record there. You will find two completed examples. Note how the student has included information that was not required, such as the patterns that follow the verb 'familiarize' and the word class of each related word. You might like to take a similar approach.

Note that you will not always be able to find related words.

Example of a completed vocabulary record

Word	Word class	Definition	Related words	Translation
pre-sessional	adjective	taking place before a course of instruction has begun	session (n.); in-session(al) (adj.)	
familiarize (yourself with something)	verb	to learn about something so that you understand it	familiar (adj.); familiarity (n.)	

➢ A blank 'vocabulary record' sheet is provided for you opposite. Make several copies of this sheet to keep in your portfolio. Alternatively, you can design your own.

➢ Review Article 2 and record 10 new words in your 'vocabulary record'. Choose words that interest you and/or which you think will be particularly useful for you. You can also use the key words provided in boxes in this book, if you wish.

➢ Add any other new words that you have studied while completing Chapters 1 and 2.

E.3 Annotating

Effective students are able to annotate articles and take useful notes.

Annotation is what you do when you add your own critical comments or observations to an article, often in the margin. It is one way of responding to, or interacting with, the text. Here is an example from Article 2:

Interesting – I thought all EAP would be pre-sessional. This must have implications for the content of such courses.

EAP courses can also be in-sessional courses. That is, they are taken at the same time as the students' main academic course. In-sessional courses can take one of two forms. They can be seen as language support classes – these are usually free drop-in classes held at lunch-times or Wednesday afternoons and students attend when they are able. Increasingly, it is also becoming possible for international students to take credit-bearing EAP courses as part of their degree.

Strategy for Success #15:
Annotate as you read

Annotating an article can help you to engage with and learn from texts. Annotations can also be added to your notes.

▶ VOCABULARY RECORD

Page no. ———

Word	Word class	Definition	Related words	Translation

© SAGE Publications Ltd 2009

➤   Select a section from Article 2 and annotate it. Compare your annotations to those of another student. Remember to keep your comments critical: that is, make a judgement about the quality of the ideas, and/or identify what is unique about the content.

E.4 Note-taking

The ability to take good notes is also an essential skill for effective study. Here are four approaches. You can:

1   take notes in a linear way, in a notebook
2   take notes on index cards, one for each topic or area
3   use a word-processing program to record your notes
4   take a 'spider diagram' approach in which you place your main topic in the centre of the page and work outwards, making connections and adding ideas and information.

➤   Discuss with another student. What are the advantages and disadvantages of each note-taking approach? Which do you personally prefer, and why?
➤   Never forget to include the bibliographic details for any note you make.

Strategy for Success #16:
Take effective notes

Effective notes are those that you can make use of at a later stage. They can act as reminders to you of the key points to include in your own writing, and can help you to learn.

▶ FOCUS F: APPLYING TO YOUR OWN SUBJECT

F.1 Locating subject-related articles

➤   Using the internet or a library, find a short article (in a newsletter or similar source, if you can) that you would like to read, or that describes your subject, part of your subject, or an area that is closely related to it.
➤   Read your article and answer the following questions about it:

1   How helpful did you find the headings when selecting the article?
2   What other aspects of the article helped you to identify it as being of potential interest?
3   How easy or difficult was it to read?
4   Would you recommend the article to another student in your field? Why/why not?

> ➤ Describe your article to another student. Tell him/her why you chose the article and what you liked/did not like about it.
> ➤ If you found the article useful, add the bibliographic information to your annotated bibliography. Include a comment that explains why the article is useful.

F.2 Applying word analysis to a subject-related article

> ➤ Find five unknown words in your article that lend themselves to the 'word analysis' approach. Share your ideas with another student and then check your work in an English–English dictionary. Were you right?

F.3 Finding and recording new subject-related words

> ➤ Highlight 10 unknown words in your article, and, using an English–English dictionary to help you, add them to your personal record.

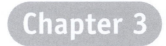

Chapter 3

Entering Higher Education

In this chapter, you can read a **discussion paper**. The paper is about the experience of entering higher education as a first-year student.

You can develop your skills in these areas:

Focus A: Reading

A.1   Looking ahead
A.2   Understanding gist
A.3   Understanding and responding

Focus B: Learning language

B.1   Discourse markers
B.2   Academic vocabulary: related words

Focus C: Writing

C.1   Using discourse markers
C.2   Writing introductions

Focus D: Researching

D.1   Understanding the purpose of abstracts
D.2   Identifying sources of information

Focus E: Studying

E.1   Expectations and norms of behaviour in higher education institutions
E.2   Recording related words

Focus F: Applying to your own subject

F.1   Identifying various sources of subject-related information
F.2   Locating and reading abstracts and introductions
F.3   Recording related words in subject-related articles

FOCUS A: READING

A.1 Looking ahead

The text for this chapter is a **discussion paper** entitled 'Addressing the issues of social and academic integration for first-year students', by Professor Sharon Beder. The paper was written for the Faculty of Arts at the University of Wollongong in New South Wales, Australia.

> Discuss these questions before you read Article 3:

1 A number of **keywords** are provided at the start of Professor Beder's article, as follows:

Keywords: First-year experience, freshman, transition, school to university, identity, drop-out rates, retention, social integration, mentoring, peer tutoring, learning skills, generic skills, curriculum, Orientation Course, Faculty of Arts (Beder, 1997).

What is the purpose of including such keywords at the beginning of a text?

2 Use your English–English dictionary to find the meaning of any words you do not know in the list above. What do they tell you about the text?

3 What do you understand by the phrase 'social and academic integration', and why do you think this might be important for first-year students?

4 Discuss your own experience of being a new student with another student. What have you found easy about the process? What have you found difficult?

---

discussion paper (noun phrase) [C] 'A discussion paper may originate from various sources, including commissions/committees and staff, and is produced for the purpose of providing balanced information on a particular topic without espousing a particular [...] position.' American Academy of Family Physicians, Policy and Advocacy (2007)

---

keyword *n.* [C]
A word that you type into the computer so that it will search for that word on the internet. *You can find the site by entering the keyword 'quark'.*

Strategy for Success #17:
Make use of keywords

Use the keywords that are sometimes provided at the beginning of articles to help you to decide how useful it is likely to be.

'Article 3 is long, but don't be discouraged – it's very readable.' Moutaz Bassam Falih Saleh

(first-year student)

➤ Article 3 may be longer than you are used to reading – it has 3890 words. Do you think longer articles require a different reading approach to shorter ones? Discuss with another student.

➤ Read and annotate Article 3.

Strategy for Success #18:
Do not be deterred by long articles

Consider scanning long articles rather than not reading them at all.

► ARTICLE 3: ADDRESSING THE ISSUES OF SOCIAL AND ACADEMIC INTEGRATION FOR FIRST-YEAR STUDENTS: A DISCUSSION PAPER

Dr Sharon Beder

University of Wollongong

Abstract

First-year students face a number of problems in adjusting to university life. These include developing an appropriate identity and becoming socially integrated into the university, as well as attaining learning and generic skills and qualities such as critical thinking and intellectual rigour. Some of these problems, 5 especially those of social integration, are particularly pertinent to arts students. Some options that faculties might consider to address these problems are covered in this discussion paper. These include the introduction of a one week orientation course for arts students; the development of a first-year introductory subject to enhance academic and social integration, improve retention rates and 10 improve academic success; the implementation of a mentoring or peer tutoring scheme to provide guidance and advice to first-year arts students; or adaptation of the existing first-year arts curriculum.

The first-year experience

The experiences of first-year university students have become a major focus of concern in the US, the UK and Australia. This has been prompted by factors such as increasing student numbers, widening diversity in the backgrounds of students, high student drop-out rates in first year, and the accelerating implementation of teaching technologies and flexible course delivery [1]. In 1995, there were three international conferences held on the topic. In the US, where first-year students of 20 both genders are referred to as 'freshmen', a National Research Centre for the Freshman Year Experience has been set up at the University of South Carolina [2] and *The Journal of The Freshman Year Experience* was established in 1989 [3].

In 1994, the Committee for Advancement of University Teaching (CAUT) commissioned a study by the Centre for the Study of Higher Education into the first-year 25 experience in Australia, mainly because of concerns about 'the rapid growth of student participation levels in universities' and the diversity of the first-year student population that resulted. It sought to identify 'ways in which the first-year teaching and learning environment for on-campus students could be enhanced [4].' Authors Craig McInnis and Richard James with Carmel McNaught argued: 30

It is in the first year that students are most likely to form lasting outlooks, values and patterns of behaviour with respect to higher education and lifelong learning. Alternatively,

they may conclude that university is not for them. The amount of time and energy
invested by both students and universities in this formative period is likely to increase in
35   the more competitive market environment that has emerged since the higher education
reforms of the 1980s. Universities will be concerned to protect their investment in the
students selected, and students will be more selective and demanding of quality in their
initial undergraduate years. In this respect, the first year is becoming pivotal for the
major stake holders. [...]

40   Their study identified a number of issues for first-year students. Another international study by Caroline Baillie of Imperial College, London, of first-year
experiences in engineering education identified similar issues [5]. Some of these
issues are especially relevant to Arts students and these are outlined below.

Social Integration

45 The first year is important in the social integration of a person into the academic and
social fabric of the university and in the adoption of the role of university student [6].
Social integration is more than a simple matter of the student having social interactions. It requires students to see themselves as a 'competent member of an academic
or social community' within the university, such as the Faculty of Arts, and may be
50 aided by 'rites of passage' whereby students move from membership of one community to another; from school, childrearing or work, for example, to university [7].
   The process of integration is an interactive process in which the student takes
an active part. The CAUT study identified three categories that affect this social
integration:

55 1   the students' 'background characteristics and experiences' which influence their
     expectations of, perceptions of, and behavioural responses to university
  2   'contextual factors' such as accommodation and financial resources
  3   a range of factors for which the university is responsible. These include curricu-
     lum and timetable issues and the teaching/learning environment [8].

60 For students to be fully integrated and involved in university life they need to develop
a sense of belonging and an appropriate identity as a university student. In a 1982
study of Australian university students, Clive Williams developed an 'Institutional
Belongingness Scale' and argued that students who achieved low scores in his survey
on this scale 'can be said to feel identified with university as an institution and to have
65 made a comfortable entry to life there [9].' However, many students do not manage
the transition to this new identity with 3–7% of students 'seriously alienated from the
university [10].'
   The 1994 CAUT survey found that 'students who had a higher academic orientation, and stronger student identity, were more satisfied with their course ...
70 happier with the teaching [11].' Students who have a stronger academic orientation,
that is, those who are 'in tune with the cultivating climate that traditionally charac-
terizes higher education' tend to perform better academically [12].

Before coming to university, most students, school leavers and those of mature age have begun to form their new identity because of the commitment and preparation required to decide to go to university. Nevertheless, the university experience requires 75 personal changes that many students are unprepared for [13]. There is often a gap between expectations of university and the reality of the experience [14]. This was recognised by surveyed academics who claimed that 'a large body of students are proceeding to university without a clear understanding of tertiary culture [15].'

Forming a student identity is closely related to feeling connected to and inte- 80 grated with the university. However, the proportion of students who manage to attain this sense of identity is likely to fall with an increase in flexible delivery and in the numbers of students who have to spend large amounts of time off campus so as to earn an income, even when studying full-time [16]. To some extent, orientation week is aimed at enhancing social integration. However, McInnes and James 'sus- 85 pect that many students, because of age, social context, cultural background or perhaps personality characteristics, are not interested [17].'

The problem of identity is a particularly vexing one in Arts faculties, where a common vocational destiny and core curriculum is missing. Williams' study of 19 universities found that Arts faculties tended to score badly on his Institutional 90 Belongingness Scale compared with other faculties [18]. The same was true for his 'Social Involvement Scale' and his 'Alienation Scale [19].' The study also found higher rates of discontinuation in generalist faculties such as Arts than in vocationally oriented courses such as medicine and engineering [20].

[...]   95

Vocational goals do not provide Arts students with a sense of belonging either, and indeed first-year Arts students often put educational goals ahead of vocational goals [21]. This was evident from the CAUT survey which found 'a reasonable level of commitment among first-year students [generally] towards the university as a place of learning for its own sake, and for personal growth balanced against vocational goals.' 100 This commitment could be reinforced with an understanding of the role, place and importance of Arts in society and by facilitating student identification with it.

Drop-out Rates

Falling retention rates have been a major incentive for the study of first-year students and ways to help them in the USA and Britain. The 1994 study of first- 105 year Australian students found that 'over a third had given serious consideration to deferring in the first six months of their courses [22].'

An early Australian study found that successful students, those who pass most of their first-year courses, had clearer objectives than those who drop out [23]. This was confirmed by the 1994 CAUT study which found that although 74% of stu- 110 dents said they were clear about why they were at university, those who said they were getting marks over 70% on average also tended to be those who were clearer about their purpose at university.

It has been argued that students are more likely to drop out if they are not suffi-
115 ciently integrated, that is if they do not 'establish sufficient ties' with the university
or if their values are incompatible with those of the university [24]. An early study
found that students were more likely to stay if they had formed some sort of relationship with a lecturer or involvement in campus activity [25]. Drop-out rates are
also associated with the extent to which students identify with their area of study.
120 North Carolina State University has found that most students dropping out of university were coping with the academic work but 'they hadn't anchored themselves
to the institution' according to the dean of undergraduate studies. They therefore
introduced a programme for first-year students that aimed to give students a sense
of identity and belonging [26].

125 ## Attainment of Learning Skills

About 45% of students in the CAUT survey found that 'the standard of work expected
at university was much higher than they expected' and most found university to be
more demanding than school. Only about a third thought that their schooling had
given them 'a very good preparation' for their university study. The required self-
130 motivation and personal responsibility for learning was the most cited difference
between school and university. Whilst students preferred this situation, the transition took some adjustment [27].

Almost half the students were unsure about 'what was required of them, or of the
direction they should take' in their university courses [28]. Their insecurity was exacer-
135 bated by initial confusion at the start of the year about timetables, expectations, how
they compared with fellow students, and university standards. Almost a third of
students also had difficulty adjusting to the style of teaching at university [29]. 'Many
adjustment problems simply amount to basic misconceptions that could be remedied
by better communication from universities and departments [30].'
140 First-year mature age students at Flinders University identified the following
problems:

- Feeling overwhelmed by one's own ignorance, lack of background knowledge,
  feelings of inadequacy, doubts about one's intellectual capacity.
- Difficulties in understanding what staff require of students – what is the purpose
145 of written assignments, tutorials? What are staff looking for in grading me?
- Inadequate or highly critical feedback from staff.
- Inability to use the library effectively.
- Feeling overwhelmed by the amount of reading and complexity of reading
  material.
150 - Little direction or help by staff on how to study.
- Feeling unable to approach staff.
- Having no idea how to tackle a long essay – choosing, researching, planning,
  organizing/selecting material, developing argument, writing, referencing … [31]

The sorts of study skills that students need to gain include problem-solving, 'time management, learning how to learn, independent learning, motivation, responsibility [32].' Most lecturers would also agree that 'student involvement in the social environment of the classroom is an important factor in the quality of the teaching–learning experience [33].' Not only do lecturers find students who do not participate a problem but students themselves can be quite anxious about that participation.   155

Many universities have preparatory programmes and special admission schemes that endeavour to give students learning skills, but they are designed for people who would not normally meet their admission requirements so as to increase access to and equity in higher education rather than for the first-year student [34]. Additionally, some universities provide some form of study skills assistance to students.   160

In general, only a small proportion of students at universities avail themselves of such services. The 1994 CAUT study found that 72.6% of students never used study skills support services and about 8% were not even aware of them [35]. There has been a trend in universities towards such services being offered within courses as faculties take on responsibility for student academic success, and there have been efforts for such support units 'to get more closely involved in the academic teaching programme during sizeable components of the first-year course [36].' The ability for them to do this depends on funding and staffing resources.   165   170

Caroline Baillie, in her study of engineering students, noted that when left to themselves, students often learn study skills that enable them to get by rather than 'to approach their studies in a deeper manner throughout their degree without getting into bad habits or survival strategies [37].' A deep approach has been defined by the Centre for the Study of Higher Education: 175

> A 'deep' approach involves the active search for meaning, leading to an outcome of a more complete understanding, while a 'surface' approach involves learning by rote and relies on memorizing [38].   180

[…]

The 1994 CAUT study of first-year Australian students in various faculties also found that whilst over 80% of students want to get good grades, over half (53%) 'said they only studied the minimum of what was actually required by their teachers [39].' Three quarters of academics interviewed in the same study agreed that 'most students only study those things that are essential to complete the course [40].'   185

Most university students do not start off with such an approach: First-year university students' orientations towards learning are in a formative stage and inextricably linked to the pursuit of identity and self-efficacy developed in the peer group context [41]. Students can learn bad habits and approaches from other students, especially in a homogenous, self-reinforcing setting. On the other hand, social involvement with other students doing the same classes can be helpful for students. However, about a third, according to the CAUT study, do not work with or consult other students when they have problems. Those that do tend to be the middle achievers, rather than the high achievers or the low achievers. Low achievers   190   195 tended not to work with other students, as well as to have less social involvement with other students [42].

The authors of the CAUT study recommend:

200   Giving attention to the social climate of learning means actively structuring opportunities for students to communicate with one another – and with their teachers – about their academic work outside the classroom. Small, vocationally oriented courses have generally worked hard and successfully at this: the challenge for large generalist courses is to take on board the importance of developing a life outside the classroom that supports and reinforces academic goals [43].

205   ## Attainment of Generic Skills

Generic skills, attributes and values were defined by the Higher Education Council (HEC) in 1992 as:

210   skills, personal attributes and values which should be acquired by all graduates regardless of their discipline or field of study. In other words, they should represent the central achievements of higher education as a process … such qualities as critical thinking, intellectual curiosity, problem-solving, logical and independent thought, effective communication and related skills in identifying, accessing and managing information; personal attributes such as intellectual rigour, creativity and imagination; and values such as ethical practice, integrity and tolerance [44].

215   […]

According to the CAUT study:

participation in higher education reaches out into communities where relatively few have been to university … for this substantial group of students, learning in social isolation denies them opportunities to develop important generic skills, such as leadership and the
220   ability to work in teams, currently valued by employers and society [45].

A related area is that of creating lifelong learners. In a report to the National Board of Employment, Education and Training, QUT academics Philip Candy, Gay Crebert and Jane O'Leary stressed the key role of higher education in generating lifelong learners. In addition to information literacy, a lifelong learner, they argued, has an inquiring mind, a sense of personal agency, a repertoire of learning skills and 'helicopter vision',
225   which they defined as incorporating 'a sense of interconnectedness of fields,' a broad vision as well as an awareness of how knowledge is created and its limitations [46].

Options Available to the Faculty of Arts

Universities have responded to the problems associated with first year in various ways.
230   Often, particular groups of students are targeted. Sometimes the aim is 'compensatory',

that is, to make up for a lack of learning skills and preparation in some students, to bring them up to the level of the average school leaver. Some university faculties provide 'foundational' programmes that aim to give students a general background in the field of endeavour before they choose their specific specialization and get started in higher education. For example, faculties such as engineering often have a common first year before students are separated into particular branches of engineering. Some universities also offer transition programmes for students coming from school to university, sometimes during the summer, that 'aim to promote integration into and affiliation with the university [47].' The options presented below are ones that could enhance the experience of all first-year students, facilitating social and academic integration and developing their academic and generic skills.

Short Orientation Course

Introductory courses or orientation courses of about a week are particularly common in the USA. The aim of such courses includes 'building "studenting" skills, instilling a sense of membership in the academic community and generating enthusiasm' for fields of study, as well as fostering good relationships between academics and students [48]. For example, Gallaudet University runs a compulsory week-long residential orientation week, during which students are put in groups, take placement tests, select their courses for the following year, attend workshops and 'fun' events and are familiarized with the university services and regional surroundings [49].

An Introductory Subject

Introductory one-session courses with credit points awarded are particularly popular in the USA. Two-thirds of US colleges have such courses, which seek to enhance academic and social integration, improve retention rates and improve academic success [50]. Additionally, such courses may attempt to get students 'to adopt new intellectual values and interests' that ensure deeper learning [51]. They endeavour to counter isolation through the development of a sense of community among first-year students [52], 'a sense of competence and social belonging [53]' and ideally through fostering 'a community of learners [54].'

Introductory courses can be voluntary or compulsory, although they are generally compulsory in engineering faculties. Some introductory subjects target students 'at risk' of academic failure and others are more general. General courses have the added advantage of being able to identify students at risk who do not fall into the group normally targeted by preparatory programmes. One example of a more general course is the subject University 101 at the University of South Carolina. This is a three-credit-hour course which is taken by 70% of first-year students at the university. Classes are small (20–25) and taught by academics who have been to a special workshop designed for the purpose. They are aided by Peer Leaders and/or Graduate

270   Student Leaders who also undergo special training. Its goals are as follows [55]:

* To promote for first-year students a positive adjustment and assimilation into the university.
* To help students learn to balance their freedom with a sense of responsibility as part of the process of enhancing self-knowledge and self-confidence.
275 * To help students learn and develop a set of adaptive study, coping, critical thinking, logical problem-solving, and survival skills.
* To help students make friends and develop a support group.
* To improve student attitudes towards the teaching/learning process and towards faculty who are responsible for providing this process.

280   [...]

Evaluations of this and other freshman courses in the USA have found that they are indeed successful in raising retention rates, grades and graduate rates of those that take them, particularly for students thought to be 'at risk' [56].

The University of Kansas runs a voluntary live-in Freshman Summer Institute
285   aimed at all undergraduate students. It is worth 5 credit points and takes four weeks over the summer break. [...] The orientation seminar description reads:

> This course will provide an introduction to the University community and the value and role of higher education in our society, strategies for successful transition to and partici-
> pation in that community, exploration of the University commitment to diversity and
290   multiculturalism, and information about University resources and procedures [57].

Mentoring and Peer Tutoring

Some universities have systems of mentors and tutors that involve academic staff or students in helping the students to be less socially isolated and to offer guidance and advice. This may involve an informal relationship where the student is free to drop in and chat
295   with the mentor/tutor or may involve a more formal relationship where small group meetings are involved [58]. For example, Georgia Southern University guarantees that students 'will develop a relationship with at least one person (a faculty, staff, or upperclass student mentor) to whom they can turn for information, guidance and support [59].' At the University of Colorado, Boulder, academics and administrators telephone
300   new students a few weeks after the start of class 'to see how they are adjusting [60]'.

Some universities limit such mentoring to disadvantaged students. John Hopkins University, Office of Multicultural Student Affairs, runs a Mentoring Assistance Peer (MAP) Program in which senior students guide incoming students (about five each) from minority groups through their first year.

305   Your peer will help you learn the JHU campus and discover its many resources. You will
> be encouraged to keep up with your studies and to complement your academic experi-
> ence by getting involved in co-curricular activities ... Beyond that, your peer will be a
> friend who will listen to your problems in a non-judgemental way and provide invaluable
> support and advice [61].

[...] Northern Illinois University hires Student Orientation Leaders who are   310
given training in public speaking, communication and leadership skills, receive free
room and board, including during the summer, and are paid $US 1720 [62]. North
Carolina State University spent $US 200,000 in 1995 on paying counsellors for
first-year students and they expect this to grow to $1 million when their First Year
College programme is fully operational. The university believes that this expendi-   315
ture will 'pay off for the university' in higher retention rates [63].

Flinders University established a 'peer group support system' for first-year
mature-age students in 1986. The idea was that the students would divide themselves into groups which would meet once a week [64]. The group leaders were
volunteer senior students, postgraduates, honours and third-year undergraduates,   320
who were given no training but were paid once funding became available. They saw
their role as keeping the group focused, helping them get the information they
wanted, making sure everyone participated, helping with basic learning skills, critical thinking, understanding basic jargon, time management, encouraging them,
sharing study strategies, and helping them get on top of their anxieties [65].   325

Student surveys found that students felt these peer support groups differed from
tutorials in that they were non-threatening and relaxed, assumed no pre-existing
knowledge, and offered encouragement and reassurance that other students suffered similar anxieties and uncertainties. This helped them to feel less isolated. They
were able to feel that they belonged to the group and therefore were part of the uni-   330
versity. The groups also offered an opportunity to acquire study skills that were
usually assumed in tutorials, in a cooperative, non-competitive atmosphere [66].

Peer tutoring is sometimes used in conjunction with introductory first-year
courses. However, at least one study of a first-year freshman course showed no difference in student evaluations, whether or not undergraduate teaching assistants   335
were used [67]. This indicates that peer tutoring and first-year introductory courses
are alternative ways of dealing with first-year problems.

Entire Curriculum Change

One or two universities have overhauled the whole first year of particular degrees to
address the problems associated with first-year students. Some engineering schools   340
in the USA have done this in an effort to integrate 'learning activities from several
connected disciplines [68].' Mechanical Engineering at UTS has also completely
rethought their first-year offerings to encourage a more problem-based approach
[69]. This option requires a strong commitment from the whole faculty, careful
thought in development, and resources and educational support to achieve [70].   345

Recommendation

That the Faculties of Arts examine the options available for enhancing the first
year experience of Arts students, in particular, to aid their social and academic

350 integration and the development of the generic skills identified by the Higher Education Council.

References

1 C. McInnis and R. James with C. McNaught, *First Year on Campus: Diversity in the Initial Experiences of Australian Undergraduates*, Centre for the Study of Higher Education, University of Melbourne, September 1995, 1.1.

2 B. Gose, 'A New Approach to Ease the Way for Freshmen', *The Chronicle of Higher Education*, 8 Sept 1995, pp. A57–8.

3 *The Journal of the Freshman Year Experience* 1(1), 1989.

4 McInnis and James, op.cit., 1.1.

5 C. Baillie, 'First Year Experiences in Engineering Education – A Comparative Study', paper presented at Teaching Science for Technology at Tertiary Level Conference, Stockholm, 1997.

6 Anon., 'Philosophical Basis for the First Year Experience', Georgia Southern University, undated.

7 N. Christie and S. Dinham, 'Institutional and External Influences on Social Integration in the Freshman Year', *Journal of Higher Education* 62 (4), 1991, p. 413.

8 McInnis and James, op.cit., 2.1.

9 C. Williams, with T. Pepe, *The Early Experiences of Students on Australian University Campuses*, University of Sydney, 1982, p. 63.

10 McInnis and James, op.cit., 5.1.

11 Ibid., 5.10.

12 Ibid., 5.2.

13 Ibid., 4.0.

14 Ibid., 1.1.

15 Ibid., 4.0.

16 Ibid., 10.1.

17 Ibid., 5.2.

18 Williams, op.cit., pp. 63–4.

19 Ibid., pp. 67–68.

20 Ibid., p. 118.

21 McInnis and James, op.cit., 4.1.

22 Ibid., 1.1.

23 Williams, op.cit., p. 70.

24 Christie and Dinham, op.cit., pp. 412, 429.

25 Cited in E. Ness, F. Rhodes and G. Rhodes, 'University Studies: The Genesis of an Orientation Class', *NASPA Journal* 26(3), p. 202.

26 Gose, op.cit., p. A57.

27 McInnis and James, op.cit., 4.3.

28 Ibid., 4.3.

29 Ibid., 4.4.

30 Ibid., 4.6.

31 M. Griffiths, 'Peer Group Support: A report upon a pilot peer group support system for first year university students', report commissioned by the Flinders University Equity Program, 1986, pp. 20–21.

32 Baillie, op.cit.

33 McInnis and James, op.cit., 5.6.

34 D. M. Cobbin and J. Paul Gostelow, *1994 National Register of Higher Education Preparatory Programs and Special Admission Schemes*, AGPS, Canberra, 1993.

35 McInnis and James, op.cit., 10.3.

36 Ibid., 10.3.

37 Baillie, op.cit.

38 P. Candy, G. Crebert and J. O'Leary, *Developing Lifelong Learners through Undergraduate Education*, National Board of Employment, Education and Training, AGPS, Canberra, 1994, p. 99.

39 McInnis and James, op.cit., 1.1.

40 Ibid., 1.1.

41 Ibid., 10.5.

42 Ibid., 5.6.

43 Ibid., 10.5.

44 Quoted in J. Clanchy and B. Ballard, 'Generic Skills in the Context of Higher Education', *Higher Education Research and Development* 14 (2), 1995, pp. 155, 157.

45 McInnis and James, op.cit., 10.1.

46 Candy et al., op.cit., p. 43.

47 Ibid., 10.2.

48 Baillie, op.cit.

49 Gallaudet University, World Wide Web home page, 1997.

50 Gose, op.cit., p. A57.

51 Anon., op.cit.

52 Seton Hall University, World Wide Web home page, 1997.

53 S. Robbins and L. Smith, 'Enhancement programs for entering university majority and minority freshmen', *Journal of Counselling and Development* 71(5), pp. 510.

54 General Studies Office, Montana State University, World Wide Web, 1995.

55 University of South Carolina, 'The Freshman Year Experience: University 101', World Wide Web, 1996, web.csd.sc.edu/fye/infopeic.html

56 Ibid., A. L. Cone, 'Sophomore academic retention associate with a freshman study skills and college adjustment course', *Psychological Reports* 69(1), 1991, pp. 312–314. Robbins and Smith, op.cit., pp. 510–514.

57 Freshman Summer Institute, University of Kansas, World Wide Web home page, 1996.

58 Baillie, op.cit.

59 Anon., op.cit.

60 Gose, op.cit., p. A57.

61 *John Hopkins University*, Office of Multicultural Student Affairs, World Wide Web home page, 1997.

62 Office of Orientation and Campus Information, Northern Illinois University, World Wide Web home page, 1997.

63 Gose, op.cit., p. A57.

64 Griffiths, op.cit., 1986.

65 Ibid., pp. 37–40.

66 Ibid., pp. 28–31.

67 Robbins and Smith, op.cit., pp. 510–514.

68 B. Olds and R. Miller, 'Developing Meaningful Freshman Programs in Engineering Education', workshop presented at IEEE 1993 Frontiers in Education Conference, IEEE, 1994, p. 24.

69 S. Johnston and H. McGregor, 'Practice-Based Engineering Education at UTS', paper presented at Teaching Technology to Tertiary Students Conference, Stockholm, 1997.

70 Baillie, op.cit.

A.2 Understanding gist

> **gist** *n.*
> The main idea and meaning of what someone has said or written. *Don't worry about all the details as long as you get the gist.*

> ➤ Before you read this text, you were asked to study the keywords that were provided at the beginning. How did these help you to understand the text?

> ➤ Studying keywords provided at the start of a text like this one is a good way to help you understand the gist of a text. Below, you will find a list of other ways to help you 'get the gist' of a text. Choose one, and apply it to any other article that you wish in this book. Then share your understanding of the **gist** of your article with another student.

- skimming the headings and sub-headings
- reading the abstract
- reading the introduction and the conclusion
- skimming the article and reading a few phrases that catch your eye
- reading the first and last lines of paragraphs.

➤ Reflect upon the technique you used to 'get the gist' of the article you selected. Discuss. How successful was it? Would you use it again? Why (not)?

➤ Before you read Article 3, you were also asked to answer this question:

What do you understand by 'social and academic integration', and why do you think this might be important for students in their first year of higher education?

How has 'getting the gist' of the text helped you to expand your ideas on this subject? Describe what you understood to another student, and listen to another student's description. As you share your ideas, try to relate them to your own experiences.

Strategy for Success #19:
Quickly reject unsuitable articles

Skim an article for its gist and use the information to help you to decide if the article is useful for your purposes. This can save you a great deal of time, as you won't waste time reading in detail articles that are not helpful.

A.3 Understanding and responding

➤ Read Article 3 again and, working with another student, choose some of the following questions to answer. [ANSWERS] Make a note of your answers in your portfolio.

1   In the abstract, Professor Beder mentions some problems that first-year students face, and four solutions. What are they? Do any of the solutions suggested apply to your context? If not, how are first-year students in your context provided with support?

2   What is meant by the phrase 'this formative period' (line 34)? Can you think of some ways in which your current experience may be 'formative'?

3   The author refers to a 'more competitive market environment' (line 35). Has your own context become more competitive? Can you give some examples?

4   'Social integration [...] requires students to see themselves as a 'competent member of an academic or social community' within the university' (lines 47–49). What things happen to you in the course of your studies that help you to see yourself as 'competent'? Give a few examples.

5   In line 50–51, a number of life transitions are mentioned. Can you think of further examples?

6   In lines 52–53, 'the process of integration' is described as 'an interactive process in which the student takes an active part'. In what ways would you say your current experience contributes towards integration and is (inter)active?

7   What word in the same paragraph has the opposite meaning to 'integrated' (line 60)?

8   'There is often a gap between expectations of university and the reality of the experience' (lines 76–77). Is this your experience? Give some examples to support your answer.

9   What do you understand by the phrase 'flexible delivery' (line 82)? Are you studying in 'flexible delivery' mode? Give some examples from your current experience to show that you are or are not studying in flexible delivery mode.

10   Did you attend an 'orientation week' (lines 84–85) or something similar? If so, how did it help you to orientate yourself towards higher education?

11   What do you understand by the phrase 'vocational destiny' (line 89)? Do you have one?

12   The author refers to the role of schooling in preparing students for higher education (line 129). What did your school do to help you to prepare for higher education?

13   In your experience, how does the 'style of teaching' (line 137) at university differ from that at school? Why do you think some people might have trouble adjusting to the former?

14   Do any of the problems listed in lines 142–153 apply to you? If so, discuss what strategies you can use to help you to address the problems you are experiencing.

15   Lecturers identify 'student involvement in the social environment of the class-room' (lines 156–157) as being an important factor in the quality of your experience. What do you understand by this phrase? How important is such involvement for you personally?

16   'A related area is that of creating lifelong learners' (line 221). What is meant by the phrase 'lifelong learner'? Is this how you see yourself? Why/why not?

17   What do you understand by 'information literacy' (line 224)? How 'information literate' do you consider yourself? Give some examples.

18   What is meant by the phrase 'repertoire of learning skills'? Can you provide some examples from your own 'repertoire'?

19   The word 'generic' is used a number of times in the text. Find any or all of these examples: lines 4, 205, 206, 219, 241, 349. What do you understand by it? How could you use this word in other areas of life?

20   The writer discusses four ways in which tertiary institutions could enhance the experience of all first-year students. These are:

- offering a short orientation course
- creating an introductory course that addresses transition issues
- mentoring and peer tutoring
- changes to the curriculum.

What in your opinion would be the most effective way of improving the transition experience?

▶ FOCUS B: LEARNING LANGUAGE

B.1 Discourse markers

> **discourse** n. [U] *formal*
> The language used in particular types of speech or writing.
> *A study of spoken discourse.*

In written academic English, you will find many examples of words or phrases that enable the writer to develop his or her ideas, or show how they are connected to one another. Such words or phrases are often called '**discourse** markers' because they mark, or signal, the direction that the discourse, or text, is taking. They help you to understand the relationship between parts of the text.

These words or phrases are particularly useful when you are writing about complex ideas. They may be organized into groups according to their function.

Here are some of the most useful functions they perform:

1   Focusing attention on what follows
2   Adding supporting information
3   Providing an example
4   Clarifying
5   Showing that ideas contrast, but do not contradict, each other
6   Showing that ideas contrast each other
7   Showing cause and effect.

➤   Below, you will find seven groups of words or phrases (A–G) that perform functions 1–7 above. If a word or phrase has been used in the text, you will see a line number provided next to it. Read the example or examples in context. Then match the groups of discourse markers A–G to functions 1–7 above   ANSWERS . Note your answers in your portfolio, like this:

Function: ————————————————————

Discourse markers: ————————————————————
—————————————————————————————————————

Group A	Group B
with respect to (line 32) in this respect with regard to (line 38) regarding as for as regards as far as … is concerned	such as (lines 49, 213) for example (lines 51, 235) one example of … is (line 265) namely to illustrate
Group C	**Group D**
as a result so hence thus consequently accordingly therefore (lines 122, 330)	in other words that is (lines 71, 231)
Group E	**Group F**
as well as (lines 4, 227) moreover furthermore besides in addition to (line 224) additionally (lines 163, 256)	on the other hand (line 191) while (line 179) whilst (lines 131, 183) whereas

Group G
however (lines 65, 193) nonetheless nevertheless (line 75)

➢ Check your work with another student. Discuss your reasons for your choice of answer. If you do not have the same answers, ask your tutor. You will return to the lists you have made later.

B.2 Academic vocabulary: related words

A useful skill for expanding your vocabulary is finding related words, and a form for you to use to record related words in your portfolio is provided on p. 74. Many words that occur frequently in academic writing are used in several different forms. Examples of this are the words 'integrated' (lines 3–4), 'assumed' (line 327), and 'evident' (line 98) which may also be found in the following forms:

• integrate	• assume	• evidenced
• integrates	• assumes	• evidential
• integrating	• assuming	• evidence
• integration	• assumption	• evidently
	• assumptions	

➢ What other groups of related words can you think of? Brainstorm this with another student. Make a note of your ideas and share them with another pair of students.

Strategy for Success #20:
Learn related words

When you encounter a word for the first time, learn any related words at the same time. This approach can often help you to learn two or more words for the price of one!

➢ A useful list of 'related words' is freely available on the internet, called the 'Academic Word List'. Type the phrase 'Academic Word List' into your computer's search engine and search till you find a site that mentions Averil Coxhead, the writer and researcher who prepared this list (and, incidentally, the author of the text used in the next chapter of this book). Make sure your site tells you about Averil Coxhead's research (Coxhead, 2000). Read the information available and answer the following questions ⌐ANSWERS¬ (you may need to refer to more than one site to find all the answers):

1 What is the 'Academic Word List'?
2 Where was it developed?
3 Why was it developed?
4 What four groups of words does the list *not* include?
5 How many groups of related words does it include?
6 How many sublists are there?

7 Why is one word in each sublist in italics?

8 Why have some words been placed into sublist 1, while others appear in sublists, 2, 3, 4 and so forth?

9 How did Averil Coxhead identify the words in the 'Academic Word List'?

10 From which disciplines did Averil Coxhead gather her data for the research that led to the identification of the 'Academic Word List'?

11 Name five different kinds of writing that were used as data in the research.

12 How many words did the database for the research include?

13 How will you make use of the 'Academic Word List'? Discuss your ideas.

14 Print out the list of headwords and add it to your portfolio for reference and study.

➤ Work with another student. Take a different section of Article 3 each and find words that you think might be included in the 'Academic Word List'. Note them down in your portfolio. Compare your list with the other student's. Put a question mark against any word that you are not sure would belong to the list. Then check your headword list to confirm that they are considered 'academic'. Were you surprised by any that were excluded? Discuss.

Strategy for Success #21:
Use the internet as a resource

Use the resources available to you on the internet. You can search for anything from 'discourse markers' to 'transition from high school to university'. You can also use an online dictionary and thesaurus.

▶ FOCUS C: WRITING

C.1 Using discourse markers ANSWERS

➤ The sentences below are all taken from the texts used in Chapters 1–3 of this book. Use a suitable word or phrase from the groups of discourse markers on p.67 to complete them. When you have finished, compare your answers to those of another student. There may be more than one possible answer. If you have made different choices, discuss whether both are possible.

1 This book is for students who will be studying or are studying within any discipline (an area or branch of knowledge or teaching, _____ arts or science) or academic subject (_____, one where an emphasis is placed on reading, researching and writing), at college or university.

2 The big difficulty with reading is the amount involved. These classes _____ aim to assist the non-native speaker of English studying in the medium of English at tertiary level to use a wide range of reading strategies in order to receive more benefit from the course.

3   General efficient reading strategies such as scanning to find the book or chapter, skimming to get the gist and careful reading of important passages (Wallace, 2004, pp. 9–38) are necessary, _____ vocabulary building exercises in the student's own area.

4   EAP is thus an important area of ESP, accounting for a large amount of the ESP activity worldwide. Most of the work, _____, takes place, unknown to much of the English language teaching world, in universities.

5   Social integration is more than a simple matter of the student having social interactions. It requires students to see themselves as a 'competent member of an academic or social community' within the university, such as the Faculty of Arts, and may be aided by 'rites of passage' whereby students move from membership of one community to another; from school, child rearing or work, _____, to university.

6   North Carolina State University has found that most students dropping out of university were coping with the academic work but 'they hadn't anchored themselves to the institution' according to the dean of undergraduate studies. They _____ introduced a program for first-year students that aimed to give students a sense of identity and belonging.

7   Students can learn bad habits and approaches from other students, especially in a homogenous, self-reinforcing setting. _____, social involvement with other students doing the same classes can be helpful for students.

8   Before coming to university, most students, school leavers and those of mature age, have begun to form their new identity because of the commitment and preparation required to decide to go to university. _____, the university experience requires personal changes that many students are unprepared for.

9   _____ information literacy, a lifelong learner, they argued, has an inquiring mind, a sense of personal agency, a repertoire of learning skills and 'helicopter vision', which they defined as incorporating 'a sense of interconnectedness of fields,' a broad vision as well as an awareness of how knowledge is created and its limitations.

C.2 Writing introductions

A good introduction to an article performs a number of functions. It should do much of the following:

- Stimulate the reader's interest
- Outline the background to, and context of, the research

- Indicate the purpose and focus of the article
- Indicate assumptions
- Provide a **thesis statement**
- Indicate the overall scope and direction of the paper
- Outline the methods used.

> Note the use of the word 'indicate' above (one of the words in the 'Academic Word List'). What does it mean? Why has it been used here in preference to, say, 'describe'?

> Read the introduction to the article in Chapter 7. Identify which sentence or sentences:

- describe the background to, and context of, the research
- indicate the focus of the article
- provide a thesis statement
- indicate the overall scope and direction of the paper.

Did the introduction successfully stimulate your interest? Share your thoughts with another student.

> When you are writing an introduction, keep in mind these eight key points to include: background, context, direction, method, purpose, focus, scope and thesis.

Make a note of them in your portfolio, but rearrange them into a sensible order for a good introduction.

thesis *n. plural* theses [C] **1** A long piece of writing about a particular subject that you do as part of an advanced university degree such as an MA or a PhD. *Cynthia's still working on her thesis.*
thesis statement AmE In writing, the thesis is the sentence or group of sentences which state what the main idea of an essay is. *a paragraph introducing your thesis statement...*

▷ FOCUS D: RESEARCHING

D.1 Understanding the purpose of abstracts

> A number of the articles in this book provide an **abstract** at the beginning. Read them and skim the article to which the abstract belongs. Then work with another student and discuss the purpose of abstracts. Share your ideas with your tutor and then make a list in your portfolio.

> A good abstract will represent the entire article and indicate its purpose, topic, main sections, and conclusions. Work with another student. Choose one or more of the abstracts in this book. Work together to identify which part or parts of the abstract tell you about its:

abstract *n.* [C] A short written statement containing only the most important ideas in a speech, article, etc.

- purpose
- topic
- main sections
- conclusions.

➤ When writing an article, at which stage should you write the abstract, and why? Discuss with another student and check your ideas with your tutor.

D.2 Identifying sources of information

➤ As a student, you will often need to use various sources of information. Some sources of information are obvious, such as textbooks and journal articles, but there are many others. Brainstorm this topic with other students and make a list. Be as detailed as you can. For example, do not simply write down 'books'. Instead, consider different types of books, such as encyclopaedias, atlases, edited collections of articles, and so forth. Ask your tutor for his or her contributions.

➤ Your institution may provide online access to its library, and it may subscribe to an online library database such as EBSCOhost. Visit your library and find out what is available, and how to use it.

➤ In your discussion above, you will almost certainly have mentioned the internet as a source of information. A useful **portal** is available at bubl.ac.uk/index. html. This is an online catalogue of links to selected resources covering approximately 140 different subjects, from accounting to zoology. Visit it when you can, and look up the resources available for your own subject.

portal *n*. [C]
A website that helps you to find other websites.

▶ FOCUS E: STUDYING

E.1 Expectations and norms of behaviour in higher education institutions

➤ Work with another student. What would you tell a new student about university life to help him or her to prepare for it? Brainstorm points to include. You may like to use these points to write an article for your institution's newsletter.

Strategy for Success #22:
Explore the wide range of resources that are available to you

In your studies, do not limit yourself to books or the internet as sources of information and ideas. Learn about the full range of resources at your disposal and make regular use of them.

E.2 Recording related words

Making a record of related words can help you to expand your vocabulary.

The 'Academic Word List' discussed above provides all forms of words (for example, different forms of verbs such as 'define': 'defines', 'defined' and 'defining'), and this area is certainly worth thinking about when you encounter a new word. However, you can also focus on different parts of speech: in particular, noun, adjective, verb, and adverb.

➤ Here is one way of making such a record. It includes different prefixes, something you may wish to do. Study the examples, which are all taken from sublist 1 of the 'Academic Word List':

Nouns	Verbs	Adjectives	Adverbs
Significance Insignificance	Signify	Significant Insignificant	Significantly Insignificantly
Response Respondent	Respond	Responsive Unresponsive	Responsively
Similarity	–	Similar Dissimilar	Similarly

➤ A blank 'related words record' sheet is provided for you on page 74. Make several copies of this sheet to keep in your portfolio. Add the words below to it. Note that, as in the example above, it is not always possible to find examples for each heading. When you have completed this task, compare your results to those of another student. Use your dictionary and the 'Academic Word List' to help you.

1	analyse	5	evident	9	proceed
2	research	6	define	10	interpret
3	approach	7	establish	11	theory
4	concept	8	identify	12	require

RELATED WORDS RECORD

Page no. ____

Nouns	Verbs	Adjectives	Adverbs

This page may be photocopied for personal use only.

© SAGE Publications Ltd 2009

▌ FOCUS F: APPLYING TO YOUR OWN SUBJECT

F.1 Identifying various sources of subject-related information

➢ Visit bubl.ac.uk/index.html. Tick which of the following you can find for your subject. You may also like to look at the resources available for other subjects. Explore some of the resources.

- A journal
- A database or online library
- A report
- A magazine
- A society, agency, professional organization or association

- A dictionary
- A review
- A guide
- A biography
- A catalogue or index

> 'bubl.ac.uk is like Google, but with an academic filter.'
>
> Saoud Ali Abdulla Fadhel Al Maamari (first-year student)

F.2 Locating and reading abstracts and introductions

➢ Use bubl.ac.uk/index.html to help you to locate two or more journal articles that are related to your subject and that interest you. Read their abstracts and/or introductions and identify as many of the following features as possible:

Abstracts: purpose, topic, main sections, conclusions.

Introductions: background, context, direction, method, purpose, focus, scope, thesis.

➢ Discuss. Why are the articles of interest to you? Discuss with another student. Why did he/she find his/her articles of interest?

F.3 Recording related words in subject-related articles

➢ Make a record of words related to those you have found in your subject-related texts. Use the form on page 74 to help you to record your work.

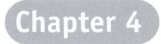

Chapter 4

Reading in Higher Education

In this chapter, you can read a **review of a book** about the reading skills needed to succeed in higher education.

You can develop your skills in these areas:

Focus A: Reading

A.1   Looking ahead
A.2   Understanding and responding
A.3   Reading with a purpose
A.4   Features of informal writing

Focus B: Learning language

B.1   Concrete and abstract meanings
B.2   Collocations

Focus C: Writing

C.1   Paragraphs
C.2   Conclusions

Focus D: Researching

D.1   Identifying genre
D.2   Thinking critically about sources of information

Focus E: Studying

E.1   Reading efficiently and effectively
E.2   Recording collocations

Focus F: Applying to your own subject

F.1   Locating and reading reviews of subject-related books
F.2   Identifying collocations in subject-related articles
F.3   Identifying concrete and abstract language in subject-related articles

FOCUS A: READING

A.1 Looking ahead

Below, you can read a **review** of a book called *Reading Skills for Success: A Guide to Academic Texts*. This book was written in 2004 by Thomas A. Upton, but the review was written in 2005 by Averil Coxhead, who is a lecturer in English for Academic Purposes, in the School of Language Studies at Massey University, Palmerston North, Aotearoa/New Zealand. She is the author of the 'Academic Word List' which you read about in Chapter 3.

> **review** n. [C]
> An article in a newspaper or magazine that gives an opinion about a new play, book, film, etc. *A film review.*

➤ Think about or discuss any or all of the following points before you read the article:

1   Do you like to read book reviews? Why/why not? If you do, what kinds of books do you like to read about?
2   Have you read a review of a book or article recently? If so, how did it help you?
3   What would you expect to learn from reading a book review?
4   Why do you think it might be useful to read a review of an academic text?

➤ Read and take notes on Article 4. Note that the paragraphs have been numbered to help you to complete the tasks below.

▶ ARTICLE 4: READING SKILLS FOR SUCCESS: A GUIDE TO ACADEMIC TEXTS (2004)

by Thomas A. Upton
Reviewer:
Averil Coxhead
Massey University, New Zealand

1   The gap between assisted or scaffolded reading materials for English as a second language (ESL) learners preparing for higher education at university or college and authentic academic textbooks is a particular challenge to teachers and learners alike. Why does this discrepancy exist? There are a number of possible reasons:
5   learners come from a variety of educational backgrounds, speak and read many different languages at different levels, may not have much experience with written academic texts and, while they share a similar goal in terms of matriculation and success at higher learning, they are preparing for study in different subject areas. Add to this the complexity of the task of considering the many aspects of L2 read-
10 ing and readers (Grabe and Stoller, 2002) and for some learners and teachers the gap is practically a chasm.

2   *Reading Skills for Success* by Thomas A. Upton is a textbook that attempts to go some way towards bridging this gap. Upton aims to have the textbook used 'as an adjunct text to assist learners in comprehending the materials they are expected to
15 read in college 'content' classes' (p.iii). The book presupposes that readers and teachers are aware of the current view of reading being 'an interactive and constructive process in which the reader uses personal and cultural knowledge to interpret the information presented in a text in order to 'create' meaning' (p. iv).

3   The book is organized into three distinct parts. Part One contains '*Word-level*
20 *clues to meaning*' including a focus on context clues, a 300-word list extracted from the Academic Word List (Coxhead, 2000), ways to develop awareness of technical terms in text, and to identify continuous ideas through pronoun use. Part Two, 'Understanding expository structures', focuses on connectors, main ideas, enumeration, classification, comparison and contrast, time order, and cause and effect. Part
25 Three is called 'Reading to study' and focuses on reading strategies, SQ3R (S = Survey, Q = Question, R = Read, R = Recite, R = Review) and note-taking when reading using the Cornell method. Each part is introduced by a short overview describing the focus and goals of each chapter.

4   An important innovation in *Reading Skills for Success* is the inclusion of two
30 chapters from published North American textbooks in their original format. The first chapter is on *ecosystems* and is from an environmental science textbook by B. J. Nebel, published in 1998. The second chapter is on *language diffusion* from a textbook on human geography by H. J. de Blij and A. B. Murphy, published in 1999. These chapters are important because they provide authentic academic reading practice in a
35 supportive environment. Learners are asked to examine these chapters using many of

the skills introduced in this book as a step towards dealing with their own academic textbooks.

5   Another feature of the book is the inclusion of short supplements comprising several pages each that follow after the two textbook chapters. The supplements contain extra activities for reading for pleasure, exercises on affixes, the remaining 270 words from the Academic Word List (Coxhead, 2000) and word card practice, as well as additional main ideas and organizational structure practice.

6   Let's now look at the chapters in *Reading Skills for Success* in general. Each chapter begins with a brief explanation of its focus, that is, a particular strategy, text structure or skills. Key terms such as *enumeration, technical terms* and *cause-and-effect relationship* are described in these sections, for example. This introduction is followed by explanation and examples where the writer expands on the main focus of the chapter and provides instances from academic textbooks to exemplify the main points. The explanations on the whole are clearly presented and well written with examples for support. In some instances, the information is put forward in a non-linear way to positive effect, as in Chapter Six, where enumeration and classification are presented and practised.

7   One of the major strengths of this book is the inclusion of excerpts from academic textbooks in each chapter that are drawn on for analyses and examples. Most of these extracts come from a variety of arts and sciences textbooks published recently in North America. They represent reading for academic purposes in disciplines such as Biology, Human Geography, Anthropology, and Environmental Sciences. There are a small number of business-based texts, in Economics and Business Communication. The exercises based on the skills that are highlighted and these textbook snippets are varied in each chapter, ranging from Chapter 2 where learners practise recognizing definitions of technical terms in textbooks, to Chapter 11 where they practise taking notes from a textbook chapter included at the end of the book. The activities and texts appear to be graded for difficulty at times, for example, in Chapter 3 where learners are encouraged to deal with increasingly difficult examples and to process larger chunks of text while identifying continuing ideas in texts (pp. 21–22). In addition, answer keys are provided at the end of the textbook and are easy to use.

8   The final exercise for each chapter is to apply the reading skill or strategy in focus to a wider context – that of the learner themselves in their own academic study. In Chapter 3, for example, learners are asked to scan a chapter of a textbook they are using and find examples of writers' use of pronouns in texts so as to restate ideas in several ways. Upton carefully manages the workload in a chapter to ensure that learners are not overloaded and attempts to ensure that each learning point is carefully practised.

9   This textbook addresses many of the issues related to reading in a second language, such as the need to enlarge one's vocabulary, locate and understand the main idea in a text, develop and practise strategies and gain a wide exposure to print (Grabe and Stoller, 2002). However, I am concerned about the lack of acknowledgement

of what the ESL learner reader brings to this textbook and to L2 reading overall.

80 Grabe and Stoller (2002) describe contextual factors that are important for preparing for L2 teaching. These factors include the knowledge readers bring to bear on texts, their reading ability in their first language, their proficiency and experience in reading in their second language, their background cultural knowledge and L1 influence. An example of Upton's approach is advising learners to focus immediately on content on

85 reading a new text and to first ask the question 'Who or what is this about?' (p. 34). One way to build on this perfectly good question further might be to ask 'What do I want to know? Why am I reading this? What do I know already?' As Alderson (2000: 121) states, 'background knowledge should be recognised as influencing all comprehension.'

90 10   Similarly, the social nature of reading and the importance of interaction do not seem to filter through the Upton text until Chapter 9, where learners are asked to discuss their self-awareness and habits as readers. In the earlier chapters, readers are focused on practising skills and strategies such as word cards as individuals dealing directly with text. Furthermore, there are very few direct links between the chapters

95 in *Reading Skills for Success*. This separation may make it easier for learners and teachers to focus on one particular aspect of reading at a time or for users to dip into the textbook. However, this approach causes some strain as the interactive nature between the different skills in reading is not reinforced. Table 4.1 on relationship connectors (pp. 27–29), for example, is complex and cognitively

100 demanding to work with. The table is difficult to process in a meaningful way in a short amount of time, but would be useful for reference at a later time. Later in the textbook, Upton refers the reader back to Table 4.1 to re-examine this material (p. 52) but this kind of linking is few and far between. Chapter 9 also contains a large table, this time on reading strategies (pp. 66–68). In Chapter 11, the strategy

105 table is referred to again but this is the only time learners revisit this rich resource.

11   Another possibly problematic area is how the Academic Word List (AWL) (Coxhead, 2000) is broken into two separate lists for inclusion into this book. The first 300 words (Sublists 1–5 of the AWL) are presented in Chapter 1 in an alphabetical list (pp. 5–6), while the rest of the arbitrarily divided list is presented in a supplement

110 at the end of the book. The learners are asked to make word cards for any 25 words they do not know from the AWL for studying. Studying from word cards is a well-documented and effective method for learning words (see Nation, 2001). However, in this book the AWL words are presented in a list without the context of the principles of frequency and range that is behind the selection of the words for the list. There is a

115 lack of context surrounding the learning of the words themselves which must beg a number of questions for learners and teachers alike. Why should the learners focus on learning AWL words out of context? Which of the words should learners choose first in the AWL and why? Why combine the ten sublists in the AWL in this way when they were already divided according to frequency in the first place? The original distinc-

120 tion made between the words in the sublists is lost in this textbook.

12   What are the strengths of this book? First of all, the links to the learners' own reading are well managed. For example, in Chapter 2 where the focus is the strategy

of guessing meaning from context, the learner readers are directed to reading a
chapter of their own textbook in order to find ten non-technical words and practise
the strategy with the words they have found.   125

13   Furthermore, I would agree wholeheartedly with Upton when he states that
one major strength of this book is the use of authentic materials. He has been very
successful in bridging between this reading textbook, the reading from other academic textbooks and the learners' own reading. Another helpful innovation is that in
some chapters, learners are encouraged to visualize ideas in texts through developing   130
charts or maps of chapters. This visual interpretation of text allows learners to
process their reading in a different way and it also breaks up the somewhat linear
nature of the book.

14   How useful would this textbook be in learning and teaching contexts outside
the USA? Many of the textbook excerpts used in the book and strategies covered   135
would potentially pertain to many other ESL learners worldwide, even though there
are several times when specialized background knowledge about North America is
needed to unpack examples and explanations. For example, on page 41, the US
government system is used as an example and broken down into the legislative,
executive and judicial branches.   140

15   *Reading Skills for Success* does not attempt to conceal how difficult academic
reading can be and is. Instead, it offers techniques for dealing with academic
reading in bite-sized chunks, supported by well-chosen examples of authentic texts
and links to further reading outside the language classroom. It would serve as a
springboard for teachers looking for ways to bring learners, academic reading, skills   145
and practice together.

References

Alderson, J. C. (2000). *Assessing reading*. Cambridge: Cambridge University Press.
Coxhead, A. (2000). A new academic word list. *TESOL Quarterly*, 34(2): 213–38.
Grabe, W. and Stoller, F. (2002). *Teaching and researching reading*. Harlow:
    Longman.
Nation, I. S. P. (2001). *Learning Vocabulary in another Language*. Cambridge:
    Cambridge University Press.

**Strategy for Success #23:
Be a selective and flexible learner**

Choose questions or activities that you feel will be most helpful to you at any particular point in your learning career. This means that you do not have to work
methodically through this book (or any other) if you do not need or want to.

A.2 Understanding and responding

➤ Read the following questions. Select 10–15 that you would like to answer, and do so, working alone. Make a note of your answers in your portfolio.

1   Skim the paragraphs. At a glance, how does its layout differ from the articles used in previous chapters? Why do you think this might be?
2   Read the review more thoroughly. Did you find it interesting? Would you want to read the book *Reading Skills for Success: A Guide to Academic Texts*? Why/ why not?
3   The author refers to two different types of reading material in paragraph 1. What are they? Which type of material does *Read, Research and Write* use?
4   What do you understand by 'discrepancy' in line 4? Which word in line 1 has a similar meaning? Which word would you expect to see more often in academic writing?
5   What reasons for the discrepancy referred to in line 4 does the author give? Do any of these reasons apply to your class?

> 'I like the "Strategy for Success" boxes.
> They open my mind to important strategies in reading, researching and writing academic articles.'
>
> Yasmine Hedi Guefrachi
> (first-year student)

6   What phrase does the author use in paragraph 2 that suggests she is slightly critical of *Reading Skills for Success: A Guide to Academic Texts*?
7   What does Upton mean by the phrase 'an adjunct text'? Are you using this book as an adjunct text?
8   In paragraph 2, the author identifies an assumption that Upton made when he wrote *Reading Skills for Success: A Guide to Academic Texts*. What is it? What words are used to suggest the assumption?
9   In paragraph 2, reading is described as 'an interactive and constructive process in which the reader uses personal and cultural knowledge to interpret the information presented in a text in order to "create" meaning'. Express the same idea in your own words. Do you agree with this definition? Would you alter it in any way?
10   In paragraph 3, three parts to *Reading Skills for Success: A Guide to Academic Texts* are identified. Part 3 focuses on reading strategies. What five strategies are mentioned here? Are any of them surprising to you?
11   Why does the writer suggest in paragraph 4 that 'the inclusion of two chapters from published North American textbooks in their original format' is important?
12   Is the overall message of the writing in paragraphs 4 and 5 generally positive or negative? Identify features of the writing that support your decision.
13   What is the effect of the phrase beginning paragraph 6, 'Let's now look … '?
14   The description of the book in paragraph 6 is expressed in mostly positive terms. One phrase is used to qualify this positive view. What is it? What is its effect?
15   Upton's book includes texts from subjects such as 'Biology, Human Geography, Anthropology, and Environmental Sciences […] Economics and Business Communication' (lines 57–59). How does that approach differ from the one taken in *Read, Research and Write*?

16   Find four tasks or activities that Upton's book requires readers to do.

17   In paragraph 8, the author observes that 'the final exercise for each chapter is to apply the reading skill or strategy in focus to a wider context – that of the learner themselves in their own academic study.' *Read, Research and Write* takes a similar approach. How does it do this?

18   In paragraph 8, what danger or pitfall does the author note that Upton avoids, and how does he do this?

19   In paragraph 9, the author refers to the need to 'gain a wide exposure to print'. What do you understand by this? Do you do this yourself? How?

20   What word does the author use to introduce a criticism of the book *Reading Skills for Success: A Guide to Academic Texts*? What is the criticism?

21   The author suggests that before reading something you should consider what you know already, your experience, and/or what you can do. Without looking back, can you remember how this was achieved at the start of this chapter? Is this approach useful?

22   Paragraph 10 contains two criticisms of *Reading Skills for Success: A Guide to Academic Texts*. Summarize them.

23   What does the author mean by the phrase 'the table is difficult to process…' (line 100)?

24   Paragraph 11 outlines one criticism. Describe it in your own words.

25   In paragraphs 12 and 13, the author identifies three positive features of *Reading Skills for Success: A Guide to Academic Texts*. Summarize them.

26   What do you understand by the phrase 'to visualize ideas' (line 130)? Would you find this strategy helpful?

27   What criticism of *Reading Skills for Success: A Guide to Academic Texts* is made in paragraph 14? Would this be a problem for you in your context?

28   What do you understand by the phrase 'bite-sized chunks' (line 143)? Is this phrase more likely to be described as 'academic' or 'informal' English?

29   Does the author finish her review on a positive or negative note? Justify your choice.

30   Is this review broadly positive or broadly negative? Justify your decision. Would you be happy if you were the author of *Reading Skills for Success: A Guide to Academic Texts*? Why/why not?

➢   Work with another student. Exchange your answers to the questions you each selected. Make notes from the other student's answers.

Strategy for Success #24:
Identify assumptions

Always consider what assumptions the author may be making. Assumptions may be about you, the audience, or about his or her topic.

A.3 Reading with a purpose

Knowing exactly why you are reading something can help you to read more efficiently.

> **evaluation** *n.* [C, U]
> A judgement about how good, useful or successful something is. *We need to carry out a proper evaluation of the new system.*

➢ Think about all of the reading you do in the course of a normal week. Prepare a table with two columns. On the left, note down the material you read. On the right, make a note of why you read each one. It is quite possible that you will find that you read something for more than one purpose. Here are two examples that I would include:

Reading material	Purpose
Newspaper	Information; pleasure; to pass the time; as a source of potential class material
Advertising leaflet	Information; **evaluation**

➢ Compare your list with that of another student. In each case you have noted, discuss how your purpose might influence how you read. Would you, for example, want to skim it (to get the gist) or scan it (to locate specific information)?

➢ Consider Article 4 above. What do you think were the author's (Averil Coxhead's) purposes when she read Upton's *Reading Skills for Success: A Guide to Academic Texts*? How do you think these purposes influenced her approach to the book? How would you approach such a task?

A.4 Features of informal writing

> **informal** *n.* [adj.]
> **1** Relaxed and friendly without being restricted by rules of correct behaviour. *The atmosphere at work is fairly informal.*
> **2** An informal style of writing or speaking is suitable for ordinary conversations or letters to friends.

Some features of Article 4 add a degree of informality to the writing, and some of the questions above point to this informality. Take a look again, for example, at Questions 4, 13 and 28.

➢ Read the article again and highlight features that you would consider examples of **informal** language, including those above. Then discuss with your group why the author does this, and what the overall effect is.

➢ Use your English–English dictionary and look up some of the words and phrases that you think may be considered informal. Does your dictionary indicate that the words are informal? If so, how does it do this?

▶ FOCUS B: LEARNING LANGUAGE

B.1 Concrete and abstract meanings

You may find that sometimes you know the meaning of a word in one context, but that when you find it being used in academic writing, it seems to have a slightly different meaning. However, thinking about the meaning of the word in other contexts can help you to understand it in the current context in which you find it. This is because sometimes writers use a word from one context with the intention that some of the original meaning is transferred to the new context.

Strategy for Success #25:
Use the meaning of a word in one
context to help you to understand it in another context

If you are familiar with a word in one context, this can sometimes help you to understand it in another context. Think in particular about possible 'concrete' meanings and 'abstract' meanings.

➢ Study these examples:

A gap = a space between two objects or two parts of an object, especially because something is missing
A gap (line 1) = a big difference between two situations, amounts, groups of people, etc.
Focus = the clearness of the picture seen through an instrument such as a camera
A focus (line 20) = the thing, person, situation, etc. that people pay special attention to.

In each example above, the meaning of the word in one situation can help you to understand what it means in the new situation.

A 'gap' has the idea of space, or separation; while 'gap' as it is used in Article 4 has the idea of difference. If you know the first meaning (as in, for example, a 'gap between her teeth'), it can help you to understand the other meaning – and vice versa.

> **concrete** *adj.*
> Definite and specific. *The lack of any concrete evidence.*

> **abstract** *adj.*
> Existing only as an idea or quality rather than as something real that you can see or touch. *The abstract nature of beauty.*

'Focus' is used in photography to refer to clearness of a picture; while 'focus' as it is used in Article 4 means an object of particular attention. If you are a photographer, you may know the word as it is used in that field, and this can help you to understand what it means in academic English.

It is sometimes the case that one meaning is **concrete**, while the other meaning is **abstract**. In the two examples above, which meanings are concrete?

➤ Study these further examples from Article 4. In each case, identify a concrete meaning and an abstract meaning, and decide which meaning the author of Article 4 intended.

Scaffolded (line 1)
Goal (line 7)
Chasm (line 11)
Bridging (lines 13 and 128)
Step (line 36)
Key (lines 45 and 66)
Overloaded (line 73)

Build (line 86)
Filter (line 91)
Dip (line 96)
Unpack (line 138)
Bite-sized (line 143)
Springboard (line 145)

➤ Can you think of any other words that you have studied recently that have concrete and abstract meanings?

B.2 Collocations

'Students with good ideas often lose marks because they don't know the four or five most important collocations of a key word that is central to what they are writing about.' (Hill, 1999: 5)

> **collocation** *n.* [C, U] *technical*
> The way in which some words are often used together or a particular combination of words used in this way.
> *'Commit a crime' is a typical collocation in English.*

You will sometimes come across words that are found together more often than would be expected if left to chance, and usually in a particular order. It is a good idea to learn these groups of words as groups, that is, as **collocations**, rather than as individual words. This is because these collocations may be more or less fixed in terms of their order, grammar, and choice of word, so if you change one of these features, it may sound unusual. An example of this from Article 4 is the phrase 'rich resource' (line 105) – 'a wealthy resource' would be unusual, although in other contexts, 'rich' and 'wealthy' may be considered very similar in meaning.

➢ Study these examples of collocations from Article 4 below. Read them in context, then, with your group, (1) identify their grammatical pattern (see some possible patterns below); and (2) discuss what they mean.

- bridge the gap (line 13)
- to develop awareness of (line 21)
- human geography (line 33)
- brief explanation (line 44)
- positive effect (lines 51)
- major strength (line 53)

Possible grammatical patterns are listed below (words in parentheses are optional):

- verb + (adjective) + noun
- (preposition) + adjective + noun
- adverb + verb or verb + adverb
- adverb + adjective + (noun)
- adjective + preposition
- noun + noun
- noun + preposition

Strategy for Success #26:
Let words that go together, stay together

Make an effort to notice collocations, and keep a record of them. Then try to use them in your own writing and speaking.

➢ Work with another student. In Article 4, find other examples of collocation that follow these patterns:

- adjective + noun
- verb + noun
- verb + adverb

➢ To 'test' any collocation, that is, find out if it is indeed an example of a collocation, visit a useful resource called 'Just the word':

193.133.140.102/JustTheWord/index.html.

For example, entering the word 'educational' will show you that it collocates strongly with several nouns including 'background', 'administration', 'approach', 'circle', and 'practice'.

Note that the green line after the collocation shows you how strong the collocation is, that is, the longer the line, the more frequently the collocation appears.

Entering the word 'bridge' will show you that it collocates strongly with 'gap', and if, having entered 'bridge', you click on 'bridge gap', you will be able to see several examples of the phrase in use, such as:

- '...bridges the gap between description and interpretation...'
- '...views in some borderlands had bridged the psychological gap between town and country...'
- 'He said he would be trying to bridge the gap between the board and the counties...'

(all examples are from 'Just the word',
193.133.140.102/JustTheWord/Scripts/show_examples.pl?triple=bridge_V+obj+ga
p_N, April 2007)

➤ Experiment with other words from Article 4, using 'Just the Word'.

Strategy for Success #27:
Use a concordancer to test your collocations

A concordancer is a computer programme or search engine that searches large quantities of language (known as a corpus (s) or corpora (pl)), from which it generates lists of words along with the contexts in which they appear. This can help you to see what words are commonly found together. There are several available on the internet. Use the one suggested above, or ask for your tutor's recommendation.

▌ FOCUS C: WRITING

C.1 Paragraphs

All of the articles that you have read so far (and all 10 articles in this book) are organized into paragraphs. Paragraphs usually contain a main idea that is expressed in the form of a topic sentence, and some supporting detail.

➤ Discuss with another student. Why do writers do this? What are the purposes of paragraphs?

> **Strategy for Success #28:**
> **Identify the main idea or topic sentence of each paragraph as you read**
>
> Paragraphs usually present one main idea and some supporting detail. Identifying the main idea will help you to learn the most important information that the writer wants to convey.

➤ Read the following ideas. They are the main ideas of each paragraph in Article 4. Which do you think will come near the beginning of the article? Which in the middle? Which near the end? Discuss these questions with another student.

Write 'B' for beginning, 'M' for middle, and 'E' for end after each one:

a)   A summary of what the book offers and one way in which it could be used.
b)   A criticism of particular interest and relevance to Averil Coxhead.
c)   The suitability of the book in different contexts.
d)   A significant new feature.
e)   Some significant criticisms concerned with the book's organization.
f)   An overview of all the chapters.
g)   A particularly positive feature (you will find two paragraphs with this idea).
h)   How the book relates to what is already known about learning to read in a second language.
i)   Why there is a need for the book being reviewed.
j)   An interesting feature of the book.
k)   The broad aims of the book.
l)   How each chapter ends.
m)   Two additional positive features.
n)   How the book is arranged.

➤ Now read Article 4 again and work out which idea matches which paragraph [ANSWERS]. Write paragraph 1, 2, 3, etc., and the corresponding letter from the list above, like this:

1 – i

➤ Select three or four paragraphs that you like. Identify the topic sentence (that is, the words that express the main idea) and those that provide supporting detail. Exchange your analysis with another student.

C.2 Conclusions

The conclusion is perhaps the most important part of students' writing, but most students don't seem to realize this – they just rush through it. (Tutor, Hong Kong)

➤ Why is the conclusion to your writing so important? Here are some ideas to help you. Which are correct? Discuss with another student, then check your ideas with your tutor.

A conclusion:

- synthesizes the main ideas and the supporting points of your writing
- should include one new piece of information
- reminds the reader why your ideas are useful, significant, important
- may include a question
- should leave the reader with more questions about the topic that he or she wants to answer
- is an opportunity to make a positive final impression
- adds completion, bringing a reader full circle
- can suggest some broader implications of your writing
- may be provocative and challenging
- shows the reader how your key ideas are related
- can link to your introduction through the use of key concepts, or key words and phrases
- may prompt the reader to think about the future
- always begins with a phrase such as 'to conclude' or 'in conclusion'
- echoes the introduction to your writing.

Strategy for Success #29:
Avoid clichés in your writing

A cliché occurs in language when a word or phrase is so overused that it tends to lose its strength or credibility. Examples include: 'time is money'; 'better late than never'; 'double-edged sword'; 'in conclusion'; 'to conclude'.

➤ Find some examples of conclusions, on any topic you like, or use those in the articles in Chapters 6, 7 and 9. Match the functions above to the language that is used. Some examples follow.

From Article 2:

'EAP is thus an important area of ESP, accounting for a large amount of the ESP activity worldwide' = reminds the reader why your ideas are useful, significant, important.

'There have been several EAP-related articles in this newsletter, and maybe there would be interest in more' = prompts the reader to think about the future.

From Article 4:

'It would serve as a springboard for teachers looking for ways to bring learners, academic reading, skills and practice together' = makes a positive final impression.

➢ Make a list of any useful phrases to include in your writing for your portfolio.

▶ FOCUS D: RESEARCHING

D.1 Identifying genres

'Genre' is the term used to refer to a number of examples of language that have several shared features, which together form a distinct variety of language use. Features that are shared relate to:

- the purpose of the language
- the place, time and/or circumstances in which the language is appropriate
- the people who use the language.

In academic writing, genres include:

- book reviews
- reports
- proposals
- term papers
- abstracts.

➢ What other academic genres can you think of? Discuss this with another student. Then select three that interest you and note down some of the features that distinguish them from other genres. Compare your work with that of other students, and add their ideas to your list, where they differ from your own. (Article 1 may help you here!)

D.2 Thinking critically about sources of information

In Chapter 1, the acronym 'ACAREA' was provided to help you to recognize a good-quality article.

➢ Can you remember what the acronym stands for? Make a note.

As well as the criteria above, you should also think **critically** about the source of an article, as suggested by the title to this section.

➢ Note down a few different sources of information. Use your ideas from Chapter 3, section D2, to help you.

> **critically** *adv.*
> Thinking about something and giving a careful judgement about how good or bad it is.
> *We teach students to think critically about the texts they are reading.*

➢ Show your list to another student. Discuss the following questions:

- How reliable is each source?
- What makes one source more reliable than another?
- Why does reliability matter?
- What sources are less likely to be reliable, and why?

➢ Expanding the acronym ACAREA to include 'source' gives us 'ACAREAS'. Memorize it, and what it stands for.

Strategy for Success #30:
Think critically

Don't assume that all academic writing is good. Instead, approach all writing with an open mind, asking such questions as: What features suggest that this is a good article? What assumptions does the author make? Where was it published? What's included in the article, and what's excluded? Does the author address an important issue? Are his or her conclusions logical, and supported in the writing?

FOCUS E: STUDYING

E.1 Reading efficiently and effectively

Efficient, effective reading is the result of a number of skills. An efficient reader:

scan *v.*
Look through [T]; to read something quickly = skim

skim *v.* [I, T]
To read something quickly to find the main facts or ideas in it = scan

- reads selectively
- reads with a clear purpose
- reads with a critical eye
- **scans** for general idea
- **skims** for specific information
- uses context to help him or her to infer the meaning of new words
- surveys the texts as a whole to extract the general idea from the title and headings.

➢ What are your strengths and weaknesses in relation to the skills above?
➢ Add to the list above. Discuss your ideas with a partner.

E.2 Recording collocations

Keeping a record of collocations is a useful way to expand your vocabulary. There are three useful approaches you could take. You can:

- make a record of new collocations as you notice them in your reading;
  or
- select any word you are interested in, and explore its collocations, making a record of some that you might like to use in the future;
  or
- search for alternatives to a collocation that you already know.

All three approaches above can be taken with the help of 'Just the word' 193.133.140.102/JustTheWord/index.html), and all three can be recorded using the table provided below.

Note these features of 'Just the word':

a) The green lines show you the strength, or frequency, of the collocation. This gives you the opportunity to focus on learning those collocations that are most frequent.

b) The collocations are 'clustered' or 'unclustered'. Clustered collocations have similar meanings (for example, 'carry out research' and 'conduct research' belong to the same cluster), while those that are unclustered do not. Note, however, that this does not mean that clustered collocations are synonymous.

c) Clicking on the underlined collocation will take you to a list of examples of that collocation in use, drawn from the website's extensive database of authentic text. You can add any example from this list to your record if you need to.

d) Using this programme, you will find that many collocations are provided. You will need to be selective: add collocations to your record that you think you could use in the near future in your own writing. Then refer to your record later – use it as a reminder.

e) Click on 'help' for a full explanation of the software and its features.

➢ Study the completed example of a 'Collocation record' on page 94. It has four columns: the first is for the 'core' word (the word you have looked up); you can note its word class in the second column; the third column provides space for some of its collocates, and in the last column you can add an example of the collocate in actual use.

Core word	Word class	Collocates with...	Example in use
performance	noun	high performance	The plan involves the creation of high performance materials.
research	noun	carry out	...group also condemns the Government for failing to carry out research into its effectiveness...
		conduct	Researchers rarely conduct research with a finished model of the causal process...
tool	noun	machine tool	Machine tools are examples of power-using machines.

(Examples from a subject-related article were provided by first-year student Ibrahim Ali Al Kodssi.)

➤ A blank 'collocation record' sheet is provided for you on page 95. Make several copies of this sheet to keep in your portfolio.
➤ Add the collocations you identified in section B2 above to this record in your portfolio.

▶ FOCUS F: APPLYING TO YOUR OWN SUBJECT

F.1 Locating and reading reviews of subject-related books

➤ Using ACAREAS to help you to identify quality information, find two reviews of books in your field.
➤ Read your reviews, and annotate them to identify (a) positive features of the book under review; and (b) criticisms or reservations that the review author has about it.
➤ Describe the positive features and criticisms of the book under review to another student. Explain why you would or would not want to read the book as a result.

F.2 Identifying collocations in subject-related articles

➤ Choose one of your two reviews. Identify possible collocations in it. Use 'Just the Word' to confirm that they are collocations and to find out their strength. Use them to complete your record of collocations and add the information about strength. Use S = strong and W = weak.

COLLOCATION RECORD

Page no. _____

Core word	Word class	Collocates with...	Example in use

© SAGE Publications Ltd 2009

F.3 Identifying concrete and abstract language in subject-related articles

➢ Read the other one of your two reviews. Find examples of words with concrete and abstract meanings. Describe your pairs of words to another student, and exchange lists.

Writing in Higher Education

In this chapter, you can read an extract from a **chapter from a book** about developing students' writing skills for higher education.

You can develop your skills in these areas:

Focus A: Reading

A.1   Looking ahead
A.2   Understanding and responding
A.3   Identifying sides of an argument

Focus B: Learning language

B.1   Presenting sides of an argument
B.2   Reference words
B.3   Synonyms, superordinates and hyponyms

Focus C: Writing

C.1   Writing summaries
C.2   Critiquing peer writing

Focus D: Researching

D.1   The research cycle
D.2   The purpose of literature reviews

Focus E: Studying

E.1   Preparing an outline of an assignment

Focus F: Applying to your own subject

F.1   Locating, reading and summarizing a subject-related book chapter
F.2   Locating, reading and note-taking from a subject-related literature review
F.3   Identifying subject-related issues

▶ FOCUS A: READING

A.1 Looking ahead

The article in this chapter is an abridged extract from a chapter in a book. The book is called *Negotiating Academic Literacies*, while the chapter is called '**Initiating** ESL Students into the Academic Discourse Community: How Far Should We Go?'

---

initiate *v.*
To arrange for something important to start, such as an official process or a new plan.
Intellectuals have initiated a debate on terrorism.

---

contradict *v.*
To disagree with something, especially by saying that the opposite is true.
The article flatly contradicts their claims.

➢ Discuss the chapter and book titles with other students and your tutor. What do they mean to you? What do you think the article will be about?

➢ Scan the headings used in the article. Do they correspond to or **contradict** the ideas you had during your discussion?

➢ The article appears to have been written in 1998. How can you tell that it is in fact older than this? Approximately when do you think it was written? How has this happened? Do you think it matters?

➢ Read and annotate Article 5. The paragraphs have been numbered to help you to complete the tasks that follow.

Strategy for Success #31:
Scan the headings and subheadings in an article

Headings and subheadings are a guide to the usefulness of an article.

▶ ARTICLE 5: 'INITIATING ESL STUDENTS INTO THE ACADEMIC DISCOURSE COMMUNITY: HOW FAR SHOULD WE GO?'

(abridged extract)

Ruth Spack

(Chapter 8, *Negotiating Academic Literacies* (1998) by
Zamel, V. and Spack, R. (eds))

Studies of writing programs in the disciplines and their implications

1   Several Ll programs have been instituted to introduce students to the methods of inquiry in various disciplines. In typical programs, English teachers have collaborated with teachers in other disciplines, such as biology (Wilkinson, 1985), psychology (Faigley and Hansen, 1985), and sociology (Faigley and Hansen,   5
1985), linking the compositions to subject matter in the other course. Investigations of these programs reveal some obvious advantages: Students learn new forms of writing which as professionals they might need; they have more time to write, since there is less reading due to the fact that one subject matter is employed for two courses; and their discussions of student papers are more informative, since knowledge   10
is shared among class members.

2   However, the disadvantages of such a program are equally, if not more, significant, as Wilkinson (1985) and others show, and should be of great concern to the English teacher. First of all, it is difficult for a writing course to have a carefully planned pedagogical or rhetorical rationale when it is dependent on another content   15
course; furthermore, the timing of assignments is not always optimal. Second, the program can raise false expectations among the faculty as well as among the students. English faculty, even when they collaborate with content teachers, find they have little basis for dealing with the content. They therefore find themselves in the uncomfortable position of being less knowledgeable than their students. Students   20
likewise can resent finding themselves in a situation in which their instructor cannot fully explain or answer questions about the subject matter. Faigley and Hansen (1985) observed collaborative courses in which completely different criteria for evaluation were applied to students' papers by the two teachers, because the English teacher did not recognize when a student failed to demonstrate adequate knowledge   25
of a discipline or show a good grasp of new knowledge.

3   The same phenomenon can hold true in L2 writing instruction. Pearson (1983) finds that 'the instructor cannot always conveniently divorce the teaching of form from the understanding of content' (pp. 396–397). This drawback is often mentioned only in passing in articles recommending that English teachers use tech-   30
nical and scientific materials they are not familiar with (see Hill, Soppelsa, and West, 1982). But the lack of control over content on the part of English teachers who teach in the other disciplines is a serious problem. This concern is reflected in a state-of-the-art article on English for medical purposes (EMP):

35 4 A sense of insecurity and uncertainty can sometimes be observed amongst EMP
teachers regarding their effective roles as lay persons teaching 'medical English' among
medical professionals…

[….] Consider the view of the Finnish Medical Society team of doctors: 'We believe
that it is essential to have teachers entirely at home in medicine and English and who
40 have some experience in writing and lecturing' (Collan, 1974: 629). (Maher, 1986,
p. 138)

5 In spite of these drawbacks, some investigators claim that it is possible for an
English teacher to conduct a course that focuses on writing in a particular discipline if the teacher learns how a discipline creates and transmits knowledge. This
45 is accomplished by examining the kinds of issues a discipline considers important, why certain methods of inquiry and not others are sanctioned, how the
conventions of a discipline shape text in that discipline, how individual writers
represent themselves in a text, how texts are read and disseminated within the
discipline, and how one text influences subsequent texts (Faigley and Hansen,
50 1985; Herrington, 1985).

6 This exploration, of course, would involve a great deal of commitment, as anyone who has studied a particular field or discipline knows. Specialists in second
language instruction, for example, have spent years acquiring the knowledge and
understanding that enable them to recognize the issues that dominate discussion in
55 the field (e.g. communicative competence), the methods of inquiry employed (e.g.
ethnography), the structure of manuscripts focusing on those issues (e.g. the
TESOL Quarterly format), the names associated with various issues (e.g.
Krashen/lnput Hypothesis; Carrell/schema theory; Zamel/writing process), and the
impact a given article might have on thinking and research in the field.

60 7 It seems that only the rare individual teacher can learn another discipline, for
each discipline offers a different system for examining experience, a different angle
for looking at subject matter, a different kind of thinking (Maimon et al., 1981).
Furthermore, whereas the transmission of a discipline within content courses primarily requires that students comprehend, recall, and display information in
65 examinations, writing in the disciplines:

8 requires a complete, active, struggling engagement with the facts and principles of a
discipline, an encounter with the discipline's texts and the incorporation of them into
one's own work, the framing of one's knowledge within the myriad conventions that help
define a discipline, the persuading of other investigators that one's knowledge is legiti-
70 mate. (Rose, 1985, p. 359)

9 The teaching of writing in a discipline, then, involves even more specialized
knowledge and skills than does the teaching of the subject matter itself.

10 The difficulty of teaching writing in another discipline is compounded when
we realize that within each discipline, such as the social sciences, there are subdis-
75 ciplines, each with its own set of conventions. Reflection on personal events, for
example, is considered legitimate evidence in sociology and anthropology, but not
in behavioral psychology (Rose, 1983). Even within the subdisciplines, such as

anthropology, there are other subdisciplines with their own sets of conventions. The articles of physical anthropologists, for example, resemble those of natural scientists, whereas those of cultural anthropologists sometimes resemble those of 80 literary scholars (Faigley and Hansen, 1985).

11   To further complicate matters, no discipline is static. In virtually all academic disciplines, there is controversy concerning the validity of approaches, controversy that non-specialists are usually unaware of until it is covered in the popular media (see, for example, Silk, 1987, for a discussion of the recent debate 85 between political and anthropological historians). In addition, the principles of reasoning in a discipline may change over time, even in science, which is affected by the emergence of new mathematical techniques, new items of apparatus, and even new philosophical precepts (Yearley, 1981). Formal scientific papers, then, though often considered final statements of facts, are primarily contributions to 90 scientific debate (Yearley, 1981).

12   Even studying a finished product [...] cannot prepare English teachers to teach students how writers in other disciplines write. A written product such as a scientific report is merely a representation of a research process, which is finally summarized for peers; it is not a representation of a writing process. To teach writ- 95 ing, writing teachers should teach the writing process; and to teach the writing process, they should know how to write. But English teachers are not necessarily equipped to write in other disciplines. Testimony to this truth appears in the ESP literature:

13   In the author's experience, every attempt to write a passage, however satisfactory it 100 seemed on pedagogic grounds, was promptly vetoed by the Project's scientific adviser because a technical solecism of some kind had been committed. The ESP writer, however experienced, simply does not know when a mistake of this kind is being committed. (Coffey, 1984, p. 8)

14   To learn to write in any discipline, students must become immersed in the 105 subject matter; this is accomplished through reading, lectures, seminars, and so on. They learn by participating in the field, by doing, by sharing, and by talking about it with those who know more. They can also learn by observing the process through which professional academic writers produce texts or, if that is not possible, by studying that process in the type of program recommended by Swales (1987) for 110 teaching the research paper to non-native-speaking graduate students. They will learn most efficiently from teachers who have a solid grounding in the subject matter and who have been through the process themselves.

15   I do not deny that programs that instruct students to write in other disciplines can work. But a review of the L1 literature (e.g. Herrington, 1985) and the L2 115 literature (e.g. Swales, 1987) on successful programs reveals that the teachers are themselves immersed in the discipline. For example, Herrington's (1985) study is an observation of senior-level engineering courses taught by engineering faculty. And Swales's list of publications reveals a background in scientific discourse dating back at least to 1970. 120

Academic writing tasks for ESL college students

16   English teachers cannot and should not be held responsible for teaching writing in the disciplines. The best we can accomplish is to create programs in which students can learn general inquiry strategies, rhetorical principles, and tasks that
125 can transfer to other course work. This has been our traditional role, and it is a worthy one. The materials we use should be those we can fully understand. The writing projects we assign and evaluate should be those we are capable of doing ourselves. The remainder of this chapter is devoted to practical suggestions for incorporating academic writing into an English composition course designed for
130 ESL undergraduates, without the need for linking the course with another subject-area program.

Writing from other texts

17   Perhaps the most important skill English teachers can engage students in is the complex ability to write from other texts, a major part of their academic writing
135 experience. Students' 'intellectual socialization may be accomplished not only by interacting with people, but also by encountering the writing of others' (Bizzell, 1986, p. 65). As Bazerman (1980) says, 'we must cultivate various techniques of absorbing, reformulating, commenting on, and using reading' if we want to prepare our students to 'enter the written exchanges of their chosen disciplines and the var-
140 ious discussions of personal and public interest' (p. 658).
18   L1 and L2 research shows the interdependent relationship between reading and writing processes (see Krashen, 1984; Petrosky, 1982; Spack, 1985). Both processes focus on the making of meaning; they share the 'act of constructing meaning from words, text, prior knowledge, and feelings' (Petrosky, 1982, p. 22). To
145 become better writers, then, students need to become better readers.
19   Intelligent response to reading, Bazerman (1980) reminds us, begins with an accurate understanding of a text – not just the facts and ideas, but also what the author is trying to achieve. But this is not easy for second language readers. Even advanced, highly literate students struggle in a way that their NS counterparts do
150 not. First, there are linguistic difficulties. Overcoming them is not simply a matter of learning specialists' language because often the more general use of language causes the greatest problem. Given the complexity of reading in a second language, it is necessary for L2 writing teachers to become familiar with theories and techniques of L2 reading instruction (see, for example, Dubin, Eskey, and Grabe, 1986) if they
155 are to guide their students to become better academic writers.
20   Some of those techniques are already part of L1 and L2 composition instruction. Marginal notes, note-taking, working journals (see Spack and Sadow, 1983), and response statements (Petrosky, 1982) can train students to discover and record their own reactions to a text. Exercises that focus on the processes of summarizing,
160 paraphrasing, and quoting can encourage precise understanding of an author's style and purpose. But these techniques should not be ends unto themselves. Rather, paraphrase, summary, and quotation become part of students' texts as they incorporate

key ideas and relevant facts from their reading into their own writing. In this way, students can develop informed views on the issues they pursue, building on what has already been written.   165

21   Readings can be content based, grouped by themes, and can be expressive or literary as well as informative. They can be drawn from a specific field, if the area of study is one that the instructor is well versed in, or from several fields, if the articles are written by professionals for a general audience. Although these articles may not be considered academic since they were not written for academic/professional audiences, they can give   170
students an understanding of how writers from different disciplines approach the same subject. Most important, they allow instructors to avoid placing themselves in the awkward position of presenting materials they do not fully understand. But whatever readings are chosen, teachers of ESL students should always consider the background knowledge that readers are expected to bring to written texts (e.g. knowledge of   175
American history, recognition of the publications in which the texts originally appeared, discernment of organizational formats, etc.) and help their students establish a frame of reference that will facilitate comprehension (Dubin et al., 1986).

22   Writing tasks should build upon knowledge students already possess but should also be designed to allow new learning to occur. Students can initially write about their   180
own experiences or views, then read, discuss, and respond informally in writing to the assigned readings. They can next be assigned the task of evaluating, testing the truth of, or otherwise illuminating the texts. Students can be directed to compare the ideas discussed in one or more of the readings with their own experiences, or they can be asked to agree or disagree or take a mixed position toward one of the readings. Making spe-   185
cific references to the readings, they can develop ideas by giving examples, citing experiences, and/or providing evidence from other texts on the subject.

23   By sequencing assignments, the teacher can move the students away from a primarily personal approach to a more critical approach to the readings. The goal should not be regurgitation of others' ideas, but the development of an independent   190
viewpoint. Students can develop the ability to acknowledge the points of view of others but still 'question and critique established authorities in a field of knowledge' (Coles and Wall, 1987, p. 299). This is a particularly important skill for foreign students, many of whom are 'products of educational systems where unquestioning acceptance of books and teachers as the ultimate authority is the norm' (Horowitz   195
and McKee, 1984, p. 5).

24   Yet other assignments, such as research projects utilizing the library and perhaps data from interviews and/or observations, can ask students to evaluate and synthesize material from a number of sources in order to establish a perspective on a given subject or area of controversy. Like the assignments   200
discussed above, this type of assignment allows for demonstration of knowledge and prompts the 'independent thinking, researching, and learning' (Shih, 1986, p. 621) often required when students write for their other university courses. Such an assignment also builds on skills students have already practiced: reading, note-taking, summarizing, paraphrasing, quoting, evaluating, comparing, agreeing/   205
disagreeing, and so on.

25   These skills are transferable to many writing tasks that students will be required
to perform in other courses when they write for academic audiences. The content
will vary from course to course, and the format will vary from discipline to discipline
210   and within disciplines, depending on the particular constraints of individual assignments and the particular concerns of individual teachers. But students should have a
fairly good sense of how to focus on a subject, provide evidence to support a point or
discovery, and examine the implications of the material discussed.

References

Bazerman, C. (1980). A relationship between reading and writing: The conversa-
tional model. *College English*, 41, 656–661.

Bizzell, P. (1986). Composing processes: An overview. In A. R. Petrosky &
D. Bartholomae (Eds), *The Teaching of Writing* (pp. 49–70). Chicago: The National
Society for the Study of Education.

Coffey, B. (1984). ESP-English for specific purposes [State-of-the-art article].
*Language Teaching: The International Abstracting Journal for Language Teachers and
Applied Linguists*, 17, 2–16.

Coles, N., & Wall, S. V. (1987). Conflict and power in the reader-responses of adult
basic writers. *College English*, 49, 298–314.

Dubin, F., Eskey, D. E., & Grabe, W. (1986). *Teaching Second Language Reading for
Academic Purposes*. Reading, MA: Addison-Wesley.

Faigley, L., & Hansen, K. (1985). Learning to write in the social sciences. *College
Composition and Communication*, 36, 140–149.

Herrington, A. J. (1985). Classrooms as forums for reasoning and writing. *College
Composition and Communication*, 36, 404–413.

Hill, S. S., Soppelsa, B. F., & West, G. K. (1982). Teaching ESL students to read and
write experimental-research papers. *TESOL Quarterly*, 16, 333–347.

Horowitz, D. M., & McKee, M. B. (1984). Methods for teaching academic writing.
TECFORS 7, 5–11.

Krashen, S. D. (1984). *Writing: Research, theory and applications*. Oxford: Pergamon
Press.

Maher, J. (1986). English for medical purposes [State-of-the-art article]. *Language
Teaching: The International Abstracting Journal for Language Teachers and Applied
Linguists*, 19, 112–145.

Maimon, E. P., Belcher, C. L., Hearn, C. W., Nodine, B. F., & O'Connor, F. B.
(1981). *Writing in the arts and sciences*. Boston: Little, Brown.

Pearson, S. (1983). The challenge of Mai Chung: Teaching technical writing to the
foreign-born professional in industry. *TESOL Quarterly*, 17, 383–399.

Petrosky, A. R. (1982). From story to essay: Reading and writing. *College English*,
46, 19–36.

Rose, M. (1983). Remedial writing courses: A critique and a proposal. *College
English*, 45, 109–126.

Rose, M. (1985). The language of exclusion: Writing instruction at the university. *College English*, 47, 341–359.

Shih, M. (1986). Content-based approaches to teaching academic writing. *TESOL Quarterly*, 20, 617–648.

Silk, M. (1987, April 19). The hot history department. *The New York Times Magazine*, pp. 41, 43, 46–7, 50, 56, 63, 64.

Spack, R. (1985). Literature, reading, writing, and ESL: Bridging the *gaps. TESOL Quarterly*, 19, 703–725.

Spack, R., & Sadow, C. (1983). Student-teacher working journals in ESL composition. *TESOL Quarterly*, 17, 575–593.

Swales, J. (1987). Utilizing the literatures in teaching the research paper. *TESOL Quarterly*, 21, 41–68.

Wilkinson, A. M. (1985). A freshman writing course in parallel with a science course. *Composition and Communication*, 36, 160–165.

Year!ey, S. (1981). Textual persuasion: The role of social accounting in the construction of scientific arguments. *Philosophy of Social Sciences*, 11, 409–435.

A.2 Understanding and responding

➢ Read the following collocations in their contexts. Work with another student and your tutor, and discuss what they mean, as they are used:

a) 'methods of enquiry' (lines 1–2)
b) 'raise false expectations' (line 17)
c) 'the same phenomenon can hold true' (line 27)
d) 'mentioned only in passing' (line 30)
e) 'state-of-the-art' (line 34)
f) 'entirely at home' (line 39)
g) 'the issues that dominate discussion' (line 54)
h) 'engagement with the facts' (line 66)
i) 'myriad conventions that define a discipline' (lines 68–69)
j) 'the difficulty … is compounded' (line 73)
k) 'ends unto themselves' (line 161)
l) 'well versed in' (line 168)
m) 'a frame of reference' (lines 177–178)
n) 'a more critical approach' (line 190)
o) 'regurgitation of others' ideas' (line 191)
p) 'to establish a perspective on' (line 200)
q) to 'examine the implications of' (line 213)

➢ Many of the phrases in question 1 are useful in a range of contexts. Make a note of a few that you would like to try to use in your next writing assignment.
➢ Read the article and answer the following questions.

1   In lines 2–3, the author refers to English teachers collaborating with teachers of other disciplines. What do you think might be the benefits of such collaboration (a) for language students; and (b) for the teachers themselves? Discuss, then check your ideas with the information given in paragraph 1.

2   In lines 18–19, the writer suggests that English faculty teach language, while content teachers teach content. Do you see a clear division between language and content? Can you give some examples?

3   'It seems that only the rare individual teacher can learn another discipline, for each discipline offers a different system for examining experience, a different angle for looking at subject matter, a different kind of thinking (Maimon et al., 1981).' (Lines 60–62). Discuss this assertion with your tutor. Does he or she agree? How familiar is he or she with another discipline and all that it entails, as suggested in paragraph 7?

4   EAP may be considered a 'subdiscipline' (line 74) which in turn may be seen as a 'subdiscipline' of English Language Teaching (ELT) or teaching English to Speakers of Other Languages (TESOL). What other subdisciplines within ELT/TESOL do you know of?

5   'No discipline is static. In virtually all academic disciplines there is controversy concerning the validity of approaches' (lines 82–83). Discuss this with your tutor in relation to ELT/TESOL. What changes has he or she seen during the course of his or her career? What controversies is he or she aware of?

6   Paragraph 11 refers to 'a research process' and 'a writing process' (lines 94–95). Describe what you think each process might involve.

7   Under what conditions does the author suggest that 'programs that instruct students to write in other disciplines' (line 114) can work?

8   In paragraph 16, the author suggests that students need to develop 'the complex ability to write from other texts' (line 134) . What does she mean by this, and why does she believe it?

9   What do the acts of reading and writing have in common, according to the author?

10   What particular difficulties do second language readers face? What does the author suggest that teachers need to do to help students overcome these difficulties?

11   What techniques mentioned in paragraph 19 are you familiar with? What techniques have you used so far while using *Read, Research and Write*?

12   In paragraph 20, the author suggests using articles 'from a specific field, if the area of study is one that the instructor is well versed in, or from several fields, if the articles are written by professionals for a general audience.' (lines 167–169) What benefits does she identify for the student and the teacher with this approach?

13   What do you understand by the phrase 'take a mixed position' in paragraph 21? What are the alternatives to such a position?

14   Why does the author think that the goal of taking 'a more critical approach' to reading is particularly important for foreign students? Does her observation here relate to your own experience?

15 What does the author suggest are the benefits of doing a research project for students? What areas in EAP could make interesting research projects for students?

16 In paragraph 25, the author describes the ultimate goal of EAP writing courses. What is it?

A.3 Identifying sides of an argument

Academic **argument** occurs when different sides of a discussion are presented. In writing, the author will usually present ideas that support or refute one side, in order to establish his or her own position.

> **argument** *n*. [C]
> A set of reasons that show that something is true or untrue, right or wrong, etc.
> *We need to provide a convincing argument as to why the system should be changed.*

➤ Paragraph 3 contributes further to the author's discussion about language and content, and describes a problem. What is it?

➤ In paragraph 16, the author states her own position in relation to the ideas presented. What is her position? What are your own views? Does your tutor hold the same view?

Strategy for Success #32:
Identify the 'sides' in an academic discussion

Clearly identify the sides, or positions, in an academic discussion, and consider your own position in relation to those presented. Where do *you* stand?

FOCUS B: LEARNING LANGUAGE

B.1 Presenting sides of an argument

Various words and phrases help the author to introduce and discuss contrasting ideas in her writing.

> 'Section B.1 in Chapter 5 really helps the reader to identify the sides of an argument and therefore have a better understanding of any text.'
>
> Tariq Ibrahim Abdul Rahim Al Jallad (first-year student)

➤ Read the examples below in context and answer the questions that follow:

1 'However, the disadvantages of ... are equally, if not more, significant' (lines 12–13). What disadvantages does the author identify? What is the effect of the phrase 'if not more' here?

2 'This drawback ...' (line 29). What is the drawback referred to? How serious is a 'drawback'?

3   'But …. is a serious problem' (lines 32–33). What is the serious problem?

4   'This concern… '(line 33). Which concern?

5   'In spite of these drawbacks …' (line 42). What drawbacks is the author refer-ring to?

6   'Some investigators claim that …' (line 42). What is the effect of the word 'claim' in this sentence?

7   'To further complicate matters' (line 82). What does this phrase tell us about what we are about to read?

8   'I do not deny that' (line 114). What is the effect of the use of the word 'I' here? Why is the use of 'I' rare in such articles?

9   'But a review of the literature reveals …' (line 115). What is suggested by the word 'reveal'?

Other words and phrases that may be used to introduce and discuss contrasting ideas include the following:

however	in contrast
on the one hand … on the other hand	on the contrary
nevertheless	still
nonetheless	despite (the above/such arguments)
notwithstanding	in spite of

➤   Make a note of a few words or phrases that you would like to include in the next writing assignment in which you are asked to present sides of an argument.

B.2 Reference words

Various words and phrases help the author to avoid repeating words or ideas in her writing.

For example, the phrase 'These programs' in line 7 means that the author avoids repeating the information about programmes in which English teachers have col-laborated with teachers in other disciplines, of which she provides three examples. We can say that the phrase 'These programs' *refers to* all of the information provided in lines 2–6. The relationship can be shown like this:

In typical programs, English teachers have collaborated with teachers in other disciplines, such as biology (Wilkinson, 1985), psychology (Faigley and Hansen, 1985), and sociology (Faigley and Hansen, 1985), linking the compositions to subject matter in the other course. Investigations of these programs reveal some obvious advantages …

… refers to …

Words that refer in this way may be called 'reference words'. Some common reference words include:

- this
- that
- these
- those
- pronouns such as 'he' or 'they'.

➤   Read the examples below in context and identify what the word or phrase is referring to. Discuss your ideas with another student:

Strategy for Success #33:
Notice reference words, and what they refer to

Good academic writing will contain many reference words. Take note of them and make sure you can identify what they refer to. Try to use them unambiguously yourself in your own writing.

---

1   Such a program (line 12)
2   It (line 15)
3   Their (line 20)
4   The two teachers (line 24)
5   The same phenomenon (line 27)
6   This (line 45)
7   This exploration (line 51)
8   Those (× 2) (line 84)
9   It (line 84)
10   This truth (line 98)

➤   Now find 10 more examples in the article for other students in your class. Ask them to identify exactly what the word or phrase is referring to, and do another student's list yourself.

➤   Make an effort in your own writing to use reference words and phrases. Make sure they are **unambiguous**.

> **ambiguous** *adj.*
> Something that is ambiguous is unclear, confusing, or not certain, or things that produce this effect.
> *There was an element of ambiguity in the president's reply.*

B.3 Synonyms, superordinates and hyponyms

Another way of adding variety and avoiding repetition of words or ideas in writing is to use synonyms, superordinates and hyponyms.

Synonyms are words with similar or closely related meanings, such as 'drawback', 'concern' and 'problem', as they are used in paragraph 3.

Superordinates are general terms that can be used instead of specific examples, which are called 'hyponyms'. 'Discipline' is a superordinate term, while 'biology', 'sociology' and 'psychology' are all hyponyms.

➢ Copy the table below into your portfolio. Find synonyms for the words or phrases provided. Each pair of synonyms appears in the same paragraph, except where indicated otherwise. In three cases, you need to find two possible synonyms. One has been completed for you as an example. ANSWERS

Paragraph	Word or phrase		Synonym	Instruction
1	student	=	class member	–
1	program	=		–
1	composition	=		Look in paragraphs 1 and 2
2	faculty	=		Find two examples
2	demonstrate	=		–
6	discipline	=		–
17	skill	=		Find two examples
18	making	=		–
21	article	=		Find two examples
21	understanding	=		–
22	directed to	=		–
23	development of an individual viewpoint	=		Look in paragraph 24

➢ Choose an appropriate synonym from the list below to replace the highlighted words in the following paragraph from Article 5:

5. In spite of these drawbacks, some investigators claim that it is possible for an English teacher to conduct a course that focuses on writing in a particular discipline if the teacher learns how a discipline creates and transmits knowledge. This is accomplished by examining the kinds of issues a discipline considers important, why certain methods of inquiry and not others are sanctioned, how the conventions of a discipline shape text in that discipline, how individual writers represent themselves in a text, how texts are read and disseminated within the discipline, and how one text influences subsequent texts (Faigley and Hansen, 1985; Herrington, 1985).

Choose from these words:

approved	concentrates	run	significant
researchers	circulated	instructor	difficulties

➢ Think of an appropriate synonym for the eight highlighted words and phrases in the following paragraph from Article 5. Check your ideas with another student.

11. To further complicate matters, no discipline is static. In virtually all academic disciplines there is controversy concerning the validity of approaches, controversy that non-specialists are usually unaware of until it is covered in the popular media (see, for example, Silk, 1987, for a discussion of the recent debate between political and anthropological historians). In addition, the principles of reasoning in a discipline may change over time, even in science, which is affected by the emergence of new mathematical techniques, new items of apparatus, and even new philosophical precepts (Yearley, 1981). Formal scientific papers, then, though often considered final statements of facts, are primarily contributions to scientific debate (Yearley, 1981).

➢ Superordinates and hyponyms can also provide variety in writing, and can be useful when you are summarizing or paraphrasing someone else's writing. Copy the table below into your portfolio. Find hyponyms in the paragraph indicated in column 1 for the superordinates provided ⬚ANSWERS⬚. One has been completed for you as an example.

Paragraph	Superordinate	Hyponyms	Instruction
1	discipline	biology, psychology, sociology	Find 3 examples
6	field or discipline		–
6	issues that dominate discussion		–
6	manuscript		–
6	name		–
10	discipline		–
10	subdisciplines		Find 3 examples
12	a finished product		–
20	techniques		Find 7 examples
24	skills		Find 9 examples

➢   Notice other writers' use of synonyms, superordinates, and hyponyms when you read, and think about adding variety to your own writing by deliberately including some examples of each type of relationship.

FOCUS C: WRITING

C.1 Writing summaries

As part of your course, you may be asked to write a summary of an article you have read. There are a number of different kinds of summaries, and they may be just one or two sentences long, or they may run to several pages. Factors influencing the exact length and form of a summary are the length and type of the original article and your reasons for summarizing it. In all cases, however, your task is to restate in general terms the main information provided in another article. The skills required to do this are similar to those you need for writing a literature review.

Writing a summary can do two things – the process can help you to understand the article you have read in greater depth, and the result – your summary – can show your tutor how well you have understood it.

To write a good summary, take the 'prepare, write, check, avoid' approach:

1 **Prepare...**
   a. Read the original article or chapter thoroughly. Highlight key points and make annotations.
   b. Identify the writer's purpose (to describe, persuade, explain...?). This will help you to recognize key information.
   c. Identify the overall thesis. What does the author say or argue for?
   d. Identify the main points that he or she has made in support of his or her thesis.

2 **Write...**
   a. Use your own words
   b. Write a sentence that summarizes the writer's argument. Use this sentence to begin your summary.
   c. Describe each main point. Show how the ideas are connected or develop.
   d. When referring to a writer's ideas, use the author's last name and the present tense, as in these examples from Article 5 'as Wilkinson (1985) and others show' (line 13); 'Pearson (1983) finds that...' (lines 27–28)

3 **Check...**
   a. Compare the content of your draft with the original text. Make sure you have represented the writer's ideas accurately.
   b. Revise and rewrite as needed.
   c. Proofread for errors of form and rewrite as needed.

4   **Avoid…**
   a) Quoting too much; where you do quote, keep it short, use inverted commas
       ('…') and include the quote in the main body of your writing, that is, do not
       separate it and indent it.
   b) Adding your own ideas or critiquing the writer's ideas.
   c) Including minor details.
   d) Giving too many examples (one or two may be acceptable depending on
       your own purposes).

➤   Work with another student or students. Follow the steps above to write a sum-
    mary of Article 5. You may like to divide the work up among yourselves. Write
    the final version either on an overhead transparency or word process it, if there
    is a computer and a projector in your classroom.

Before you write, remember to agree with your tutor upon a subset of annotations
from the companion website which you would like him or her to use when marking your work.

C.2 Critiquing peer writing

The ability to give and receive constructive feedback
is an essential skill for success in higher education. As
a student, you probably expect to receive feedback
from your tutor on your written assignments. Other
students are a useful source of feedback too. However,
feedback content needs to be **constructive** and its
delivery sensitive. Follow these keys to successful
feedback:

> **constructive** *adj*.
> Useful and helpful, or likely to
> produce good results.
> *We welcome any constructive
> criticism.*

Keys to constructive feedback:

1   **Constructive content is:**
   a) focused
   b) relevant
   c) based upon evidence
   d) descriptive rather than evaluative

2   **Sensitive delivery is:**
   a. supportive and friendly
   b. collaborative, encouraging dialogue and discussion
   c. able to offer feedback in the form of a question, such as 'have you thought
       about…?'

> **Strategy for Success #34:**
> **Give, receive and benefit from constructive criticism from tutors and peers**
>
> Giving feedback, receiving feedback, and acting upon it, are all essential skills to develop, both for a higher education context and for the workplace.

➤ Which phrases in the list below could you use to give constructive feedback? Make a note in your portfolio, and make an effort to use them in the next activity.

'Critiquing is very important and this section is a great idea because to have to do this is very common in university life.'
Tariq Ibrahim Abdul Rahim Al Jallad (first-year student)

- I like the way you …
- I found this section very useful because…
- I don't like this explanation.
- You could perhaps think about adding…
- I was wondering if you needed to expand your introduction, because…
- This isn't clear at all.
- This is all wrong.
- In my own work, I added … and I received positive feedback from our tutor.

- You can't do it like this.
- Have you considered including/expanding/editing …
- You have too many spelling mistakes here.
- You haven't used a spellchecker, have you?
- I would like to read more information about this … because …
- I think this conclusion could be improved, if you…
- You've included too many quotes.

➤ Add some more ideas of your own to your list of useful phrases for giving constructive feedback. Show your list to another student and read his or her list. Then give each other constructive feedback on your lists!

critique *v.*
To say how good or bad a book, play, painting, or set of ideas is.
He offered to critique our plans.

➤ Read a summary of Article 5 prepared by other students in your class and **critique** it by offering constructive feedback. Listen to or read constructive feedback on your own work, and improve it accordingly.

FOCUS D: RESEARCHING

D.1 The research cycle

Research involves identifying a research question, selecting appropriate methods to help you to answer the question, gathering data, analysing data, discussing the results and making recommendations. These stages are often reflected in the headings used in articles, particularly when articles are research reports.

➢ Study 'The research cycle: from question to recommendation' on the next page. With another student, take it in turns to describe the process, from identification of research question to informing stakeholders of your recommendations.

➢ Scan the articles in this book and find examples of research stages reflected in headings or subheadings.

➢ Discuss with another student some possible topics for research within the field of EAP. Choose topics that are relevant to you in your current circumstances.

➢ Photocopy the research cycle and pin it up above your desk.

D.2 The purpose of literature reviews

➢ With another student, consider the role of the literature review in the research process. Read the comments about its function in the 'research cycle'. Then discuss the meaning of any of the following phrases with your tutor, or use your English–English dictionary. Identify three verb phrases that *do not* describe the functions of a literature review in the list below: `ANSWERS`

- to synthesize ideas
- to report on research methods used
- to appraise critically
- to identify areas of controversy
- to identify questions for further research
- to make recommendations
- to identify the gaps in the research to date
- to avoid reinventing the wheel
- to present results of a project
- to locate relevant ideas and methods
- to build on the platform of existing knowledge.

➢ Discuss with other students: What is the function of a literature review as part of a research cycle? Use the phrases above, as well as those in the diagram of the research cycle, to help you to **elaborate** your answer.

➢ As well as being part of the research process, a literature review may also stand alone. Such a review may provide an analysis of the current state of research into an area or topic. Discuss with another student:

| **elaborate** *v.* [I, T] |
| To give more details or new information about something |
| *He said he had new evidence, but refused to elaborate any further.* |

How could you make use of such a review in your field? How would you locate a stand-alone literature review?

The research cycle: from question to recommendation

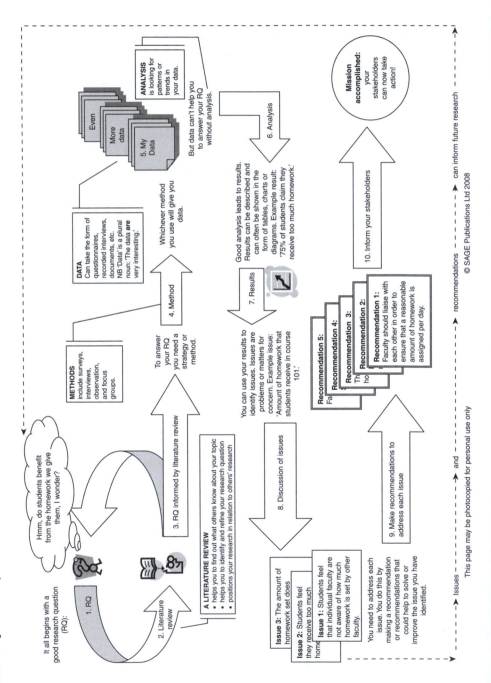

It all begins with a good research question (RQ):

Hmm, do students benefit from the homework we give them, I wonder?

1. RQ

2. Literature review

A LITERATURE REVIEW
• helps you to find out what others know about your topic
• helps you to identify and refine your research question
• positions your research in relation to others' research

3. RQ informed by literature review

To answer your RQ you need a strategy or method.

METHODS
include surveys, interviews, observation, and focus groups.

4. Method

Whichever method you use will give you data.

DATA
Can take the form of questionnaires, recorded interviews, documents, etc.
NB 'Data' is a plural noun: 'The data **are** very interesting.'

5. My Data
More data
Even

ANALYSIS
is looking for patterns or trends in your data.

But data can't help you to answer your RQ without analysis.

6. Analysis

Good analysis leads to results. Results can be described and can often be shown in the form of tables, charts or diagrams. Example result: '75% of students claim they receive too much homework.'

7. Results

You can use your results to identify issues. Issues are problems or matters for concern. Example issue: 'Amount of homework that students receive in course 101.'

8. Discussion of issues

Issue 3: The amount of homework set does

Issue 2: Students feel they receive too much hom

Issue 1: Students feel that individual faculty are not aware of how much homework is set by other faculty.

You need to address each issue. You do this by making a recommendation or recommendations that could help to solve or improve the issue you have identified.

9. Make recommendations to address each issue

Recommendation 5:
Recommendation 4:
Recommendation 3:
Recommendation 2:
Recommendation 1:
Faculty should liaise with each other in order to ensure that a reasonable amount of homework is assigned per day.

10. Inform your stakeholders

Mission accomplished: your stakeholders can now take action!

FOCUS E: STUDYING

E.1 Preparing an outline of an assignment

Preparing an outline of what you are going to write is an essential part of the writing process.

➢   Discuss with another student. Why is it a good idea to prepare an outline before you begin to write?
➢   Compare your ideas with those of other students and make an expanded list on your classroom whiteboard. Copy this longer list into your portfolio.

Different genres will affect the types of outline you need to prepare. For example, you may be asked to write the kind of essay that requires the traditional structure of:

* Introduction
* Body (organized into one main point per paragraph, possibly with topical headings)
* Conclusion
* References.

Alternatively, a research report may require:

* Introduction
* Literature review
* Methods
* Results
* Discussion
* Conclusion
* Recommendations
* References.

While this structure may work for a book review:

* Summary of book being reviewed
* Discussion
* Evaluation
* References.

However, you may find that there is no recommended structure for the type of essay you have been asked to write. In this case, you need to prepare a structure that best conveys your message. You can select from the headings provided above or use your own. If in doubt, check your outline with your tutor before you begin to write your first draft.

> **Strategy for Success #35:**
> **Always plan and prepare an outline before writing your first draft**
>
> Good preparation and outlining will help you to organize your thoughts, present your ideas logically, and answer the question.

➤ Follow these steps to preparing a useful outline:

1 **Prepare...**

    a. Consider the question or assignment. Break it down into its parts. What do you need to do in order to fulfil the requirements of the task?

    b. Consider the genre. Is it the kind of genre that has a standard structure, such as a research report?

2 **Write...**

    a. Headings

    b. Subheadings

    c. Notes under each heading to reflect the essential points that you want to make; one main point per paragraph.

3 **Check...**

    a. Have you covered all parts of the question?

    b. Have you included all the sections you need?

    c. Does your outline present your information in a logical way?

    d. Are your ideas presented convincingly?

4 **Avoid...**

    a. Including too much information.

➤ Work with another student. Prepare what is sometimes called a 'reverse outline'. Take one of the articles in this book that you have read and write an outline of it, as the author might have prepared before he or she started to write.

➤ Work with another student. Prepare an outline for an essay in answer to the following question:

What writing skills do students need for effective study in higher education? In answering this question, give examples from your own experience.

FOCUS F: APPLYING TO YOUR OWN SUBJECT

F.1 Locating, reading and summarizing a subject-related book chapter

➤ Locate and read a subject-related book chapter. Identify five pairs or sets of synonyms in the chapter and add them to your portfolio. Summarize your chapter.

Before you write, with your tutor, remember to agree upon a subset of annotations from the companion website which you would like him or her to use when marking your work.

F.2 Locating, reading and note-taking from a subject-related literature review

➤ Locate and read a subject-related literature review. Identify as many sets of superordinates and hyponyms in the review as you can. Make notes.

F.3 Identifying subject-related issues

➤ Read paragraphs 6, 10 and 11 of Article 5 again. Then interview, informally, a lecturer in your field. Ask him or her:

1   What issues currently dominate discussion in our field?
2   What methods of inquiry are employed?
3   What journals do you know of that focus on those issues?
4   What names are associated with various issues in our field?
5   Which articles or books do you think have had significant impact in our field?
6   What subdisciplines (and subdisciplines of subdisciplines) are there?
7   What current controversies are there in our field?

Make notes of the answers he or she provides.

Strategy for Success #36:
Gather data and use these to inform your writing

Good writing is based upon evidence, so, with your assignment in mind, gather data about your topics before you begin to write.

➢ Use your summary, notes and the data you have gathered through your interview to write a short article for a newsletter. Remember to agree with your tutor upon a subset of annotations from the companion website which you would like him or her to use when marking your work. Prepare an outline of your writing before you begin. Show your outline to your tutor. Give your article a heading, such as:

Economics: an introduction to current issues and controversies

or

A discussion of current issues and controversies in the field of …

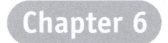

Documenting Skills

In this chapter, you can read an extract from a **journal article** about plagiarism. You can develop your skills in these areas:

Focus A: Reading

A.1　Looking ahead
A.2　Understanding and responding

Focus B: Learning language

B.1　Identifying citations
B.2　Paraphrasing
B.3　Introducing short quotes
B.4　Introducing long quotes

Focus C: Writing

C.1　Citations
C.2　Writing a list of references
C.3　Using sources in your own writing
C.4　Critiquing peer writing

Focus D: Researching

D.1　Different citation systems
D.2　Identifying your discipline's citation system

Focus E: Studying

E.1　Recording sources

Focus F: Applying to your own subject

F.1　Identifying citations in a subject-related article

▶ FOCUS A: READING

A.1 Looking ahead

---

abridged *adj.* [usually before noun]
An abridged book, play, etc., has been made shorter but keeps its basic structure and meaning.
The abridged edition was published in 1988.

'What I like about this chapter is that I found out about plagiarism and how understandings may differ from one culture to another. This gave me a chance to think about it. Also, I learned how to use two kinds of citation systems.'

Khawla Abdulla AL Manthari
(first-year student)

Below, you can read an **abridged** extract from a journal article about plagiarism.

➤   Before you read, discuss what you know about this topic with other students and your tutor. What does the word 'plagiarism' mean? To what extent does it occur in your context? Do you believe that it is a problem?

➤   Read the abstract. The phrase 'Pandora's Box', which is used in the title, is explained as referring to something where 'the elements contained inside are too frightening to allow escape for fear of the havoc that may result'. The author then gives a number of examples of such 'havoc'. Can you find two?

➤   The phrase 'Pandora's Box' is a metaphor. How effective is it in this context? Find out what it makes your tutor think of.

➤   Read and take notes on Article 6. The paragraphs have been numbered to help you to complete the tasks below.

ARTICLE 6: PANDORA'S BOX: ACADEMIC PERCEPTIONS OF STUDENT PLAGIARISM IN WRITING

Wendy Sutherland-Smith
(Abridged extract from Sutherland-Smith, W. (2005) 'Pandora's box:
academic perceptions of student plagiarism in writing. *Journal of English for
Academic Purposes*, 4, 83–95.)

Abstract

Plagiarism is viewed by many academics as a 'kind of Pandora's box' – the elements contained inside are too frightening to allow escape for fear of the havoc that may result. Reluctance by academic members of staff to discuss student plagiarism openly may contribute to the often untenable situations we, as teachers, face when dealing with student plagiarism issues. In this article, I examine the dilemmas English for Academic Purposes (EAP) staff face when dealing with student plagiarism in the tertiary classroom. The perceptions of all 11 teachers involved in teaching a first-year EAP writing subject at South-Coast University are detailed in light of the university's policy on plagiarism. My research indicates that not only is an agreed definition of plagiarism difficult to reach by members of staff teaching the same subject, but plagiarism is a multi-layered phenomenon encompassing a spectrum of human intention. Evaluating the spectrum can lead to differences in the implementation of university plagiarism policy, the result of which embodies issues of equity. The aim of the article is to encourage policy-makers and academic staff to acknowledge the concerns about implementation of plagiarism policy. Collaborative, cross-disciplinary re-thinking of plagiarism is needed to reach workable solutions.

5

10

15

Keywords: EAP writing classrooms; plagiarism; policy; teacher perceptions; university

20

Plagiarism: an ESL perception

1   A number of research studies undertaken in tertiary classrooms around the globe characterize perceptions of plagiarism both by students and teachers. Some studies survey the attitudes of students towards plagiarism and academic dishonesty (Dant, 1986; Deckert, 1993; Drum, 1986; Kroll, 1988; Matalene, 1985; Myers, 1998; Pennycook, 1996). Other studies attempted to ascertain teaching methods to overcome the problem of plagiarism in student writing (Belcher, 1995; Bloch & Chi, 1995; Braine, 1995; Howard, 1995, 1999). These studies found that there were widely differing conceptions of plagiarism by students, staff and institutions.

2   Early studies such as those of Dant (1986) and Kroll (1988) concluded that students had differing notions of plagiarism which ranged from considering copying

25

30

text as a legitimate activity to plagiarism as a moral wrong. Matalene (1985) argues that broader understandings of non-Western writing traditions are necessary. She asserts that 'ethnocentrism is a less and less appropriate response, we need to under-
35 stand and appreciate rhetorical systems that are different from our own' (p. 790), based on interview data from 50 undergraduate Chinese students at Shanzi Daxue University. Similarly, Myers (1998, p. 13) contends that traditional Western notions of plagiarism 'splinter on close examination … and a new order is needed'. This order is inclusive of the writing traditions of non-western backgrounds.

40 3   Sherman (1992) noted that first-year students in an Italian university gave verbatim answers without analysis or sourcing. She observed that 'what we all saw as plagiarism, they clearly saw as not only legitimate but correct and proper' (1992, p. 191). Sherman concluded that Italians value mimetic practice in written text whilst promoting oral debate for spoken text. Interestingly, Sherman's study high-
45 lights the fact that strategies such as rote learning and recounting tracts of text from the original are seen not only as acceptable, but desired. Bloch and Chi (1995) agree that cultural traditions shape preferred writing styles. They state that 'each form of rhetoric reflects the cultural traditions in which it is developed' in their study of Chinese students' use of citations in academic writing (p. 271). The
50 authors add that simplistic views of Western and Eastern views of differences in citation methods should be cautioned and that 'Chinese rhetoric is as complex and ever changing as is Western rhetoric' (p. 271). Deckert's (1993) survey of 170 first-year Chinese students' attitude to plagiarism makes similar findings. He notes that 'the student is simply pursuing the writing task in a manner consistent with her edu-
55 cational background and broader cultural experience' (p. 95). It is in this sense that the student is engaging in what Deckert terms 'learned plagiarism' (p. 95). Although supporting the idea that cultural context influenced his students' writing, he added:

4   They are the proverbial rote memorizers or recyclers. In other words, egocentric
60 concerns of learning well and feeling right about oneself together far exceed concern for either the college, the original writer, one's own classmates, or one's relationship with the teacher. (p. 104)

5   This conclusion drew criticism from Pennycook (1996), who suggests that Deckert (1993) operated within Western notions of value within academic writing.
65 Pennycook considers that Western notions of plagiarism are not cross-culturally applicable. He argues that in cultures where rote learning and huge feats of memory are regarded as displaying intellectual superiority, notions of Western citation styles are inapplicable or inappropriate. Pennycook claims that Deckert's Western framing of the notion of plagiarism and ownership of authorial work has been protected by
70 laws of intellectual property. He observes that:

6   Given the emphasis on the creative individual as producer and owner of his or her thoughts, it seems that the borrowing of words is often discussed in terms of *stealing* (author's emphasis) or committing a crime against the author of a text. This particular

connection presumably has its origins in the peculiarly Western conjunction between the growth of the notion of human rights and the stress on individual property, thus making the reuse of language already used by others a crime against the inalienable property rights of the individual. (1996, p. 214) 75

7   Pennycook's view that Western notions of plagiarism are merely one way of viewing the issue has received widespread support from other academics, particularly those writing in the cross-cultural studies area. Shen (1989) observes, when he 80 was instructed to 'write what you think and be yourself' when learning English in the USA, that:

8   To be truly myself, which I knew was the key to my success in learning English composition, meant not to be my Chinese self at all. That is to say, when I write in English I have to wrestle with and abandon (at least temporarily) the whole system of ideology 85 which previously defined me in myself ... I had to put aside an ideology of collectivism and adopt the values of individualism. (p. 461)

9   Many academics (Angelil-Carter, 2000; Howard, 1995, 1999, 2000, 2002; Lunsford & Ede, 1994; Pennycook, 1996; Scollon, 1994; Woodmansee & Jaszi, 1995) consider that plagiarism is not a simple matter of ascertaining whether text 90 was copied or not by students without attribution. There are deeper issues underlying such practices, which will be explored in this paper.

The study

10   The aims of the study were to explore the perceptions of plagiarism by 11 EAP teachers at South-Coast University. Specifically, these EAP professionals 95 teach an introductory writing subject in the Faculty of Business and Law. A further aim was to probe the EAP staff's attitude to the university plagiarism policy and their experiences in its implementation.

11   *Data collection*

Data were collected during Semester One 2002, from the 11 EAP staff who teach 100 the subject Writing for Academic Success at South-Coast University. The subject is a preparatory academic skills unit for first-year international students in the Faculty of Business and Law. Its aim is to prepare students for academic writing tasks such as case study reports and research essays as well as legal and business citation methods. The subject is offered at three campuses within Australia, two metropolitan and 105 one rural, as well as campuses in Indonesia and Malaysia. Data were collected by questionnaire survey and semi-structured interviews.

12   *Questionnaire*

Questionnaires were distributed to staff by internal mail and e-mail. Questionnaires contained mostly closed questions requiring yes/no or multiple-choice responses. 110

This design was adopted to make the document short and quick to answer, thus encouraging staff to take the time to complete it. Staff returned questionnaires via mail. From the overall questionnaire responses, a list of 10 interview questions was drawn up.

115 ### 13 *Interviews*

Ten semi-structured questions formed the basis of interviews as these questions focus on individual perceptions of plagiarism, definitions and teaching strategies to overcome plagiarism. Teachers were asked the same questions, in the same order for interview consistency. Interviews were intended to last approximately 40 minutes, 120 but some ran longer due to lengthy responses. Interviews were tape-recorded and then transcribed.

14 *Data analysis*

For data analysis, both interview transcriptions and survey responses were examined. An initial reading of interview transcripts gave a general impression of 125 responses. Interviews were then coded using the N*Vivo computer software program, which allows rich text documents to be coded and comparisons across transcripts to be made. Patterns of response may emerge which are then coded as nodes or themes across texts. In this study, common issues for teachers about plagiarism were sought and they are identified as elements in this paper.

130 ## Results and discussion

15 The discussion below indicates some of the areas in which EAP teaching staff experience problems in implementing South-Coast University's plagiarism policy. University Regulation 4.1(1) states:

16 Plagiarism is the copying of another person's ideas or expressions without appro-
135 priate acknowledgment and presenting these ideas or forms of expression as your own. It includes not only written works such as books or journals, but data or images that may be presented in tables, diagrams, designs, plans, photographs, film, music, formulae, websites and computer programs. Plagiarism also includes the use of (or passing off) the work of lecturers or other students as your own. The University regards plagiarism as an
140 extremely serious academic offence.

17 The following section presents teacher perceptions which emerged from the coding of teacher responses.

18 *Intention*

Staff at South-Coast University are divided on the issue of intentional and uninten-
145 tional plagiarism. Nine of the 11 teachers consider that some writing is plagiarism as defined under regulation 4.1, but lack of intentional wrongdoing by the student means plagiarism is not present. Two teachers maintain that all acts of plagiarism

are, by definition, intentional, as students are well aware of the policy and know that copying texts is punishable under the regulations.

19   *Unintentional plagiarism*   150

Nine teachers feel that a distinction needs to be made in official policy between intentional and non-intentional plagiarism. These teachers characterize plagiarism as only deliberate or deceptive acts of copying, such as downloading papers from commercial websites. Other acts are unintentional plagiarism, which is not, in the teachers' eyes, a punishable offence. Comments by Dave (aged 41) typify the com-   155
ments made by the nine teachers and characterize the essential differences between these actions. Dave said:

> 20   Where a student deliberately takes an essay from an Internet papermill site and hands it in, then *that's* plagiarism. But where you've got kids with poor referencing skills and you know … no earthly idea of academic conventions and they just copy stuff out of   160
> the textbook, then that *shouldn't* be considered plagiarism in my book. (Dave's emphasis, interview, 25 June 2002).

21   Dave's view is supported by the literature. Pennycook (1996, p. 226) asserts that 'it is certainly important to distinguish between good and bad plagiarism, that is between those who reuse parts of texts very well and those who seemed to ran-   165
domly borrow'. Similarly, Howard (1995, 1999) says intention is the key. She states, 'if the plagiarism was not intentional … was it engendered by an ignorance of cita-tion conventions? By a monologic encounter with unfamiliar words and concepts?' (1999, p. 797).

22   The thrust of Dave's assertion is that academic writing genre may be unfamil-   170
iar to many EAP students. De Voss and Rosati (2002, p. 193) agree and consider that 'students aren't necessarily evil or thinking, but instead they're learning to negotiate and do research in new spaces'. Hawley (1984) contends that plagiarism is on a continuum from unintentional to intentional action by students. He believes that plagiarism can occur where 'sloppy paraphrasing to verbatim transcription   175
with no crediting of sources' is evident (p. 35) and may, in fact, come 'more from simple ignorance rather than deceit' (p. 38). Lea and Street (1999) in an examina-tion of higher education textual practices concluded that students found it 'difficult to identify their own ideas separately from sources' (p. 80). Academics such as Gardiner (2001), Hawley (1984), Howard (1995, 1999), Larkham and Manns   180
(2002), Martin (1992, 1997), and Pennycook (1996) consider that investigating the plagiarist's intention is a positive step towards decreasing plagiarism itself. They believe a closer examination of intention may reveal that cases classified as plagia-rism, may not, in fact, be so.

23   *Intentional plagiarism*   185

Two members of staff, Luke and Claire, believe all acts of copying are plagiarism, and intention is therefore automatically proven. These teachers believe that all acts

of plagiarism should be punished stringently. Claire's (aged 47) attitude is: 'Saying
that there is such a thing as unintentional plagiarism is a bit of a cop out, really. I
190 mean, how do you know what a student really intended?' Luke (aged 51) was more
adamant. He said:

> 24 When they copy verbatim from the textbook, if I'm particularly shocked by what I
> see, then I'll usually write the word PLAGIARISM across the page, usually across the
> text itself. In some cases I'm able to prove where it's come from and I share that with the
> 195 student with great glee. I don't think they're as naive as they pretend to be. (Interview, 30
> May 2002)

25 The view of plagiarism as 'intellectual murder most foul' representing a 'clear
and present danger to intellectual liberty' (Mirsky, 2002, p. 98) is also shared by
second language researchers. In Angelil-Carter's (2000, p. 3) work on plagiarism in
200 South Africa, a teacher describes plagiarism as 'the scourge of academic life'. A similar perspective is found in Le Heron's (2001) six-year study of plagiarism in an
information systems course in New Zealand, where plagiarism is characterized as a
synonym for cheating and learning dishonesty. Kolich (1983, p. 141) views plagiarism as 'the worm of reason' and contends plagiarism is morally reprehensible but
205 says it can only be prevented when teachers encourage a sense of intellectual curiosity and discovery in their students. Loveless (1994) claims that academic plagiarism
is 'the cardinal sin of academe' and argues that transgressors should be 'dealt with
harshly' (p. 510). Similarly, Laird (2001) considers plagiarism as an 'academic
felony' and to minimize the chances of plagiarism by her students, keeps 'rhetorical
210 fingerprints' of her students' writing for comparison (p. 56). For these teachers and
researchers, plagiarism is an offence of automatic admission of wrong. The teachers
interviewed in this study reflect the general division in the second language community over the issue of intention in plagiarism.

26 Burdensome administration

215 All staff note that heavier workloads, larger classes, increased pressure to publish,
lengthy grant application processes and dealing with overwhelming degrees of
administration have encroached on teaching time. When academics balance immediate tasks such as entering exam grades against pursuing plagiarists, many simply
do not have the time to invest in the often lengthy chase. Detection of plagiarism is
220 only the starting point. Verifying plagiarism, collating student work and presenting
evidence to the responsible committee takes an inordinate amount of time. The
female lecturer estimated it took her an extra 15 hours to prepare evidence for the
relevant committee. When the committee found that plagiarism had not been con-
clusively proven, and warned the student without penalty, she said she would not
225 pursue cases formally again. Such perceptions are again supported by instances in
the literature. Whiteman (2001) writes that her similar experience consumed an
'astonishing amount of time' and she 'finally gave up ... and returned to my grading
a more cynical educator' (p. 26).

27 *Is it really worth it?*

Nine of the 11 academics interviewed feel that the time, effort and 'sleepless   230
nights' utilized in deciding to take a case of student plagiarism through the correct
channels is not worth the effort. Lyn (aged 45) elaborates. She said she was
worried about a suspected case of plagiarism and sought advice from a senior
academic, who advised her that she would 'regret' the decision as 'the hassle
involved' was not worth the time taken. After 'agonizing about it for a couple of   235
days', Lyn decided not to formally report the case, and said she 'reluctantly let it
go' (interview, 7 June 2002).

28 *Teachers as judge, jury and executioner*

Nearly all teachers interviewed felt that past experience of colleagues indicated that
the relevant university committee would 'let the students off'. All teachers related   240
stories about colleagues, from different departments, who had pressed for inquiry
hearings in cases of student plagiarism. In all instances, the committee dismissed
the case against the student as not sufficiently proven. This is not to suggest that the
committee's process or procedure was incorrect, but rather the staff perceived the
committee's decision as a 'lack of professional support' and a 'waste of time'. All   245
interviewees propose that 'minor' cases of plagiarism should be handled by individual staff, although there is no agreement on what constitutes a 'minor' act of
plagiarism. Some teachers believe 'minor' means one or two sections of the writing
task are missing citations. Other staff consider a couple of copied paragraphs, or
ineffectively paraphrased text, are 'minor.' There is no synthesis of opinion on this   250
point. Most teachers consider it is 'more effective' (Luke, aged 48) if cases of plagiarism are handled by teachers and not through formal academic processes. Mark
and Claire considered the system 'fails the staff', therefore it is better to 'handle
things yourself'.

Recommendations   255

29   Patently, university departments must re-evaluate their approaches in dealing
with the issue of student plagiarism with their staff. The findings indicate that open
and intellectual engagement with the issue of plagiarism itself and individual reactions to the policy is overdue. Additionally, attempts must be made to find methods
of implementing the plagiarism policy in a more uniform manner. From the com-   260
ments of staff, it is clear that little confidence exists in current university procedures
and processes to deal with cases of alleged plagiarism. Where staff consider that the
system fails them, and are creating a sub-system of dealing with cases on their own,
the university runs the risk of allegations of inequitable treatment of individual
cases. I consider that the re-establishment of confidence in the system is a top prior-   265
ity, which requires dialogue between policy-makers and staff for effective
implementation. Increasing awareness of the importance of intellectual honesty and
endeavour may be achieved through professional development sessions for staff and

re-kindling a sense of the value that intellectual rigour has for the institution and its
270 academic reputation.

Conclusion

30 Clearly, plagiarism is a multi-faceted issue. One key observation emerging
from this research is that whilst teachers operate collaboratively in the preparation
and delivery of academic writing preparation programs, they approach issues of
275 plagiarism within those programs individually. The concerns staff raised about negative collegiate responses to involvement with plagiarism inquiries and lack of
confidence in the existing university structures require careful consideration by
institutional policy-makers and departments. As teachers, we must decide to either
ignore plagiarism completely and engender new generations of writers with a sense
280 that all writing is freely available to take and use without any attribution, or we must
decide to tackle this difficult and sensitive issue. One step towards overcoming plagiarism in tertiary environments is to open Pandora's box. Once opened, the
elements need to be publicly and effectively discussed. Until such discussion takes
place, plagiarism remains hidden in the shadows of academic discourse.

References

Angelil-Carter, S. (2000). *Stolen language? Plagiarism in writing*. London:
Longman.
Belcher, D. (1995). Writing critically across the curriculum. In D. Belcher, &
G. Braine (Eds.), *Academic writing in a second language: Essays on research and
Pedagogy* (pp. 135–154). Norwood, NJ: Ablex.
Bloch, J., & Chi, L. (1995). A comparison of the use of citations in Chinese and
English academic discourse. In D. Belcher, & G. Braine (Eds.), *Academic writing
in a second language: Essays on research and pedagogy*. Norwood, NJ: Ablex.
Braine, G. (1995). Writing in the natural sciences and engineering. In D. Belcher, &
G. Braine (Eds.), *Academic writing in a second language: Essays on research and
Pedagogy*. Norwood, NJ: Ablex.
Dant, D. (1986). Plagiarism in high school: A survey. *English Journal*, 75(2), 81–84.
De Voss, D., & Rosati, A. (2002). It wasn't me, was it? Plagiarism and the Web.
Computers and Composition, 19(2), 191–203.
Deckert, G. D. (1993). A pedagogical response to learned plagiarism among
tertiary-level ESL students. *Journal of Second Language Writing*, 2, 94–104.
Drum, A. (1986). Responding to plagiarism. *College Composition and Communication*,
37, 241–243.
Gardiner, S. (2001). Cybercheating: A new twist on an old problem. *Phi Delta
Kappan*, 83(2), 172–174.
Hawley, C. (1984). The thieves of academe: Plagiarism in the university system.
Improving College University Teaching, 32, 35–39.

Howard, R. M. (1995). Plagiarisms, authorships and the academic death penalty. *College English*, 57(7), 788–806.

Howard, R. M. (1999). *Standing in the shadow of giants: Plagiarists, authors, collaborators.* Stamford: Ablex.

Howard, R. M. (2000). Sexuality, textuality: The cultural work of plagiarism. *College English*, 62(4), 473–491.

Howard, R. M. (2002). Don't police plagiarism: Just teach! *The Education Digest,* 67(5), 46–49.

Kolich, A. M. (1983). Plagiarism: The worm of reason. *College English*, 45(2), 141–148.

Kroll, B. M. (1988). How college freshmen view plagiarism. *Written Communication,* 5(2), 203–221.

Laird, E. (2001). We all pay for Internet plagiarism. *The Education Digest,* 67(3), 56–59.

Larkham, P., & Manns, S. (2002). Plagiarism and its treatment in higher education. *Journal of Further and Higher Education,* 26(4), 339–349.

Lea, M., & Street, B. (1999). Writing as academic literacies: Understanding textual practices in higher education. In C. Candlin, & K. Hyland (Eds.), *Writing: Texts, processes and practices* (pp. 62–82). London: Longman.

Le Heron, J. (2001). Plagiarism, learning dishonesty or just plain cheating: The context and countermeasures in information systems teaching. *Australian Journal of Educational Technology,* 17(3), 244–264.

Loveless, E. (1994). A pedagogy to address plagiarism. *College Composition and Computers,* 44(4), 509–514.

Lunsford, A. A., & Ede, L. (1994). Collaborative authorship and the teaching of writing. In M. Woodmansee, & P. Jaszi (Eds.), *The construction of authorship: Textual appropriation in law and literature* (pp. 417–436). Durham: Duke University Press.

Martin, B. (1992). *Plagiarism by university students: The problem and some proposals.* Wollongong: University of Wollongong.

Martin, B. (1997). Credit where it's due. *Campus Review,* 7(21), 4–10.

Matalene, C. (1985). Contrastive rhetoric: An American writing teacher in China. *College English*, 47(8), 789–808.

Mirsky, S. (2002). Technology is making it harder for word thieves to earn outrageous fortunes. *Scientific American*, 286(4), 98–99.

Myers, S. (1998). Questioning author(ity): ESL/EFL, science, and teaching about plagiarism. *Teaching English as a Second or Foreign Language,* 3(2), 1–21.

Pennycook, A. (1996). Borrowing others' words: Text, ownership, memory and plagiarism. *TESOL Quarterly,* 30(2), 201–230.

Scollon, R. (1994). As a matter of fact: The changing ideology of authorship and responsibility in discourse. *World Englishes,* 13(1), 33–46.

Shen, F. (1989). The classroom and the wider culture: Identity as a key to learning English composition. *College Composition and Communication,* 40(1), 459–466.

Sherman, J. (1992). Your own thoughts in your own words. *ELT Journal,* 46(3), 190–198.

Whiteman, S. (2001). The price of an A: An educator's responsibility to academic honesty. *English Journal*, 91(2), 25–30.

Woodmansee, M., & Jaszi, P. (1995). The law of texts: Copyright in the academy. *College English*, 57(7), 769–787.

Wendy Sutherland-Smith is Lecturer in Business Communication in Bowater School of Management and Marketing at Deakin University, Australia. Her research interests include intellectual property and its relationship to academic writing and cross-disciplinary notions of authorship.

▶ FOCUS A: READING

A.2 Understanding and responding

➤ Find sentences or phrases in Article 6 that express the same ideas as those given below. In each case, you will find the sentence or phrase you need in the paragraph provided. | ANSWERS |

> **ethical** *adj.*
> Relating to principles of what is right and wrong.
> *The use of animals in scientific tests raises difficult ethical questions.*

1 Some research has tried to identify steps that teachers can take to address the issue of plagiarism in students' written work. (Paragraph 1)

2 Students vary in their attitudes towards plagiarism, from believing that it is acceptable practice at one end of the spectrum to believing that it is **unethical** at the other end. (Paragraph 2)

3 All language is influenced by the customs and behaviours of the society in which it was fostered. (Paragraph 3)

4 Many academics agree that Western attitudes towards plagiarism are simply one way of approaching the issue. (Paragraph 7)

5 Unless a student deliberately sets out to copy another's work, it cannot be called plagiarism. (Paragraph 18)

6 Some staff believe that plagiarism occurs only when students set out to copy something on purpose, or with the intention of misleading. (Paragraph 19)

7 According to one researcher, plagiarism may be the result of poor rewording or outright copying of another's writing, with no reference to the original text. (Paragraph 22)

8 Some researchers contend that finding out whether plagiarism was committed on purpose or not may show that writing labelled plagiarism may not actually be an example of plagiarism. (Paragraph 22)

9 On the subject of plagiarism in ESL students' writing, the research participants are unable to agree about the question of intention. (Paragraph 25)

10 All research participants suggest that insignificant examples of plagiarism can be addressed by the teacher; however, participants differ as to which examples of plagiarism may be classified as 'insignificant'. (Paragraph 28)

11   If tutors believe that they will not receive support from the organization and instead take matters into their own hands, the organization is in danger of being accused of treating different cases unfairly. (Paragraph 29)

12   Teachers work together to design and teach classes to develop ESL students' writing skills, but they address the issue of plagiarism in their students' work differently. (Paragraph 30)

➤   Read again sentences 2, 3, 4, 5 and 6 above. Discuss them with another student. Describe your own view, and listen to the other student's ideas.

▶ FOCUS B: LEARNING LANGUAGE

B.1 Identifying citations

➤   In Chapter 5, section D.2, you considered literature reviews and their purpose. Review the notes you made in relation to this section. Remind yourself of the purpose of conducting and writing up a literature review and exchange your ideas with another student.

➤   Article 6 in this chapter does not have a section called 'literature review', yet the article provides a literature review. How does it achieve this? Do you prefer one approach? If so, why?

➤   The author of Article 6 uses three different approaches to citing another author's work. They are:

- **Paraphrasing** the other author's ideas.
- Inserting a short, direct, quote (no more than two lines) from the other author's writing into Article 6.
- Inserting a longer, direct, quote (more than two lines) from the other author's writing into Article 6.

> **paraphrase** *v.* [T]
> To express in a shorter, clearer, or different way what someone has said or written.
> *To paraphrase Finkelstein, mathematics is a language, like English*

Work with another student. Find and highlight three examples of each of the above in Article 6.

➤   Why does the author paraphrase sometimes, and provide a direct quote at other times? What is the effect of each? Why do writers paraphrase and quote? Discuss these questions with another student.

Strategy for Success #37

Use evidence from other sources in the form of paraphrasing or direct quotes to support and give weight to the ideas you are writing about.

B.2 Paraphrasing

The ability to paraphrase is a similar skill to the ability to summarize (see section C.1 in Chapter 5).

To paraphrase, you need to:

- identify ideas that will be useful in your own writing
- use your own words to express these ideas
- acknowledge the original source of the idea by providing a reference to it.

Strategy for Success #38

As you read and identify the main ideas of paragraphs, try to express them in writing using your own words. Add these to your notes.

➤ Work with another student. One should read paragraphs 1, 2, 9 and 22. The other should read paragraphs 25, 27, 28 and 29. Identify the main idea of each paragraph, and use your own words to express it ⬚ANSWERS⬚. Make notes and use these notes to help you to exchange your 'main ideas' with the other student. Discuss the eight ideas. Do you agree/disagree with them?

➤ Work with another student. Paraphrase each of the 4 ideas from Article 6 below. Follow these steps:

1 Identify the main idea. What is the author saying?
2 Discuss and describe the idea in your own words. Use synonyms, superordinates and hyponyms (see section B.3 in Chapter 5 to help you here).
3 Make notes.
4 Use your notes to express the idea in your own words in writing. Do not refer to the author's original words at this point.
5 Add the appropriate reference, as in this example: (Pennycook, 1996).

Idea 1

Given the emphasis on the creative individual as producer and owner of his or her thoughts, it seems that the borrowing of words is often discussed in terms of *stealing* (author's emphasis) or committing a crime against the author of a text. This particular connection presumably has its origins in the peculiarly Western conjunction between the growth of the notion of human rights and the stress on individual property, thus making the reuse of language already used by others a crime against the inalienable property rights of the individual. (Paragraph 6)

Idea 2

The teachers interviewed in this study reflect the general division in the second language community over the issue of intention in plagiarism. (Paragraph 25)

Idea 3

All staff note that heavier workloads, larger classes, increased pressure to publish, lengthy grant application processes and dealing with overwhelming degrees of administration have encroached on teaching time. When academics balance immediate tasks such as entering exam grades against pursuing plagiarists, many simply do not have the time to invest in the often lengthy chase. (Paragraph 26)

Idea 4

Detection of plagiarism is only the starting point. Verifying plagiarism, collating student work and presenting evidence to the responsible committee takes an inordinate amount of time. (Paragraph 26)

B.3 Introducing short quotes

➢ In order to include a direct quote from another's writing in your own work, you need to **integrate** it into your own writing. This means that any writing which includes a quote must flow grammatically and logically. Study the examples below from Article 6:

> **integrate** *v.* [I, T]
> If two or more things integrate, or if you integrate them, they combine or work together in a way that makes something more effective.
> *Colourful illustrations are integrated into the text.*

1 She asserts that 'ethnocentrism is a less and less appropriate response, we need to understand and appreciate rhetorical systems that are different from our own'. (Paragraph 2)
2 She observed that 'what we all saw as plagiarism, they clearly saw as not only legitimate but correct and proper'. (Paragraph 3)
3 They state that 'each form of rhetoric reflects the cultural traditions in which it is developed'. (Paragraph 3)
4 He notes that 'the student is simply pursuing the writing task in a manner consistent with her educational background and broader cultural experience'. (Paragraph 3)

➢ In each case above, identify who the pronoun (she, they) refers to.
➢ In each case above, identify the tense used to introduce the quote. Why is this particular tense used? Is it always used when introducing a quote? Find other examples in this book and discuss this point with your tutor.

➢ Four verbs are used to introduce the quote that follows. They are:

- assert
- observe
- state
- note.

Work with another student to expand this list. Brainstorm your own ideas and skim Article 6 (and the other articles in this book if you wish) to help you – you will find other verbs that are used to introduce quotes. Compare your list with those of other students, and create a 'master' list to add to your portfolio.

B.4 Introducing long quotes

➢ Long quotes are treated differently from short quotes when they are integrated into writing. Work with another student and study the three examples you highlighted in section B.2 above. Scan this book for other examples of long quotes. Discuss: how are long quotes treated? Apart from their length, what differences do you observe between the treatment of short quotes and that of long ones? What similarities do you notice? Make a list of differences. Compare your list with those of other students and make a 'master' list.

➢ Discuss. Why do you think long and short quotes are treated differently?

▶ FOCUS C: WRITING

C.1 Citations

➢ Read the answers to a student's questions about **citations** below:

> **citation** *n*. [C]
> A line taken from a book, speech, etc. = quotation.
> *The essay begins with a citation from 'Hamlet'.*

What is a citation?
A citation is a reference to any published item that gives the details needed to identify the item accurately.

What is the numerical system of citation?
When you include a paraphrase or quote, you need to provide information about where your paraphrase or quote comes from. You can do this by numbering each paraphrase or quote in parentheses. Then, at the end of your writing, you write the number, and note the full citation next to it in a section entitled 'References' or 'Works cited'. This system, known as the numerical system, is the one used in Article 3.

Here is an example. In Article 3, we find:

> This has been prompted by factors such as increasing student numbers, widening diversity in the backgrounds of students, high student drop-out rates in first year, and the accelerating implementation of teaching technologies and flexible course delivery [1]. (Extract from Article, 3, lines 16–19)

At the end of Article 3, we find:

> 1 C. McInnis and R. James with C. McNaught, *First Year on Campus: Diversity in the Initial Experiences of Australian Under-graduates,* Centre for the Study of Higher Education, University of Melbourne, September 1995, 1.1.

What is the author–date system of citation?

In the author–date system, you write the author's name and year of publication at the end of the paraphrase or quote. Full citation information for all of your sources is then provided at the end of your writing, in alphabetical order by author surname, in a section entitled 'References' or 'Works cited'. The author–date system is in widespread use. Articles 1, 2, 4, 5 and 6 are based upon this system.
Here is an example. In Article 6, we find:

> Pennycook (1996, p. 226) asserts that 'it is certainly important to distinguish between good and bad plagiarism, that is between those who reuse parts of texts very well and those who seemed to randomly borrow'. (Extract from Article 6, paragraph 21)

At the end of Article 6, we find:

> Pennycook, A. (1996). Borrowing others' words: Text, ownership, memory and plagiarism. *TESOL Quarterly*, 30(2), 201–230.

What about page numbers?

In all cases, if you are providing the citation for a quote, you need to include the page numbers to help the reader find the quote in its original form if he or she so wishes.

In the numerical system, page numbers appear only in the list of references.

In an author–date system, they appear in the text, usually after the year of publication, like this:

> Similarly, Myers (1998, p. 13) contends that traditional Western notions of plagiarism 'splinter on close examination ... and a new order is needed'. (Extract from Article 6, Paragraph 2).

What do 'ibid' and 'op. cit' mean?

Both phrases are used to avoid repeating a citation.

'Ibid' means 'in the same place' and is used when the work has been cited immediately above.

'Op. cit' means 'in the work cited' and it is used when the work has been cited somewhere else in the list of references, but not immediately above.

There is no need to use these phrases (they help the writer more than the reader) but you might read them (see the reference list for Article 3, for example), so it is useful to know what they mean.

➢ Prepare your own questions to ask your tutor. Ask about:

- the difference between a list of 'references' and a 'bibliography'
- the advantages and the disadvantages of numerical and author–date systems
- secondary sources: what they are and how to refer to them
- any other related issues or areas you would like to know about.

C.2 Writing a list of references

➢ This is an extract from the list of references provided for Article 6:

Matalene, C. (1985). Contrastive rhetoric: An American writing teacher in China. *College English*, 47(8), 789–808.

Mirsky, S. (2002). Technology is making it harder for word thieves to earn outrageous fortunes. *Scientific American*, 286(4), 98–99.

Myers, S. (1998). Questioning author(ity): ESL/EFL, science, and teaching about plagiarism. *Teaching English as a Second or Foreign Language*, 3(2), 1–21.

Pennycook, A. (1996). Borrowing others' words: Text, ownership, memory and plagiarism. *TESOL Quarterly*, 30(2), 201–230.

Scollon, R. (1994). As a matter of fact: The changing ideology of authorship and responsibility in discourse. *World Englishes*, 13(1), 33–46.

They are all references to journal articles. Note the order of information:

1 Surname
2 Initial
3 Year of publication
4 Article title
5 Journal title
6 Volume
7 Issue
8 Page numbers for the article.

Note the use of punctuation (full stops and commas) and formatting (indentation, italics and parentheses). Does this look familiar to you? Where else was a similar approach taken in this book?

➤ Skim some of the lists of references at the end of the articles in this book. Find and highlight two examples of each of the following that are mentioned in the reference lists.

- A book
- A chapter in a book
- A journal article
- A website.

For each text type, make a note of the order of information, the punctuation used and how it has been formatted.

➤ A useful online programme can help you to write your references using the Harvard system. Visit Neil's Toolbox (2007): www.neilstoolbox.com/bibliography-creator/index.htm.

Strategy for Success #39

Always make a note of the full bibliographic details of useful books or articles, when you consult them.

C.3 Using sources in your own writing

➤ Work with another student. Write an essay (around 800 words) either in favour or against this statement:

Statement

'Academic plagiarism is the cardinal sin of academe and transgressors should be dealt with harshly.'

(Adapted from Article 6, paragraph 25)

Your essay should have an introduction and conclusion, and you should include at least one example of each of the following:

- paraphrase
- short quote
- long quote.

You may quote from any text in this book, or from your own sources. Provide a list of references at the end of your writing. Use an author–date system unless your tutor suggests otherwise.

Before you write, with your tutor, remember to agree upon a subset of annotations from the companion web site which you would like him or her to use when marking your work.

➤ Proofread your work when you have finished, and read it out loud to your partner. Remember that doing this can help you to hear errors or ambiguities that you may not be able to see.

C.4 Critiquing peer writing

➤ Read other students' writing and critique it by offering constructive written feedback. Read the constructive feedback on your own work, and improve it accordingly, before submitting your work to your tutor.

▶ FOCUS D: RESEARCHING

D.1 Different citation systems

Different organizations within disciplines use different citation systems. Some of the more widely used systems are listed below:

Abbreviation/name of citation system	Organization	Discipline/subject area
ACS	American Chemical Society	Chemistry
APA	American Psychological Association	Social sciences
APSA	American Political Science Association	Political Science
ASA	American Sociological Association	Sociology
CBE	Council of Biology Editors	Science
IEEE	Institute of Electrical and Electronics Engineers	Technology
MHRA	Modern Humanities Research Association	Humanities; Arts
MLA	Modern Language Association	Humanities; Language studies

➤ Discuss these with your tutor. Which is he or she familiar with? Which one does he or she use? Which ones follow an author–date system?

D.2 Identifying your discipline's citation system

➤ Find out which reference system your tutors expect you to use. If you are a first-year student and you are taking a range of different subjects, you may find that you will have to use more than one citation system.

For example, your EAP tutor may want you to use the APA system, while your chemistry tutor may prefer another. However, it is important to use the same system consistently throughout the same piece of work.

Strategy for Success #40

Become familiar with the preferred citation system within your discipline at an early stage in your student life. This will save you a lot of time and effort later.

➤ Find out as much as you can about the system that you are expected to use. Go online to help you do this.
➤ Obtain a copy of your department or university style guide. Add this to your portfolio and refer to it as needed.
➤ If you are writing an article for a magazine, newsletter or journal, you will probably find that you are required to use their citation system. Find out what this is before you begin writing.

Strategy for Success #41

Add a copy of your department or university style guide to your portfolio, and refer to it as needed.

▶ FOCUS E: STUDYING

E.1 Recording sources

Index card *n*. [C]
A small card for writing on, used especially in an index.

➤ Read Strategy for Success #39. Discuss with other students and your tutor: Why is this strategy recommended?
➤ Keeping an annotated bibliography as mentioned in Chapter 1, section D.2, is an ideal way of recording sources or potential sources. However, many people prefer an **index card** approach to using a computer. Here is an example:

Index *n. pl.* indexes. [C]
A set of cards or a database containing information, usually arranged in alphabetical order and used especially in a library.

Subject area: _____

Author(s): _____

Year of publication: _____

Title of article: _____

Title of book/journal: _____

_____

Place of publication: _____

Publisher: _____

Other information (e.g. URL): _____

Date retrieved: _____

Comments: _____

_____

➤ Design your own card if you would like to use this approach. Then decide how you would like to organize your cards – by author or by subject area.

▶ FOCUS F: APPLYING TO YOUR OWN SUBJECT

F.1 Identifying citations in a subject-related article

➤ Locate a subject-related journal article on a topic that interests you. Using a set of highlighter pens in the colours suggested, identify as many as possible of the citation types below in your article. Highlight both in-text citations and the corresponding reference in the reference list. Here is an example from Article 6:

Lea and Street (1999) in an examination of higher education textual practices concluded that students found it 'difficult to identify their own ideas separately from sources' (p. 80). (Extract from Article 6, paragraph 22)

In the list of references:

Lea, M., & Street, B. (1999). Writing as academic literacies: Understanding textual practices in higher education. In C. Candlin, & K. Hyland (Eds.), *Writing: Texts, processes and practices* (pp. 62–82). London: Longman.

Find examples of:

- books (highlight in yellow)
- book chapters (highlight in grey)
- journal articles (highlight in green)
- conference proceedings (highlight in turquoise)
- websites (highlight in pink).

➤ Exchange your article with another student and check his or her work.

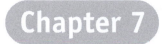

Chapter 7

Researching Skills

In this chapter, you can read a **journal article** about the research that informed the development of this book.

You can develop your skills in these areas:

Focus A: Reading

A.1   Looking ahead
A.2   Understanding and responding
A.3   Identifying steps in a process
A.4   Alternatives in data presentation

Focus B: Learning language

B.1   Words commonly used in descriptions of research
B.2   First person, singular and plural
B.3   Using the passive voice
B.4   Referring to data presented graphically

Focus C: Writing

C.1   Summarizing a research process
C.2   Paraphrasing and synthesizing ideas

Focus D: Researching

D.1   Understanding qualitative and quantitative research

Focus E: Studying

E.1   The 'prepare, draft, evaluate, proofread, improve, reflect' cycle

Focus F: Applying to your own subject

F.1   Presenting subject-related data
F.2   Summarizing a subject-related research process

▶ FOCUS A: READING

A.1 Looking ahead

In this chapter, you can read an abridged journal article about the research that this book is based upon. The full version is available in *Learning and Teaching in Higher Education: Gulf Perspectives*, Vol. 5, No. 1, January 2008.

➤ The research was mentioned briefly in Chapter 1. What can you remember about it? Discuss this with other students and your tutor. Use the headings below to help you. Then check your ideas by returning to Chapter 1 and scanning for information. Make a note under each heading.

What the research set out to do

Criteria for tutors taking part in the research

Two areas which outcomes suggested students need to develop

A feature of this book that represents a new approach to teaching EAP

Students' ultimate purpose in studying a book such as this one

➤ Study the title of the article in this chapter. Can you identify a deliberate ambiguity?
➤ Scan the headings used in the article. Discuss what you think will be included under each one.
➤ Discuss or remind yourself of the meaning of some or all of these words as they might be used within an academic context:

1	discipline (n.)	11	interdisciplinary (adj.)
2	outcome (n.)	12	predicate on (v.)
3	practitioner (n.)	13	phase (n.)
4	deploy (v.)	14	data (n.)
5	humanities (n.)	15	discursive (adj.)
6	qualitative (adj.)	16	collate (v.)
7	heterogeneous (adj.)	17	elective (n.)
8	homogeneous (adj.)	18	pedagogical (adj.)
9	rational (adj.)	19	induct into (v.)
10	specific (adj.)	20	genre (n.)

➤ Read and annotate Article 7. Include some of the definitions above in your annotations. As you read, consider what comments the reviewer might have made if he or she had received this abridged version of the article.

ARTICLE 7: MATERIAL MATTERS: THE CASE FOR EAP AS SUBJECT MATTER OF EAP COURSES

Caroline Brandt

Assistant Professor,

The Petroleum Institute, Abu Dhabi, United Arab Emirates

Abstract

Recent research investigated English as a Second Language (ESL) undergraduate preparation through 'English for Academic Purposes' courses in relation to recipient subject lecturers' expectations. Qualitative data were gathered from 36 faculty teaching ESL undergraduates in nine countries. A two-phase approach included seeking discursive responses to questionnaires from faculty and information about curricula. Outcomes highlighted difficulties with material selection for EAP tutors. Tutors chose between 'general interest' or 'discipline-specific' material, but reported that the former could lead to oversimplification or discipline irrelevance, while the latter usually requires some specialized subject knowledge which may be beyond tutors' remit.

Addressing this, it is suggested that articles about EAP-related topics can form the subject matter of EAP courses with significant benefits. In particular, they can simultaneously provide students with models of academic writing, while the content reinforces skills needed for successful study.

Discipline specificity, and the degree to which EAP/ESP tutors and programmes should accommodate it, has been at the heart of much recent research and debate in the fields of EAP/ESP (e.g. Spack, 1988; Gaffield-Vile, 1996; Hyland, 2002; Pulverness, 2002). This paper reports on outcomes of recent research which suggests that practitioners continue to experience difficulties in relation to the degree of discipline specificity of their teaching materials. Prompted by this situation, change in practice at one institution, involving the use of EAP-related materials, is described. It is suggested that the deployment of EAP-related materials can address many of the problems identified in the research.

The research investigated the practice and expectations of faculty employed in tertiary institutions in relation to ESL students. The faculty at the centre of the study fell into two groups: those teaching English for Academic or Specific Purposes (EA/SP) and those teaching different subjects in disciplines that included humanities and science (for convenience, those teaching EA/SP are referred to as 'tutors' below while those teaching other subjects are referred to as 'lecturers', though in practice this distinction was not always maintained in the data; when referring to both groups, the term 'faculty' is used. Likewise, alternative terminology was also evident in the data, such as the use of 'EGAP' or 'English for General Academic Purposes', where I have used 'EAP'. The terms most commonly encountered in the data are employed

35   here). Specifically, the research set out to investigate tutors' practice vis-à-vis lecturers' expectations of their ESL students. Qualitative methods sought data on the views of faculty and included questionnaires sent to both groups.

Several outcomes related to the 'carrier' content of EA/SP courses, that is, the material that forms the object of study. The choice was found to lie between using

40   'general interest' material about topics such as global warming, generally felt to be the only option in the case of discipline-heterogeneous classes, or using 'discipline-specific' material, considered suitable in the case of more discipline-homogeneous classes. In the 'general interest' approach, the research identified several difficulties including sustaining student motivation when topics are perceived to lack discipline

45   relevance; while in a 'discipline-specific' approach, tutors felt that lack of subject knowledge meant that they were unable to deal with the topic in sufficient depth in relation to their students' capabilities, a difficulty that has been observed by others in the field (e.g. Spack, 1988).

In response to these and other issues detailed below, a change in practice was

50   introduced on a first-year course involving the use of articles drawn from the field of EAP. For several reasons discussed below, it is suggested that this is a rational response to the problem of identifying meaningful carrier content.

EAP courses

EAP courses are designed to prepare students to study their chosen discipline at

55   tertiary level through the medium of English, and as such encompass the develop-ment of a wide range of skills within broad areas such as academic writing, reading, listening, and speaking, as well as research and study skills. Courses reported on in this research included those that were described as being skills-oriented, in which case the emphasis was on the skills that all students are likely to need regardless of

60   their eventual discipline (see Jordan, 1997; Bell, 1998; Dudley-Evans & St John, 1998). All such courses adopted 'general interest' materials. Alternatively, courses could be oriented more towards a discipline such as chemistry or law; these relied to a large extent upon discipline-specific materials. One example of a course offering a combination of the two was described, and several courses provided students with

65   the opportunity to choose from a range of topics provided. However, in all cases significant commonality of skills addressed was found.

Regardless of whether courses follow a 'general interest' or a 'discipline-specific' approach, decisions must be made with regard to the 'carrier' content of courses, that is, the articles that are provided for students to study as examples of academic

70   discourse. In the case of discipline-heterogeneous student groups, general interest topics are often used on the grounds that they could reasonably be expected to interest the majority of students. This is the approach taken with a text found to be in widespread use in the data, Jordan's (1999) *Academic Writing Course: Study Skills in English*. This text includes articles on topics such as how paper and breakfast

75   cereal are made, and the physical description of Australia. Other courses investi-gated did not use published materials but developed their own, often drawing upon

the media as a source; examples of topics on these courses frequently related to social issues such as global warming. However, it has been pointed out that the use of general interest topics can lead to a situation in which the content fails to be of interest to students in itself, being seen instead simply as a prompt to communicate. 80 Such topics, particularly in cases where the material has lost its authenticity through simplification or abridgment, may also lead to '[the alienation of] students whose subject knowledge exceeds the level of the text'. (Pulverness, 2002). These, and other issues arising from a 'general interest' approach, are discussed below.

On other courses described in the data, a greater emphasis was placed on teaching 85 English within and for the target community. This approach is in accord with Hyland (2002), who argues in favour of discipline-specificity on the grounds that different disciplines have different views of knowledge, research practices, and ways of seeing the world, and that these distinct discourses need to be reflected in ESP materials, in order to enable students to engage effectively with their disciplines. Accordingly, the data 90 included reference to courses with titles such as 'English for Law' or 'English for Medicine'. Such courses are tailored towards a particular discipline or subject and were often referred to as representing an 'English for Specific Purposes' (ESP) approach.

However, it was noted that even where classes were organized according to discipline, students of one subdiscipline may not be interested in reading material 95 drawn from another subdiscipline; for example, students of one branch of engineering, such as mechanical, may have little interest in petroleum engineering. This problem has been identified elsewhere in the literature (e.g. Clapham, 2001: 99). It appears to be the case that the issue of specificity – and how specific to become – is one that cannot be avoided, regardless of the apparent homogeneity of class com- 100 position (Pulverness, 2002).

Yet others (for example, Gaffield-Vile, 1996: 108) have suggested an 'integrated EAP/subject content course' in which sociology (Gaffield-Vile's example) is used as a 'carrier' content source on the grounds that it is interdisciplinary and more likely to help students adjust to the new culture of an English-speaking country, assuming that stu- 105 dents are heading to such a context. This proposal is a useful one in that the topic, being interdisciplinary, may have wider appeal to students. The proposal presented here takes this idea a stage further by providing students with EAP-related materials, which provide opportunities for linguistic analysis and development within a context that is of immediate relevance to all ESL students studying at English-medium institutions. 110

Research base

The change in practice that this paper reports on was predicated on research which set out to investigate the following questions:

What skills do lecturers in various disciplines expect first-year university students to have, and why do they expect them to have these skills? 115

What skills do EAP tutors teach, and why do they think that these skills are important?'

Method

Research methods were organized into two phases. Phase 1 involved identifying
120   potential participants, carried out through a process termed 'generative networking'
(Brandt, 2004: 389–399), similar to 'snowball sampling' (a technique for developing a respondent base where existing respondents identify further potential
participants from among their colleagues and acquaintances) but differing slightly
from it in its reliance upon email as the medium of communication. The method
125   was taken to its third degree; that is, first-level participants identified second-level
participants, who in turn identified third-level participants. A response rate of
42.86% led to the receipt of 36 completed questionnaires (16 from subject lecturers
and 20 from EAP tutors), referring to 24 different courses in nine tertiary institutions in countries that included Indonesia, Australia, Bahrain and the UAE.

130   ### Questionnaire

To gather relevant data, questionnaires were prepared. The first section was aimed
at gathering information about the individual, the institution at which he or she
worked and the course or courses that he or she taught, or had taught in the five
years prior to participation in the research. In the second section, all faculty were
135   asked to relate their responses to the needs of students who had achieved, or were
considered to be capable of achieving, an IELTS score of five or above.

Analysis

Participants had been asked to respond discursively and so qualitative techniques
were employed to analyse these data. Initially, two data books were created, one for
140   each faculty group, and data were entered by collating all responses to the same
question, then searching for themes within the collated responses. Themes were
then coded to facilitate subsequent identification of patterns (Strauss & Corbin,
1990; Miles & Huberman, 1994; Denzin & Lincoln, 1998). Once this process had
been completed and all data had been entered, it was possible to reorganize them
145   according to the identified themes, enabling the identification of consistencies or
differences within the data.

Phase 2

In Phase 2, a small number of faculty who had not participated in the first phase
were invited to comment upon the preliminary findings. The purpose of this stage
150   was to enable, if analysis of these new data suggested it was necessary, the rejection,
modification, or supplementation of the emerging issues, analysed through a similar
process to that employed in Phase 1.

25 final outcomes were labelled 'critical issues' after completion of Phase 2 and are
likely to be of interest to anyone involved in the design of EAP courses. Those that
155   relate to oral communication skills are discussed in Brandt, 2008. Six issues are of
particular interest in relation to the content of EA/SP courses and these are discussed
below.

Critical issues for the design and content of EAP courses

Four issues are considered to be central to this paper:

1. The suitability of general interest 'carrier' content   160
The use of so-called general interest materials was heavily criticized in the data for reasons that may be summarized as follows:

(a)   Little obvious relevance to students' disciplines in some cases.
(b)   Lack of interest to students, exacerbated by (c) below.
(c)   The rationale for their use is not always made clear to students, who may be   165
      unable to understand why they are reading about the manufacture of glass
      bottles, for example, when they have registered to study psychology or law.
(d)   Material was sometimes no more challenging than late secondary level.
(e)   Some 'social issue' topics (for example, vivisection, abortion) were felt to
      reflect dilemmas specific to particular contexts which were of less concern and   170
      relevance in other contexts.
(f)   The media were cited as common sources of materials for teaching both EAP
      and ESP; however, it was noted that articles from the internet or newspapers,
      for example, tended to be 'journalistic' and as such did not represent examples
      of academic writing.   175

2. The suitability of discipline-specific 'carrier' content
Several tutors felt that they had been inadequately prepared for the task of teaching ESP. ESP seemed to be something that many tutors 'fell into because of circumstance' or were asked to do because of secondary school qualifications. Perhaps as a consequence, a number of tutors felt uncertain about their focus.   180
One noted:

> They [students] often know the subject better than I do [...]. It can be embarrassing and
> it often means I can't push them in the way I could if I was sure of my ground [...] and
> sometimes I don't know what to focus on – is it the language? Is it the concepts? They
> often seemed intertwined. (Mary, Bahrain)   185

Mary identifies a tension between language and content, and wonders where her emphasis should lie. Pennycook (1994: 17) has suggested that this problem is underpinned by the belief that language and content can exist independently of one another. He suggests that, rather than being simply a 'medium through which meanings are expressed', language in fact: 190

> ... itself has meaning, [...] it is not simply a medium through which meanings based on
> some sense of objective reality or personal intention pass [...] it may play a fundamental
> role in how we make sense of the world and how the world makes sense of us.
> (Pennycook, 1994: 17)

195   This strongly suggests that language cannot be taught as if it were an independent reality or devoid of meaning. By extension, it may be further argued that language skills cannot constructively be taught independently of one another. As Mary noted, language and content are 'intertwined'; reading and writing, for example, complementing each other as they do, are likewise intertwined.

200   A third issue identified in the data is concerned with the idea that disciplines are themselves homogeneous. However, a number of tutors reported teaching groups of students organized according to discipline, but discovering that their interests in fact differed according to their elected subdisciplines. This prompted one tutor to observe that: 'ultimately, if you take into account students' interests and electives, you

205   need to prepare different material for each individual.' Specificity, taken to its logical conclusion, means custom-made materials and programs for each individual.

3. The lack of identity of EAP as a subject

Tutors and lecturers alike observed that there was a status and credibility issue with EA/SP, which was 'often demoted to a background service provided to enhance the

210   greater good but [...] not entirely necessary.' It was felt to be 'not a proper subject' but often seen as 'scaffolding for *real* subjects like science' [italics in original]. It seems that the role can be poorly understood by those teaching other areas, and tutors reported having in some cases to explain and justify their existence at institutional levels. The problem may be exacerbated by the current options for sources of

215   material, which lie between materials that are of general interest but which may as a result suffer from the problem of '*futility:* [because] the content has little pedagogical rationale beyond serving as a medium for language learning' (Pennycook, 1994: 13, italics in original), and materials that must be 'hijacked' from other disciplines.

4. The institutional need to respond to students who wish to change

220   ### discipline after having taken a discipline-specific course

In institutions which offered ESP courses at pre-sessional level, it was noted that difficulties were created for students wishing to change discipline, having completed an ESP course or courses. For example, in one institution, students were required to take a course in English for Law, Engineering, Science, Arts, Business or

225   Humanities, depending upon their target discipline. However, the question arises: what should the institution do with students who successfully complete English for one discipline but subsequently wish to change to another? To what extent does a course in, for example, 'English for Law' assist the student who subsequently transfers to a science degree?

230   Two further issues are also of interest here though perhaps of less direct relevance to the theme of discipline-specificity:

5. The need to integrate the development of reading and writing skills

Of the 24 courses referred to in the data, eight took a 'discrete' skills approach at least some of the time, that is, individual skills were treated separately in the form of

classes or complete courses with titles such as 'Academic Reading'. Tutors felt that   235
this could lead to a 'fragmentation of language and lost teaching opportunities'.
Several tutors reported a preference to teach reading and writing combined, and
speaking and listening combined. This fragmentation may have contributed
towards critical issue 6 below, in which tutors distinguished between the study of
language for its own sake and the use of language for communication, a division   240
that echoes the language/content split described and challenged by Pennycook
(1994: 13). This situation draws into question the viability and value of attempting
to teach reading divorced from writing, or speaking divorced from listening.

6. The need for students to 'operationalize' English rather than 'examine it as an isolated entity or entities'   245

Faculty involved in teaching or receiving ESL students felt strongly that at this level
and context students did not need to study language per se, but needed instead to
apply it in situations through which they could develop and practise academic skills,
including those related to research and writing about that research. However, if
EAP students are to conduct even small-scale research, what can they most usefully   250
investigate? Clearly, the options available to them from general interest topics or
from within their own disciplines may suffer from a number of the criticisms
identified above.

Reflecting upon these students, however, it is possible to see that they themselves,
their teaching and learning in particular, could self-reflexively become their own   255
object of study, actively inquiring into their own contexts and their roles and
responses within them. A number of areas suggest themselves for this. The students
are, for example, in transition, an area that is well documented (see Yan & Peat,
2004: 79, for example); their teaching and learning is at the heart of many debates,
including the issues of what language and skills they need, what content should be   260
used, how people learn and study, as well as topics such as critical thinking, plagiarism, teamwork, presentation skills, and learner autonomy.

What would be the impact, therefore, of asking EA/SP students to read articles on
such topics, which serve to define EA/SP as an academic field, and to conduct
research into such areas? This question informed the change in practice that is   265
described next.

Changing practice

The study was conducted at a national university in South-East Asia during semester 2, 2005–2006. All students participating achieved an IELTS score of 5 or above
during the subsequent semester. English is the medium of instruction at this uni-   270
versity and students took core courses in English language during their first and
second years, normally tailored to their broad disciplines.

The study focused on 20 students taking 'English for Business 4'. Students were
studying a range of subjects related to business studies. The course ran for three

275 hours per week for 14 weeks. Aims focused on the development of academic reading, writing and speaking. Assessment was achieved through course work and a final examination. Course work required students to work in teams to carry out small-scale research projects related to their topic. Students were instructed to choose a topic from within the field of EAP or language learning. Topics selected

280 included study skills and information literacy. Having identified research questions, students were required to carry out small-scale literature reviews, construct questionnaires to elicit data, collate and analyse results, write a report and present their results.

Material matters

285 The use of EAP-related materials represented a significant departure for these students who had previously developed their skills through texts such as Jordan's (1999) *Academic Writing Course* (semester 1), and Cotton, Falvey and Kent's (2001) 'Market Leader' series (semesters 2 and 3).

These students, at the end of their fourth semester, had therefore experienced

290 three approaches to material selection: general interest (represented by Jordan's *Academic Writing Course*); discipline-specific (represented by Cotton et al.'s Market Leader series) and EAP-related materials. Clearly the opportunity for feedback on the three experiences was presented, and students were asked: which did you prefer, and why?

295 All 20 students broadly preferred the EAP-related approach. Many reasons were given, including:

'It was interesting to research ourselves and other students. I didn't think before that we were interesting [enough] for this. [...] I liked doing projects that no one had done already.'

300 'We get enough business stuff on our other courses. It was good to have a change.'
'I enjoyed reading about the reasons why we'd been learning some of the things you taught us to do.'

When asked if they would have preferred to have studied EAP-related topics during all four semesters, all responded affirmatively but six qualified their response by

305 adding that they would have liked a combination of EAP-related materials and business-related materials, with, in two cases, an emphasis on the former. No one expressed an interest in a course based upon general interest topics.

Discussion

An EAP-related approach can address the issues above and offer a number of

310 advantages to all participants in the process, that is, students, tutors, lecturers, and the institutions in which they work. These benefits, and the issues they address, are shown in Table 1 and discussed below.

Table 1   Addressing the issues: The benefits of using EAP as subject matter of EAP courses

Issue	Benefits of using EAP as subject matter for...			
	Students	**Tutors**	**Lecturers**	**Institutions**
1. The suitability of 'general interest' carrier content	Students can be provided with good examples of academic writing of different genres about relevant, appropriate topics. Students' status and confidence enhanced as they are able to participate actively in their current field of EAP. Ideas for original research will emerge	Tutors are teaching their own subject. Opportunities to learn about own field are enhanced as tutors are working with materials about EAP. Ideas for original research will emerge as a matter of course through collaboration with students	Status and credibility of colleague-tutors enhanced as they are seen to be teaching their own subject	Enhanced institutional credibility as EAP moves from status of outsider to fully fledged research-worthy subject
2. The suitability of discipline-specific 'carrier' content	Students taught by tutors who are recognized as specialists and experts in their field. Tutor credibility is improved	Minimal need for tutors to undergo specific training	Status and credibility of colleague-tutors enhanced as they become identified with a recognized subject	Less need to provide specific discipline-related training for tutors
3. Identity of EAP	Students see EAP as established, research-worthy, field. They read articles about that field which reinforces the skills required for scholarship and the workplace	Tutors recognized as experts in their field	Field of EAP more clearly established and defined in the eyes of those involved in other disciplines. Status and credibility enhanced	Field of EAP clearly established and defined within the institution; less need for departments to spend time explaining or justifying themselves
4. Students transferring from one discipline to another	Students take predominantly EAP-related course: transfer problems are eliminated			
5. Separation of skill areas	Reading and writing can constructively be addressed together in EAP-related approach			
6. Need to 'operationalize' students' existing language proficiency	An action enquiry approach allows students to read, reflect upon, research and write about their own current experiences and contexts. Relevance, authenticity, originality and immediacy of topic guaranteed. Focus is on developing self-awareness, on learning about and understanding own experience and contexts, and successfully communicating this to others.			

One of the main benefits of using EAP-related materials is their ability to reinforce through their content the skills that students are developing at this stage in their aca-

315　demic lives, and to provide the opportunity for enquiry in and through action. Critically, the approach can allow students to read, reflect upon, research and write about *their own current experiences and contexts*. Authenticity, originality, relevance and immediacy of topic are ensured through a focus which is more on responding to the content of texts, developing self-awareness, on learning about and understanding

320　their own experience and contexts, and successfully communicating this to others, than on aspects of language in relation to arbitrarily selected general interest content or discipline-specific content which may nevertheless lack relevance to students or be beyond the brief or expertise of their EAP tutors. In this approach, language and content are seen as inseparable; by reading, researching and writing, students are

325　actively engaging with academic texts, thereby 'operationalizing' the language for an entirely valid and meaningful purpose. Tutors, under less pressure to acquire discipline-specific knowledge, can concentrate on their own subject. Students can find themselves actively and democratically engaged in contributing to knowledge within their subject, a subject that should not be viewed as theirs temporarily, but as

330　a necessary aspect of all stages of their student lives.

Another significant benefit lies in the potential for enhanced status and credibility that the subject of EAP could acquire. The current perception of the field, as a support service reliant upon 'hijacking' others' material, could shift towards an understanding of EAP as a recognizable, well-defined subject in its own right, with

335　its own concepts, arguments, issues, and body of research.

Conclusion

While the use of EAP as subject matter on EAP courses could go a considerable way towards addressing the issues raised by the research, it is not suggested that discipline-related materials be entirely rejected. Rather, it would be possible and

340　constructive to complement EAP-related materials (which, following student-centred principles could be student-sourced) with discipline-specific material, by focusing on the type of article being studied, in recognition of the fact that:

> the academic language needs of our students are closely related to the purposes of the
> disciplines they are being inducted into. That is, different disciplines foreground different
345　> types of language – in terms of genre, grammar and lexis. (Cullip & Carol, 2002)

The desirability of using student-sourced material related to their specific disciplines has been raised by several writers, such as Dudley-Evans and St John (1998), and more recently by Pulverness, who noted that:

> At certain points it will no doubt be necessary to […] give students the opportunity to
350　> deal with text functions which are more subject-specific, such as describing technical
> process, for example. However, given the difficulty of identifying the right materials, the

best source for such texts may well be the students themselves, if they can provide examples [of] journal articles [...] which they have actually had to tackle – or will do so – in the course of their studies. (Pulverness, 2002)

In the EAP-related approach complemented by student-sourced, discipline-specific 355 materials that is proposed here, students could learn about issues such as needs, purposes, genre, and so forth, and then relate these understandings to their own disciplines, providing them with an opportunity to see how their own discipline 'foregrounds different types of language'.

Within such an approach, there need be no limit to the number of disciplines rep- 360 resented in each class; indeed a variety could be seen as an advantage as students seek to explain their articles to others outside their intended field, including their tutors. For example, if students read an article that introduces EAP, they could be asked to locate a comparable article in relation to their own discipline – that is, one written as an introduction to the field. Likewise with abstracts (students read an 365 EAP-related abstract and then locate a medicine-related abstract); with conference proceedings, with full journal articles, or with book reviews, for example. Why should EAP students, for example, not read this paper? This paragraph scores a Flesch-Kincaid Grade Level of 11.4, suggesting it is readable by high-school graduates, and it presents a number of ideas and issues that offer opportunities for discussion and 370 further research that could be conducted by EAP students themselves.

With this approach, we can introduce the student to different academic genres at a stage when this is most needed. EAP-related material can offer opportunities for linguistic analysis and original exploitation within a context that is of immediate relevance to all ESL students studying at English-medium institutions, acknowledging 375 their transitional status.

References

Bell, T. (1998). A description of the skill-based EAP Training for Pre-departure students at the British Council in Jakarta. *Internet TESL Journal,* Vol. 4/9, September. Available: iteslj.org/ (retrieved December 22 2006)

Brandt, C. (2004). Using generative networking to gather qualitative data. In Davidson, P., Bird, K., Al-Hamly, M., Aydelott, J., Coombe, C. & Khan, M.A. (Eds) *Proceedings of the 9th International TESOL Arabia Conference: ELT in the IT Age.* USA: TESOL Publications.

Brandt, C. (2008). Powerpoint or posters for EAP students' presentation skills development? In Stewart, T. (Ed.) (2008) *Speaking: Contexts and Innovations* (TESOL Classroom Practice Series). USA: TESOL International.

Clapham, C. (2001). Discipline specificity and EAP. In Flowerdew, J. & Peacock, M. (Eds) *Research Perspectives on English for Academic Purposes.* Cambridge: Cambridge University Press.

Cotton, D., Falvey, D. & Kent, S. (2001). *Market Leader Course Book: Upper Intermediate Business English.* UK: Pearson Education Ltd.

Cullip, P. F. & D. Carol (2002). Tailoring an EAP course to disciplinary needs: The UNIMAS effort. *Universiti Malaysia Sarawak.* Available: www.melta.org.my/ET/2002/wp05.htm (retrieved December 22 2006)

Denzin, N. K. & Y. S. Lincoln (Eds) (1998) *The Landscape of Qualitative Research.* USA: Sage Publications Inc.

Dudley-Evans, T., & M. J. St John (1998). *Developments in English for Specific Purposes.* Cambridge: Cambridge University Press.

Gaffield-Vile, N. (1996). Content-based second language instruction at the tertiary level. *English Language Teaching Journal,* Vol. 50/2, April.

Hyland, K. (2002). Specificity revisited: how far should we go now? *English for Specific Purposes,* 21 (4): 385–395.

Jordan, R. (1997). *English for Academic Purposes.* Cambridge: CUP.

Jordan, R. R. (1999) *Academic Writing Course: Study Skills in English.* UK: Pearson.

Miles, M. B. & A. M. Huberman (1994). *Qualitative Data Analysis: A Sourcebook of New Methods.* Beverly Hills, CA: Sage.

Pennycook, A. (1994). Beyond (f)utilitarianism: English *as* academic purpose. *Hong Kong Papers in Linguistics and Language Teaching,* p. 17.

Pulverness, A. (2002). Squaring the circle: teaching EAP to large mixed groups. *The English Teacher,* Vol. 28, June.

Spack, R. (1988). Initiating ESL students into the academic discourse community: how far should we go? *TESOL Quarterly,* 22 (1), 29–52.

Strauss, A. & J. Corbin (1990). *Basics of Qualitative Research.* London: Sage Publications.

Yan, D. & M. Peat (2004). Enhancing research and teaching to support students in transition from school to university. *The China Papers,* November. Available: science.uniserve.edu.au/pubs/china/vol4/CP4_I1.pdf (retrieved January 30 2007)

▶ FOCUS A: READING

A.2 Understanding and responding

➢ Find and highlight the words below in Article 7. The line number is provided to help you. Study the context of each word. Is the definition you discussed with another student before you read the article accurate? If not, modify your definition and change your annotation, if necessary.

1 discipline (line 8)	5 specific (line 8)
2 outcome (line 7)	6 interdisciplinary (line 104)
3 qualitative (line 36)	7 data (line 4)
4 rational (line 51)	8 pedagogical (lines 216–217)

➤ Read Article 7 and, working with another student, answer some or all of the following questions.

1   What do you understand by the phrase 'discipline specificity'? Have you ever taken an EAP course that used 'discipline-specific' materials?
2   Name an author mentioned in Article 7 who has written about 'discipline specificity' and find the title of his or her work. Does the title interest you? Would you want to read the work?
3   The author identifies a decision that EAP tutors have to make with regard to their teaching material. What is the decision concerned with?
4   What is meant by 'discipline-heterogeneous' and discipline-homogeneous'? Which kind of class are you attending?
5   Why was a change in practice introduced on the EAP course in question?
6   What is the general purpose of the section entitled 'EAP courses'?
7   In lines 85–106, an argument in favour of 'discipline-specificity' is presented, followed by a description of a related problem. Another researcher proposed a solution to this problem. Discuss these three stages with another student and make notes in relation to each one below:

  (a) The argument in favour of 'discipline-specificity'.
  (b) A description of a problem related to 'discipline-specificity'.
  (c) A solution suggested by another researcher.

8   Why do you think the word 'snowball' is used when describing the method in lines 119–129? What does its use suggest to you?
9   Give an example of a question that was asked in the first part of the question-naire used to gather data.
10 'Participants had been asked to respond discursively and so qualitative tech-niques were employed to analyse these data' (lines 138–139). Explain what this means to another student, or listen and respond to another student's explanation.
11 Phase 2 of the research enabled 'the rejection, modification, or supplementa-tion' of the issues that resulted from the analysis of the data. Find a synonym for each of these three words:

  (a) rejection
  (b) modification
  (c) supplementation.

12 The use of general interest content was criticized in the research for lack of relevance to students' disciplines. Do you agree that this is a problem?
13 Discuss with your tutor the extent to which he or she feels able to teach discipline-specific courses. Find out which disciplines he or she would be most interested in working with.
14 'Language and content are "intertwined"'. Do you agree with this statement? Give one or two examples from your own experience.

15 What does the author mean by a 'credibility issue'? (line 208)

16 What is the effect of the author's use of the word 'hijacked' in line 218? Why is it written in inverted commas?

17 What does the author mean by the phrase 'viability and value' (line 242)?

18 What do you think is the difference between 'operationalizing' English and 'examining it as an isolated entity'? (lines 244–245)

19 How does the course you are taking now compare with the one described in lines 268–283?

20 Why were the students who participated in the change in practice ideally placed to do so?

caveat *n.* [C] *formal*
A warning that something may not be completely true, effective, etc. *She will be offered treatment, with the caveat that it may not work.*

21 The report ends with a **caveat**, described in the conclusion. What is this caveat? Why might it be a good idea to end a report such as this in this way?

22 Read the list of references provided at the end of Article 7. Identify one or two sources that you would like to look at, if you had time. Explain your choice to another student.

Strategy for Success #42

When reading a research report, always consider the processes used to obtain results. You might want to use similar processes one day.

A.3 Identifying steps in a process

➤ All research is a process, and therefore all research reports are likely to include descriptions of the process the research went through. Working with another student or students, make notes of the main stages in the research process described in Article 7. Include both the preliminary research and the change in practice. You will use these notes in C.1, below.

➤ Compare your notes and stages to those of another pair or group of students. Identify any discrepancies and try to agree upon one set of notes. Share your ideas with your tutor.

Strategy for Success #43

Engage your tutor in discussion on a range of topics of direct or indirect relevance to your studies.

A.4 Alternatives in data presentation

➤   Article 7 presents a summary of the research outcomes in table form (see Table 1). What are the benefits of doing this, (a) for the writer and (b) for the reader?

➤   What other approaches to data presentation are you aware of? Discuss your ideas with another student and draw up a list.

FOCUS B: LEARNING LANGUAGE

B.1 Words commonly used in descriptions of research

➤   Return to the list of words in section A.1 above. Which words could be used in descriptions of other research projects? Make a list of these words in your vocabulary record. Use a new page and give this list a title such as 'words used to describe research'.

➤   In Chapter 5, you studied the 'research cycle'. What can you remember? Work with a student or students to identify the key stages. When you have finished, refer to the 'research cycle' to check your ideas. Add any missing words or phrases to your list.

➤   Using the nouns 'research' and 'data' sometimes causes difficulties for students. Find out from your tutor what these difficulties are, and how to avoid them. Highlight the issues in your vocabulary record.

B.2 First person, singular and plural

Broadly, writers in the hard sciences and engineering prefer to downplay their personal role to highlight the issue under study, while a stronger identity is claimed in the humanities and social sciences papers. (Hyland, 2002: 352)

In general, academic texts tend not to use personal constructions such as *I* (and *my* and *me*) but instead use *we* to 'reduce personal attribution' (Kuo, 1999: 125). This is due to the fact that they discuss and argue from an objective, not a subjective, perspective; that is, the data speaks for itself. (Nishina, 2007)

Many students believe that they should avoid using the first person singular in their writing. However, research (e.g. Webb, 1992; Hyland, 2002) indicates that while the use of the second person 'you' is rare, the use of the first person singular (I, me, my, etc.) can be acceptable. Its use can depend on **norms** within your discipline, as suggested by the quotes above. Its use may also depend on a need to:

> **norm** *n.* [C]
> The usual or normal situation, way of doing something, etc: be/become the norm. *Joyce's style of writing was a striking departure from the literary norm.*

•   *position yourself* within your writing. For example, sometimes you need to explain how your ideas relate to others' ideas: do they build upon others' ideas, or differ from them?

- **assert yourself** within your writing. For example, you might need to show that your perspective is a unique or personal one: are you perhaps using a concept in a unique way?
- *involve and identify* with the reader.

assert yourself *v.*
To behave in a determined way and say clearly what you think. *Women began to assert themselves politically.*

The first person may also be used in cases where an alternative would simply be too clumsy.

Nishina, 2007, suggests that the first person plural may have two different functions. Read this extract from the article 'A Corpus-Driven Approach to Genre Analysis: The Reinvestigation of Academic, Newspaper and Literary Texts', and identify the two functions:

The function of the use of *we* can be divided into two categories depending on the context: inclusive and exclusive. The former includes target readers (or hearers) while the latter does not (Kuo, 1999: 126). In addition, the use of *we* as opposed to *I* in academic texts implies an idea that 'the author' and 'the reader' or 'other researchers' agree to follow the process of the argument, and it provides a more 'objective' discussion through being inclusive. This aspect provides us an environment in which there is greater contact and greater solidarity between writer and reader; the use of *I* creates an environment which is more informal, individual and personal (Coniam, 2004: 283). (Nishina, 2007)

➤ Describe the two functions as you understand them and discuss your answers with another student and your tutor. Does your tutor agree with the claims above?

➤ The best way to find out what is appropriate in your discipline is by reading books and articles from your discipline. The next time you do this, notice any examples of use of the first person.

Strategy for Success #44

Become an aware reader. Notice both the content of a text and elements of the language used to express that content.

➤ Study the following examples of use of the first person singular. They have all been drawn from the articles in this book. Discuss the effect of the use of the first person with another student (does it allow the author to *position* or *assert* him or herself, or to *involve* the reader?)

'What is EAP? Who are EAP lecturers? What do they do? What are they interested in? I would like to try to answer some of these questions.' (Andy Gillett, Article 2, lines 2–3)

'There is often discussion whether these two terms – EAP and study skills – mean the same. I find it useful to make a distinction between general study skills that are not concerned with language and language study skills that will probably form part of an EAP course.' (Andy Gillett, Article 2, lines 32–35)

'Furthermore, I would agree wholeheartedly with Upton when he states that one major strength of this book is the use of authentic materials.' (Averil Coxhead, Article 4, lines 126–127)

'I do not deny that programs that instruct students to write in other disciplines can work.' (Ruth Spack, Article 5, lines 114–115)

➤ Study this example of the first person plural. Is the use of 'we' inclusive or exclusive?

'English teachers cannot and should not be held responsible for teaching writing in the disciplines. The best we can accomplish is to create programs in which students can learn general inquiry strategies, rhetorical principles, and tasks that can transfer to other course work. This has been our traditional role, and it is a worthy one.' (Ruth Spack, Article 5, lines 122–126)

If you wish to avoid using the first person, the use of the passive voice can help you. This is considered in the next section.

B.3 Using the passive voice

In the abstract of Article 7, you will find many examples of the passive voice, such as this one:

Data were gathered from lecturers in tertiary institutions in Australasia and the Arabian Gulf.

➤ Read the abstract again. Highlight examples of the passive voice and compare your selection with another student. Discuss: why is the passive voice common in this abstract? Ask your tutor for his or her views.
➤ Read the following statements about the use of the passive voice. Work with another student and decide which are true and which are false. Check your ideas with your tutor, and then correct those sentences which are false. ANSWERS

1 The passive voice can be useful when you do not know the agent (the agent is the person who performed the action you are writing about).
2 When using the passive voice, you must mention the agent if you know who the agent is.
3 It is possible to overuse the passive voice in academic writing.
4 The passive voice can be useful when it is not important for the reader to know who the agent is.
5 Both transitive and intransitive verbs can occur in the passive voice.
6 Mentioning the agent at the end of the sentence can be useful if you want to write about the agent in your next sentence.

7 Using the passive voice is not the only way of avoiding mention of the agent in your writing.

8 Using the passive voice can help your writing to seem more objective.

9 The passive voice can be useful if you want to emphasize what was done rather than who did it.

10 The passive voice occurs more frequently in spoken English than in written English.

B.4 Referring to data presented graphically

A summary of the research outcomes is presented in table form in Article 7.

➢ How does the author introduce this table in her writing?

Good writers always make a reference to each table or figure in their writing. This is because it would be wrong to assume that your reader will make the connection between your words and your table or figure.

➢ Study these other ways of introducing data presented graphically (i.e. tables, figures, charts, diagrams):

- See Table 1 below.
- These figures remained constant (Table 1)
- These figures remained constant (see Table 1)
- As shown in Table 1…
- …, as shown in Table 1.
- Table 1 shows …
- Table 1 indicates that …
- The information summarized in Table 1 below suggests that…
- These figures are shown in Table 1 below.

➢ Make a note of these phrases in your portfolio. You may want to use them again later.

FOCUS C: WRITING

C.1 Summarizing a research process

➢ Use the annotations you made as part of section A.1 and the notes you made in section A.3 to help you to write a summary of the research process outlined in Article 7. Use the passive voice where appropriate and some of the words and phrases that you have studied in this chapter.

 Before you write, with your tutor, remember to agree upon a subset of annotations from the companion website which you would like him or her to use when marking your work.

C.2 Paraphrasing and synthesizing ideas

In much academic writing, you are required to compare and contrast the ideas of other writers. You need to be able to do this when you write a literature review, whether it is a stand-alone review, a review that is integrated throughout your writing, or written as a separate section entitled 'Literature review'.

To write a good literature review, you need to be able to:

1 Identify the key **claims** that an author is making in his or her writing.
2 Evaluate an author's claims.
3 Paraphrase or summarize others' claims.
4 Provide evidence for others' claims.
5 Compare and contrast different authors' claims noticing where they are similar and where they **diverge**.
6 Identify what is not covered by the literature (this suggests areas for your own research).
7 Provide accurate references for your review.

> Read the literature review in Article 7 (the section is called 'EAP courses') and identify:

1 A paraphrase of a claim about how general interest materials only provide a **stimulus** for communication.
2 A criticism of the argument in favour of discipline-specific material, and the names of two authors who support this criticism.
3 A paraphrase of an approach that is similar to the one proposed by the author of Article 7.
4 What is not covered by the literature and a proposal for addressing this.

> While answering the questions above, you will have seen a number of phrases that can help you to paraphrase, evaluate, compare and contrast claims, and refer to their authors. Here is one example:

- (see Jordan, 1997; Bell, 1998; Dudley-Evans & St John, 1998) (line 60)
- However, it has been pointed out that … (line 78)
- These, and other issues arising from … (lines 83–84)
- This approach is in accord with … (line 86)
- …… argues in favour of … (lines 87)

---

claim *n.* [C]
A statement that something is true, even though it has not been proved. *The competing claims of scientists.*

---

diverge *v.* [I]
If opinions, interests, etc. diverge, they are different from each other: [+from] *Here Innocent's views diverged from Gregory's.*

---

stimulus *n. pl.* stimuli [C]
Something that makes someone or something move or react: *At this stage, the infant begins to react more to visual stimuli.*

Copy the above list into your portfolio and then read the section again. Add useful phrases to the list above.

➤   Work with two or three other students. Find a short article each on any aspect of EAP that interests you. Agree upon your topic before you begin your search and discuss what you would like to know about it. Prepare some questions that you would like to answer as a result of your reading.

If you have difficulty identifying a topic, try 'critical thinking', the topic of Chapter 9; or topics already considered in this book, such as plagiarism, reading skills, writing skills, or language learning.

You can use a website such as findarticles.com to help you. Select 'free articles only' before you perform your search, otherwise you will have to register and pay.

Scan your article before you print it, to make sure that it will help you to answer your questions.

Read, annotate, and take notes from your article. Exchange these with the other students in your group. Read the other students' articles.

Identify:

- similar claims expressed in two or more of your articles
- any claims that diverge
- what your reading has not told you about.

➤   Work alone to write a review of your three articles. Before you write, with your tutor, remember to agree upon a subset of annotations from the companion website which you would like him or her to use when marking your work.

Use the phrases you identified above to help your writing.

FOCUS D: RESEARCHING

D.1 Understanding qualitative and quantitative research

Generally speaking, qualitative research involves words, and is concerned with what people do, say, feel and believe, for example (the 'quality' part of 'qualitative').

Quantitative research, on the other hand, involves numbers, and is concerned with counting and measuring how often something happens, for example (the 'quantity' part of 'quantitative').

The two approaches are not mutually exclusive and it is quite possible to find research that uses both approaches in one project.

➤   Use a search engine to help you complete the table below. Simply enter the search terms 'quantitative research' and 'qualitative research' or something like 'a comparison of quantitative and qualitative research'. Copy the table below into your portfolio and use the information you find to complete it. Add any other points that you wish to include in the left-hand column and include the related information.

	Quantitative research	Qualitative research
Aims		
Data		
Role of the researcher		
Instruments/data gathering techniques		
Analysis		
Role of theory		
Sample size		
How easily the study can be replicated		

➢ Compare your information with that of another student. Improve your own table in the light of his or her information.

replicate *v.* 1 [T] *formal*
If you replicate someone's work, a scientific study, etc., you do it again or try to get the same results again. *There is a need for further research to replicate these findings.*

FOCUS E: STUDYING

E.1 The 'prepare, draft, evaluate, proofread, improve, reflect' cycle

➢ In Chapter 2, you were recommended to read drafts of your work aloud to another student. Can you remember why this technique was recommended? What benefit did it offer you? If you have forgotten, turn to Chapter 2, section C.2, to find out.

➢ One approach to writing involves six stages: a preparation stage, four drafting stages, and a final version stage. These six stages are shown in **bold** font below, but their steps are not in the best order. Working with another student, within each of the six stages below, arrange the steps of the writing process into an appropriate order: `ANSWERS`

Prepare
☐ Consult with your tutor: ask him or her to answer any questions you have and to check your outline.
☐ Give yourself a break for reflection (24 hours if at all possible).
☐ Using your notes and annotations, prepare an outline.
☐ Annotate and make notes from relevant articles.
☐ Study the assigned task or identify your own task/topic. Highlight key words/ phrases.
☐ Search for relevant articles.
☐ Brainstorm ideas.

First draft
☐ Evaluate, proofread and improve your outline.
☐ Give yourself a break for reflection (24 hours if at all possible).
☐ Write a first draft of the main body of your text, the introduction and the conclusion, in that order.

Second draft
☐ Evaluate, proofread and improve your first draft; prepare a second draft.
☐ Evaluate and improve your work; prepare a third draft.
☐ Give yourself a break for reflection (24 hours if at all possible).
☐ Read your second draft aloud to another student.

Third draft
☐ Evaluate, proofread and improve your third draft.

☐ Agree upon a subset of marking annotations from the companion website with another student. Exchange your third draft with another student and mark his or her work using your annotation subset.

☐ Give yourself a break for reflection (24 hours if at all possible).

Fourth draft

☐ Agree upon a subset of annotations from the companion website which you would like him or her to use when marking your work.

☐ Submit work to your tutor.

☐ Check that your writing addresses the task and make any small final improvements.

☐ Check that your writing conforms to presentation standards (font, spacing, front cover, etc).

Final version

☐ Exchange your improved writing with another student and read his or her work.

☐ Improve your writing according to your tutor's feedback and annotations.

☐ Select one annotation that appeared frequently in your work and find out more about that area. Ask your tutor for advice here. Make a particular effort to avoid this problem in your next writing assignment.

☐ Compare your final version with your first draft. Notice where you made improvements.

➤ Compare your order with those of other students. There is no one 'right' order, but you should be able to explain or justify your decisions to each other.

➤ Make a visual representation in poster form of the process described above for your classroom wall. Make a copy for your study area too.

FOCUS F: APPLYING TO YOUR OWN SUBJECT

F.1 Presenting subject-related data

➤ Find a subject-related article which describes a research process and which includes data presented graphically. Scan the article and notice how the author refers to these data within his or her own work. Expand the list of useful words and phrases that you prepared in section B.4 above.

➤ Compare your list with those of other students and use these lists to expand your own.

F.2 Summarizing a subject-related research process

➤ Read the article you used in F.1 above. Annotate it and make notes. Write a summary of the research process described in the article.

In your writing, use:

- the six-stage process described above
- words and phrases commonly used to describe research
- passive voice where appropriate.

 Before you write, remember to agree with your tutor upon a subset of annotations from the companion website which you would like him or her to use when marking your work.

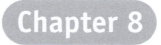

Chapter 8

Making Reasonable Claims

In this chapter, adapted from a **journal article,** you can read about the need for writers to express their claims appropriately.

You can develop your skills in these areas:

Focus A: Reading

A.1   Looking ahead
A.2   Understanding and responding

Focus B: Learning language

B.1   Different ways of expressing modality
B.2   Identifying examples of modality

Focus C: Writing

C.1   Adding appropriate degrees of caution to peer writing
C.2   Writing a newsletter article

Focus D: Researching

D.1   Using primary, secondary and tertiary sources

Focus E: Studying

E.1   Recording cautious language

Focus F: Applying to your own subject

F.1   Identifying modality in subject-related articles
F.2   Redrafting with appropriate caution

▶ FOCUS A: READING

A.1 Looking ahead

> [...] hedging assists writers to avoid overstating an assertion and to establish a relationship with readers. (Kuo, 1999: 133)

In this chapter, you can read a journal article about the need to make claims with an appropriate degree of caution in your writing. This is sometimes referred to as 'hedging'. You will also read about the kind of language that can help you to do this.

> When writers and researchers make claims, they do so based upon various **sources** or **evidence**. Sources and evidence can vary in terms of their adequacy. For example, what evidence are you aware of for the following claims? How **adequate** is this evidence?

source *n.* [C]
A person, book, or document that supplies you with information.
List all your sources at the end of your essay.

evidence *n.* [U]
Facts or signs that show clearly that something exists or is true.
There is no evidence for these claims.

adequate *adj.*
Enough in quantity or of a good enough quality for a particular purpose = sufficient.
Some creams we tested failed to give adequate protection against UV light.

complement *v.* [T]
To make a good combination with someone or something else.
The dark red walls complement the red leather chairs.

- Milk comes from cows.
- The first Coca-Cola was green.
- The penguin is the only bird that can swim but cannot fly.
- Some trees have roots that grow deep into the ground.
- Money notes are made mostly from a blend of cotton and linen, not paper.
- There are 354 steps to the crown of the Statue of Liberty.
- Honey is the only food that does not spoil.
- Women blink nearly twice as much as men.
- Some rocks grow.
- Dolphins sleep with one eye open.
- People prefer blue toothbrushes to red ones.
- Men are more likely to be struck by lightning than women.

> Do you believe all of the claims above? Work with another student. Find out which ones he or she believes to be true, and why; and find out which ones he or she doubts, and why.

> The strength of your belief in the claims above will depend on your level of confidence in the evidence for each. From the list above, select one claim that you believe in strongly and another that you have doubts about. Repeat each claim to another student, using language that indicates your degree of confidence in it.

> Work with another student and identify language that you can use when you have a high degree of confidence in the claim and language that you can use to suggest a lack of confidence. Make two lists and discuss them with another pair of students and your tutor.

> Read, annotate and take notes on Article 8. When you have finished, compare your annotations and notes to those of another student, and use his or her ideas to improve or **complement** your own.

▶ ARTICLE 8: MAKING REASONABLE CLAIMS IN ACADEMIC WRITING

Roger Nunn

Associate Professor,

The Petroleum Institute, Abu Dhabi, United Arab Emirates

Introduction

Grice's maxim of quality (1989, pp. 26–27 [1975, p. 45]) includes the statement: 'Do not say that for which you lack adequate evidence'. In academic communication, what we mean by 'adequate evidence' in support of statements about knowledge or information is of great importance. The way to talk about the quality 5 of evidence is through words like 'may', 'might', 'possibly' or 'seems'. This area of language is called 'modality'.

This paper will mainly consider the importance of 'modality' in EAP, arguing that it is a particularly useful concept for both developing academic competence and for analysing academic texts. It can help us address some of the most critical questions 10 in academic communication:

- What is the relationship between language form and language use?
- What is the relationship between the language choices that academic writers make and the content of their message?
- What is the role of evidence in supporting arguments and what means are avail- 15 able to competent writers to express their evidence?

Modality and Commitment to Knowledge Claims

Modality is defined by Halliday and Matthiessen (2004, p. 618) as 'the area of meaning that lies between yes and no – the intermediate ground between positive and negative polarity.' Modality is the way we use language to express how true our 20 claims about our research evidence are. Baggini and Stangroom (2004, p. 3) suggest that, 'in many ways the history of philosophy can be seen as the quest to establish how we can know anything at all and the extent to which such knowledge can be certain'. As Baggini and Stangroom (p. 3) point out, 'we should only seek the degree of certainty each subject matter allowed'. 25

Modality is not important only in academic writing. We meet it every day in all communication genres. It is very common in news reports, for example. We cannot *not* use modality, so whether consciously or not, journalists have to express their confidence in the truth of the stories they are reporting, and students cannot *not* express their level of confidence in the truth of their research results. Look at this 30 short example from a BBC report. The modal language in italics tells us that the reporter is not very certain about what happened:

35   What happened last night was, of course, *wrapped in secrecy* and still only a few details have emerged. *What I have been told* is that at least a hundred US special forces including army rangers entered Southern Afghanistan under cover of darkness. Now, where they came from is *classified information,* but *they could have been flown* in from warships in the Arabian Sea and then transferred to C130 aircraft at air bases nearer by. There were *apparently* two targets: an airfield near Kandahar and, some distance away, a compound belonging to the Taliban leader, Mullah Omar.

40   A careful listener or a reader needs to decide how much confidence to place in a report, whether it is news or research (See Nunn and Nunn, 2006, for a fuller discussion.) Whether a reporter or journalist is trusted will partially depend on the reader believing that the level of certainty shown in the language fits the evidence. It is possible to suggest that competence in all *academic* communication is linked to
45   the ability to evaluate the evidence of what we and others are claiming.

Thompson (2004, p. 53) links modality directly to academic report writing, suggesting modality is the extent to which a statement is 'valid' and 'the degree to which the speaker commits herself to the validity of what she is saying' (p. 69). Dudley-Evans (1994, p. 222), in his analysis of the discussion section of a research paper,
50   provides the following example:

It *is possible that* the cell reaction seen here, in which the contents condense and leave the cell walls, *may be* a characteristic of recalcitrant seeds generally, while the cells of orthodox seeds *may show* a more generalized decrease in size, without such damage to the contents. (My italics added to highlight modal language)

55   Teachers often say that students make exaggerated claims about their research findings. Awareness of modal language can help us make reasonable claims about the findings of research. It is very useful in the discussion section of a report. As Dudley-Evans points out, claims are often identified with 'hedging': 'Claims tend to be presented cautiously, that is, using modal or other hedged phrases' (p. 225). However,
60   modality cannot be limited to just 'hedging' claims. We use modality all the time to express the level of confidence that the evidence allows. Modality provides us with a range of choices from categorical (absolute) certainty to expressions of absolute doubt.

Dudley-Evans (1994, p. 225) also points out that 'claim' moves tend to be found in the company of other moves such as moves presenting findings, or moves refer-
65   ring to previous research. (A move is a unit of discourse, rather like a move in a game of chess, that helps develop the argument in combination with other moves). This means that claims are frequently followed up by a reference to the authority of previous research which then supports the claim.

The Grammar of Modality

70   One aspect of competence in a language is the ability to generate all possible forms of the verb and only those forms. This is a computational view of linguistic competence. Palmer (1987, pp. 94–95) reduces the structure of English modality to sixteen forms, using one common English verb, 'take'. It includes simple and complex active forms, such as 'will take' and 'would have been taking', and simple and complex passive
75   forms, such as 'will be taken' and 'would have been taken'. See Table 1 below:

Table 1   The English modal verb

	Modal auxiliary verb	Infinitive	Past participle of 'be'	– ing form	Past participle of main verb
1	Will	take			
2	Would	take			
3	Will	be		taking	
4	Would	be		taking	
5	Will	have			taken
6	Would	have			taken
7	Will	have	been	taking	
8	Would	have	been	taking	
9	Will	be			taken
10	Would	be			taken
11	Will	be		being	taken
12	Would	be		being	taken
13	Will	have	been		taken
14	Would	have	been		taken
15	Will	have	been	being	taken
16	Would	have	been	being	taken

In Table 1 above, Nos. 15 and 16 are labelled as 'questionable'. We might note that the nature of the main verb is not considered here. Once a verb such as 'go' is substituted, 11 and 12 must be eliminated and 15 and 16 are also more than just questionable. They are just wrong. Substitute 'die' and even further restrictions apply (13 and 14 now become unacceptable, for example, unless we accept 'a good 80 death will have been died', and there are many who will enjoy inventing a context to prove this form to be possible). In terms of competence, one relevant question is how we come to know which forms are available for use with which verb.

Different Ways of Expressing Modality

Writers have different choices available to express their degree of commitment to 85 the reliability of the information or evidence that they themselves are presenting or that they are just reporting. Fowler (1991, p. 85) suggests that 'truth modality varies in strength along a scale from absolute confidence – down through various degrees of lesser certainty.' Fowler (1991, p. 64) argues that 'writing which strives to give an

90   impression of objectivity, e.g. scientific reporting or certain traditions of "realistic" fiction, tends to minimize modal expressions'. However, Fairclough (1989, p. 129) suggests that sentences with no modal verbs still express modality. 'Ahmed is 16 years old' expresses absolute, categorical, 100% certainty. This is the strongest form of modality. It is important to point out that using an expression like 'it is certain

95   that…' is an expression of high certainty but not an expression of absolute 100% certainty. 100% certainty needs no expression that is normally labelled modal, including the word 'certain'. 'The sum of the angles of a triangle is 180°' is categorical. 'It is certain that the sum of the angles of a triangle is 180°' is no longer expressed categorically, because the issue of certainty has now been raised.

100   Modality is commonly associated with forms such as 'may' and 'might'. However, there are many other choices available, as seen in Table 2 opposite.

Reporting verbs have been added to Fowler's list for this study. Different reporting expressions lead to different levels of commitment to or detachment from the truth claims being made. Reference to external authority is also a means of sup-

105   porting an author's own truth claim. Tadros (1994, pp. 74–76) classifies reporting verbs into 'factives' (prove, show) and 'non-factives' (claim, suggest). A verb like 'claim' is a non-factive because it implies that the author is not in agreement with a statement made by an author whereas 'indicate' or 'show' expresses agreement.

Evaluating the Use of Modality in a Report by Students

110   In the following sample (1a), the writer makes an assumption that research done in the UK will automatically be relevant to a study to be done in the UAE.

> **Modality Sample 1a**
>
> In general, this research gives the statistics of the amount of plastic that are used or consumed yearly, the variety of plastic types, the advantages and disadvantages of
115 the methods and ways of recycling plastics. Here it is discussed primarily in UK, but it still relevant because each country use plastic for its importance and also for the information about recycling.

After a discussion of knowledge claims and modality in relation to this extract in class, and some language correction, the following version was produced.

120   > **Modality Sample 1b**
>
> (*Improved*) In general, this research gives the statistics of the amount of plastic that is used or consumed yearly, the variety of plastic types, the advantages and disadvantages of the methods and ways of recycling plastic. Here it is discussed primarily in the UK, **but it could still be relevant** to the UAE **to some**
125 **extent** because each country uses plastic according to its importance and some of the information about recycling **may be relevant in any context**.

Table 2   Ways of expressing modality (based on Fowler 1986, p. 132)

Ways of expressing modality	Example and comment
Categorical statements (no 'modal' language)	'The sum of the angles of a triangle is 180°.' (This does not permit doubt even to a specialist)
Modal auxiliary verbs (e.g may, might, should, etc.)	'This might mean that ...' (Labelled as 'subjective' by some specialists)
Modal adjectives, adverbs or adverbial phrases (e.g. 'probable', 'probably', 'in all probability', 'possible', 'certain', 'certainly', 'likely')	'While it is possible that these results ...' 'In all probability, these survey results can be relied upon as they are confirmed by previous research results in this field'. (Labelled as more objective by some specialists)
Evaluative adjectives and adverbs (e.g. 'fortunately', 'regrettably', 'inevitably')	'Regrettably, the conclusions are not supported by irrefutable evidence'. (Often represents value judgements)
Reporting phrases (e.g 'claim', 'is reported to have said', 'according to ...' , 'state', 'argue', 'suggest', 'imply', 'interpret this to mean that ...')	'The present author interprets this result to mean that ...' 'The survey results (appear to) suggest that ...' (Can be used to distance oneself from another researcher's statement or idea, not just to report)
Verbs of knowledge, prediction, evaluation (e.g. 'seem', 'guess', 'believe', 'appear', 'predict', 'approve')	'It seems likely that these results were not produced by chance.' 'These initial results appear to suggest that ...' (Often seen as more objective than 'may' or 'might')
Generic statements (e.g It is commonly stated that ... It cannot be denied that ... It is true that ... It is clear that ...)	'It is commonly stated that plastic waste ...' (Often used to express the author's own position or to prepare for a counter argument)

In Modality Sample 2a below, the students have used modality well. Three relatively minor linguistic errors (underlined in the text) interfere with the intelligibility of the text to a limited extent. This is not to say that the advanced-level students who wrote it do not need to work on modality more to refine their message. After re-editing and discussion, the second version (Modality Sample 2b) provides a higher level of competence.

130

Modality Sample 2a

135

Finally, as an answer to the research question, we can say that the occupants in building 2 **might be at risk** of SBS because of poor ventilation, the locations of the vents (in the northern part of the building) and the accumulation of dust on the vents and in the ducts. On the other hand, building 3 **might not be** at the same level of risk **like** building 2, because of the **less** dust and dirt accumulation on the vents in building 3 and the appropriate locations of the vents.

140

As for humidity, the records say it varies between 40–55%, which **may not trouble** the healthiness of **both** buildings in terms of SBS, according to [3].

Modality Sample 2b

(*Improved*) Finally, as an answer to the research question, [1] **it can be argued that there is some degree of risk** of SBS for the occupants in

145

building 2 because of poor ventilation, the locations of the vents (in the northern part of the building) and the accumulation of dust on the vents and in the ducts. On the other hand, building 3 **does not appear to be** at the same level of risk as building 2, because of the lower dust and dirt accumulation on the vents in building 3 and the appropriate locations of the vents. As for humidity,

150

the records say it varies between 40–55%, which **is unlikely to affect** the healthiness of either building in terms of SBS, according to [3].

Modality shows us that language and content are difficult to separate, as the degree of confidence expressed in the evidence in a research report relates to the content of the message, but depends on appropriate and subtle language choices.

155

In Modality Sample 3 below, we note the absence of evaluative acts through modal language. The statements are all categorical and present factual information with as little interpretation as possible. In contrast, the following section from the

Modality Sample 3

Figures (A & B) show a comparison between a B2 vent and a B3 vent. They

160

show that B3 vents are cleaner than those of B2, and that dust collects on the vents of B2 more than it does on the vents of B3. This is illustrated in figures (C, D, and E) which were taken from the northern part of B2. Figures (F and G) show temperature and humidity indicators. We also looked at the records of humidity level for the past few years and we found that it varied from 43% to

165

55% in building 2, and from 42% to 51% in building 3.

discussion section (Modality Sample 4 below) is presented here to support the view that appropriate levels of modality are being expressed in the evaluative 'claim' moves. The most significant evaluative moves, presented here to support this view, are highlighted in bold below. A common pattern observed in this paragraph is a factual 'result reporting' move qualified by an 'evaluative' move realized through an act of modality.   170

Modality Sample 4

However, Mr Shehada, from the General Services department, informed [neutral reporting verb] us that the ventilation systems are maintained every six months [interview result reporting move], **so we predicted that there may not be any problems related to the rate of ventilation in building 2** [evaluative claim move qualifying the result.]   175

Another example of the same pattern of a report from the findings that is then evaluated is seen in Modality Sample 5 below:

Modality Sample 5

In addition, we did not receive any complaints from the occupants we visited   180
during our investigation nor did Mr Jackson, except that workers in the northern part of the building suffered from headaches, coughing and sore throats [result report with exception]. **This is probably** (adverb) **because vents are directly over their desks, so air blows right over their heads.** [Evaluative move expressing a *possible* rather than a firmly established cause   185
through modality.]

These same examples from the discussion are presented in their broader context below (Modality Sample 6). It is then possible to identify a tentative pattern for the use of evaluative moves. Modality is particularly appropriate in a discussion section, providing the moves are accompanied by some kind of summary of a finding that   190
allows for the evaluative move to be open to a reader's own counter evaluation.

Modality Sample 6

We can (auxiliary**) conclude** from figures (1 & 2) that the respondents **think** (reporting verb) that the ventilation rate in building 2 is adequate, as an average of 93% of the occupants in the building **say** (reporting) that the air is   195
neither too much nor too little. **Unfortunately, we could not** (auxiliary)

(Continued)

(Continued)

find any records of the average rates of the ventilation in buildings 2 and 3 to assure the adequacy of ventilation. However, Mr Shehada, from the General Services department, **informed** (reporting verb) us that the ven-
200   tilation systems are maintained every six months, **so we predicted that there may not be** (auxiliary) **any problems related to the rate of ventilation in building 2.** In addition, **we did not receive any complaints from the occupants we visited** during our investigation nor did Mr Jackson, except that workers in the northern part of the building suffered
205   from headaches, coughing and sore throats. **This is probably** (adverb) **because vents are directly over their desks, so air blows right over their heads** (ventilation process – seems to remove personal responsibility). Others in the same part of the building cover their vents because of the cold, **and this might** (auxiliary) **result in poor ventilation.** Thus, they suffer
210   from headaches and runny noses, **according to [2]** (reporting expression)**.** Therefore, in the evaluation matrix, vents' locations scored 3, which **means** (verbal) that the locations **are mostly appropriate**, while number of vents and air flow scored 4, which means that both **are** appropriate.

A Summary of Modality Use in A Full Report

215   In this section, the analysis of the full research report on Sick Building Syndrome already cited and analysed in the previous section is briefly summarized.

Modality Choices Made in a Whole Text

In Figure 1 opposite, the proportional use by the authors of the different modality choices throughout the research report was calculated by the students. This result
220   underlines the importance given to reporting from authoritative sources. Furthermore, the ratio of modal verbs to verbs of knowledge, belief or evaluation, such as 'seem' or 'appear' indicates that these need to be used more. Halliday and Matthiessen (2004) suggest that modal verbs are more subjective, whereas the use of verbs of knowledge appears more objective. For example, 'Dust **could come**
225   from man-made mineral fibers' is more subjective than 'Dust **appears to come** from man-made mineral fibers', the latter expressing a more objective deduction from the data. The level of confidence expressed is of a similar level indicating that this is partly a question of formality.

The two sections of a research report in which the most frequent use of modality
230   might be expected are the background (literature review) and the discussion section. Of the 33 modals within the 823 words of the background section, 18 are reporting verbs or phrases (approximately 54.5%). This is highly predictable as reporting significant background from relevant literature is a major purpose of a

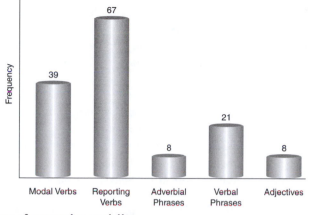

Figure 1   Ways of expressing modality

background section. In the discussion section of the SBS report, there are 73 modal uses in 1859 words, of which 26 are reporting verbs or phrases (approximately   235
35%) which supports the suggestion by Dudley-Evans (1994) that discussions also need to appeal to authority by referring back to the background section.

In the background section of the SBS dissertation, there are no uses of 'seem' or 'appear'. The frequent use of the informal 'show' (thirteen times in the background and discussion sections alone), which could be replaced by 'indicate', also suggests   240
that, while the authors are using modality correctly, they are using a limited range of choices, often selecting those which are relatively informal.

Conclusions

In this paper, several conclusions are suggested. Firstly, when we read an academic text, we need to look at the evidence carefully. Secondly, we need to look at the lan-   245
guage used to express the evidence carefully. Thirdly, as writers, we need to look at our own evidence carefully and then express an appropriate level of certainty. It is often safer to be cautious about the claims we make for our evidence. Good journal-ists and even famous philosophers do this. Competent academics tend to be modest because they are the people who know best how little they can know with absolute   250
certainty.

References

Baggini, J. and J. Stangroom (Eds) (2004) *Great thinkers.* London: Continuum.
Dudley-Evans, T. (1994) Genre analysis: an approach to text analysis for ESP. In
    Coulthard, M. (Ed.) *Advances in written text analysis,* pp. 219–228. London: Routledge.
Fairclough, N. (1989) *Language and power.* Harlow: Longman.
Fowler, R. (1986) *Linguistic criticism.* Oxford: Oxford University Press.

Fowler, R. (1991) *Language in the news.* London: Routledge.

Grice, H. P. (1975) Logic and conversation. In P. Cole and J. Morgan (Eds) *Syntax and semantics 3: speech acts.* New York: Academic Press.

Grice, H. P. (1989) *Studies in the way of words.* London: Harvard University Press.

Halliday, M. and C. Matthiessen (2004) *An introduction to functional grammar.* London: Arnold.

Nunn, F. and R. Nunn (2006) Teaching language *and* research skills through an international media project. *Asian ESP Journal,* Volume 2, Issue 2, pp. 27–53.

Palmer, F. (1987) *The English verb.* London: Longman.

Tadros, A. (1994) Predictive categories in expository text. In Coulthard, M. (Ed.) *Advances in written text analysis,* pp. 69–82. London: Routledge.

Thompson, G. (2004) (2nd edn) *Introducing functional grammar.* London: Arnold.

Roger Nunn has taught EFL and EAP for more than 30 years in seven different countries. He has a PhD in TEFL from Reading University, UK, and is currently an Associate Professor in Communication at the Petroleum Institute in Abu Dhabi where he specializes in project-based courses and teaching research skills, and research into developing academic competence. He is Senior Associate Editor of the *Asian EFL Journal.*

▶ FOCUS A: READING

A.2 Understanding and responding

➤ Read the words or phrases from Article 8 below in their contexts, and then discuss their meaning with another student. Your notes and annotations may help you here. Check your ideas with your tutor.

1   maxim of quality (line 2)
2   adequate evidence (line 4)
3   academic competence (line 9)
4   the relationship between language form and language use (line 12)
5   the intermediate ground between positive and negative polarity (lines 19–20)
6   communication genres (line 27)
7   hedged phrases (line 59)
8   categorical certainty … absolute doubt (line 62)
9   moves (line 64)
10 questionable (lines 76 and 79)
11 writing which strives to give an impression of objectivity (lines 89–90)
12 commitment to or detachment from the truth (lines 103–104)

➤ Work with another student. Make a list of words or phrases from Article 8 that you would like to understand better. Discuss these with another pair of students and then with your tutor.

➤ Read Article 8 again and, working with another student, answer some or all of the following questions:

1 'We should only seek the degree of certainty each subject matter allowed' (lines 24–25). Why do you think that different subject matters might allow different degrees of certainty? Can you think of some examples?

2 'A careful listener or a reader needs to decide how much confidence to place in a report' (lines 40–41). Are you aware of doing this? Give an example of the kind of listening or reading material that would prompt you to do this, in particular.

3 'Teachers often say that students make exaggerated claims about their research findings' (lines 55–56). Why do you think that students might be guilty of this? Has a teacher ever said this about your work?

4 'Writers have different choices available to express their degree of commitment to the reliability of the information or evidence that they themselves are presenting or that they are just reporting' (lines 85–87). If you wanted to express different degrees of commitment to the truth of the statements below, how might you do it?

> **objective** *adj.*
> Based on facts, or making a decision that is based on facts rather than on your feelings or beliefs. *Scientists need to be objective when doing research.*

(i) The first Coca-Cola was green.
(ii) Dolphins sleep with one eye open.

5 Why do you think **objectivity** (line 90) and **subjectivity** (line 223) are so important in relation to research?

> **subjective** *adj.*
> A statement, report, attitude, etc. that is subjective is influenced by personal opinion and can therefore be unfair. *The ratings were based on the subjective opinion of one person.*

6 'The two sections of a research report in which the most frequent use of modality might be expected are the background (literature review) and the discussion section.' (lines 229–231). What reason for this does the author give?

7 '... while the authors are using modality correctly, they are using a limited range of choices' (lines 241–242). Who are the 'authors' referred to here? How can you expand your personal range of choices in relation to the language area discussed in Article 8?

▶ FOCUS B: LEARNING LANGUAGE

B.1 Different ways of expressing modality

Article 8 identifies seven ways of expressing modality. They are:

1 Categorical statements (e.g. 'The sum of the angles of the triangle is ...').
2 Modal auxiliary verbs ('may', 'might', etc.).
3 Modal adjectives, adverbs or adverbial phrases (e.g. 'certain').

4   Evaluative adjectives and adverbs (e.g. 'fortunately', 'regrettably').
5   Reporting phrases (e.g. 'claim', 'is reported to have said').
6   Verbs of knowledge, prediction, evaluation (e.g. 'believe', 'appear').
7   Generic statements (e.g. 'it is commonly stated that…', 'it is true that…').

> Work with another student. Read the phrases and sentences below. Most are taken from the chapters in this book. They express varying degrees of caution. First, copy the seven ways of expressing modality, above, as headings into your portfolio. Then highlight the modal language used, and match the phrases and sentences to the correct heading, or category. Finally, check your ideas with another pair of students or your tutor. ANSWERS

(a)   Caroline Baillie, in her study of engineering students, noted that when left to themselves, students…
(b)   However, the results suggested that this is unfortunately…
(c)   In addition to information literacy, a lifelong learner, they argued, has an inquiring mind…
(d)   It is probably true that most EAP lecturers …
(e)   …the social nature of reading and the importance of interaction do not seem to filter through the Upton text until Chapter 9…
(f)   There are deeper issues underlying such practices…
(g)   It is inevitably the case that…
(h)   Perhaps the most important skill English teachers can engage students in is the complex ability to write from other texts…
(i)   … the impact a given article might have on thinking and research in the field.
(j)   The same phenomenon holds true in L2 writing instruction…
(k)   From the comments of staff, it is clear that little confidence exists in current university procedures and processes.
(l)   It seems that only the rare individual teacher can learn another discipline…
(m)   Reluctance by academic members of staff to discuss student plagiarism openly may contribute to the often untenable situations…
(n)   The object of an EAP course is to help overseas students…

Strategy for Success #45

Add variety to your writing by using different ways to express caution appropriately.

B.2 Identifying examples of modality

> Work with another student. Read Article 8 again. Highlight examples of modality which the author himself uses (that is, ignore those that appear in the

quotations, tables, and samples of students' work). Here is an example to help you:

Teachers often say that students make exaggerated claims about their research findings. Awareness of modal language can help us make reasonable claims about the findings of research. It is very useful in the discussion section of a report. As Dudley-Evans points out, claims are often identified with 'hedging': 'Claims tend to be presented cautiously, that is, using modal or other hedged phrases' (p. 225).

➤ Use your highlighted examples to add to the seven lists you began, above.

▶ FOCUS C: WRITING

C.1 Adding appropriate degrees of caution to peer writing

➤ Rewrite one or more of the following extracts from students' work so that the writing expresses the authors' claims more appropriately. The extracts are concerned with the difficulty of attracting women into engineering and retaining them.

Extract 1, Fatima Al Zaabi

All societies expect women to choose feminine jobs which are suitable for their sensitivities. This misconception is one of the problems that women face in their futures. In addition, they are discouraged from investing in a career or even participating in the occupational system. As a result, they reduce their academic aspirations in order to achieve goals and be accepted in life.

To solve the problem of attracting women into engineering, there are three solutions. Firstly, the media and books can emphasize that women can do things men cannot do. Secondly, there are different ways of attracting women at a young age, such as a trip for high school student to many universities, or holding meetings with engineering professors. Finally, nurturing women's talents by exposing them to the profession at a young age works well.

Retention is another problem that goes against women in their careers. Most women leave university after two or three years of studying in order to marry or complete their personal lives. However, if the university signs a contact with the student, they will avoid this problem. Besides, we can overcome this problem by increasing the number of the female faculty who will support them. This affects their retention and success.

Extract 2, Sara Ali Al Abadi

There is a strong connection between the image of engineering that the students have before joining the Petroleum Institute and their choice of major. Some students believe that engineering is based on calculations only. This idea has a great impact on some of the students who are not very good at math by making them avoid the majors that require strength in math.

Some other students see engineering as a career where you can earn a great deal of money after graduating. This thought is a strong motivation for these kinds of students.

Extract 3, Khawla Abdulla Al Manthari

We found that parental support has various forms which affect student achievement differently, for example emotional support has a positive effect on student achievement while frequent enquiry has a negative effect, so we recommend that parents find the type of support that best suits their children.

C.2 Writing a newsletter article

➢ Write a short article for new students explaining the need to write with caution, for a student newsletter. Give some examples of claims that are not cautiously expressed, and show your readers how to amend them so that they express the claim more cautiously.

Strategy for Success #46

Read *and* write with an appropriate degree of caution.

▶ FOCUS D: RESEARCHING

D.1 Using primary, secondary and tertiary sources

Researchers consult different sources of information. These sources may be primary, secondary or **tertiary**. While there is some disagreement as to the precise scope of these terms, broadly, they may be understood as follows:

Primary sources are *original materials* that have not been interpreted or evaluated in any way. They belong to the time period that is under investigation. Examples include diaries, correspondence such as letters and emails, interviews, documents such as birth certificates, photographs, survey data and reports.

Secondary sources are *interpretations or evaluations of primary sources*. Secondary sources filter the evidence provided by a primary source. They are one step away from the primary source.

> **tertiary** *adj.*
> Third in place, degree or order.

Academic writing may include both primary source material (e.g. the results section of a research report) and secondary source material (e.g. the literature review or the discussion section of a research report).

Tertiary sources are sources that *bring together in condensed form both primary and secondary sources*. As this often requires summarizing, they are two steps away from primary sources. Examples include school textbooks, guidebooks, encyclopaedias, almanacs and dictionaries.

➤ Work with another student. The examples of primary data on page 185–6 are all from a student project. The student, Yasmine Guefrachi, investigated the influence of peer support on student achievement. Study the 3 figures below and (a) report the results; (b) discuss what they might mean and the reasons for them. Use an appropriate level of caution when you discuss the results.

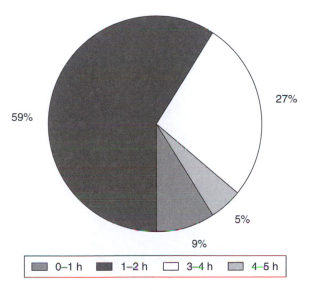

27%

59%

5%

9%

| 0–1 h | 1–2 h | 3–4 h | 4–5 h |

Figure 1   Average hours spent studing with peers

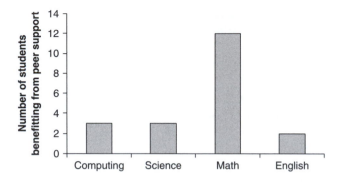

Figure 2   Usefulness of peer support according to subject

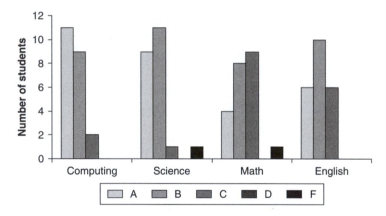

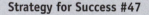

Figure 3   Final student grades in each subject

> ➤ Work with another student. Write a short description of the results above, and then discuss them. Use two headings: *Results* and *Discussion*.

Strategy for Success #47

When reading academic writing, always consider and evaluate the sources: are they primary, secondary or (less frequently) tertiary?

▶ FOCUS E: STUDYING

E.1 Recording cautious language

In section B.1 above, you arranged examples of ways of expressing modality into seven different categories.

> ➤ Your tutor will give you an article related to the field of English for Academic Purposes. Read it and highlight examples of modality used to express claims appropriately. Copy some of these examples and add them to the seven lists.

▶ FOCUS F: APPLYING TO YOUR OWN SUBJECT

F.1 Identifying modality in subject-related articles

➢   Read a subject-related article on a topic that you are studying at the moment. Highlight examples of modality used to express claims appropriately. Copy some of these examples and add them to the seven lists in your portfolio.

➢   Read another student's seven lists and use some of the phrases to expand your own.

F.2 Redrafting with appropriate caution

➢   Find an essay or other academic writing that you have recently completed, for example, the writing you did in Chapter 7, section F.3. Rewrite it, bearing in mind the need to express your claims with an appropriate degree of caution.

Before you write, remember to agree with your tutor upon a subset of annotations from the companion website which you would like him or her to use when marking your work.

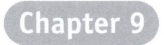

Chapter 9

Thinking Critically

In this chapter, you can read a paper published in **conference proceedings** about developing students' critical thinking skills for higher education.

You can develop your skills in these areas:

Focus A: Reading

A.1   Looking ahead
A.2   Key skills for thinking critically
A.3   Understanding and responding
A.4   Text structure

Focus B: Learning language

B.1   Language of evaluation
B.2   Keywords for thinking critically

Focus C: Writing

C.1   Writing critically
C.2   Critiquing peer writing

Focus D: Researching

D.1   Asking good questions
D.2   Evaluating internet sources

Focus E: Studying

E.1   Analysing term papers and examination questions
E.2   Responding to tutor feedback on the content of written work

Focus F: Applying to your own subject

F.1   Thinking critically about a subject-related article
F.2   Thinking critically about subject-related term papers and examination questions

▶ FOCUS A: READING

A.1 Looking ahead

This chapter is concerned with 'critical thinking'; in particular, with the need for EAP students to learn how to think critically. One definition of critical thinking is: 'reacting with systematic evaluation to what you have heard and read' (Browne and Keeley, 2004: 2).

Thinking critically can influence how people read and what they write, and so we find terms such as 'reading critically' or 'writing critically'. Reflection and critical thinking are also closely related, and so you may come across the term 'critical reflection'. Regardless of the terminology used, however, the idea of 'reacting with systematic evaluation' applies.

➢ Using Google, enter 'definition of critical thinking'. Select: 'Web definitions for critical thinking'. Read the various definitions that this search provides. Select two or three that you find interesting, **succinct** and memorable and add these to your portfolio. Compare your selection with that of another student.

> **succinct** *adj.*
> Clearly expressed in a few words.
> *A succinct explanation.*

➢ The need to be able to think critically was first introduced in Chapter 4 in relation to sources of information. Your sources – journal articles, textbooks, encyclopaedias, atlases, edited collections, etc. – should all be considered critically. However, critical thinking is not only useful in relation to your studies – it can help you in many other areas of your life too.

Work with another student. Make a list of things that you encounter in your lives as students which you should think critically about. You can think about things you read as well as things you hear. Compare your list with that of another pair of students. Highlight three things that you will make an effort to think critically about, in particular, next time you encounter them.

A.2 Key skills for thinking critically

➢ Thinking critically requires a number of skills. Study the list of skills below and discuss the meaning of any new words or phrases. Then consider: which of the following do you think are *not* involved in critical thinking? (Check your answer in the key when you have finished.) ANSWERS

- Describing
- Justifying
- Categorizing
- Evaluating evidence for claims
- Predicting

- Identifying assumptions
- Interpreting
- Asking questions
- Reflecting
- Suspending judgement

- Identifying cause and effect
- Identifying implications and issues
- Recognizing what may have been omitted
- Synthesizing
- Comparing and contrasting
- Analysing
- Identifying problems and solutions
- Identifying similarities and differences
- Understanding
- Processing
- Exploring ideas
- Recognizing **bias**
- Avoiding overgeneralization
- Recognizing **contradictions**
- Distinguishing fact from opinion
- Analysing the meanings of words and phrases
- Identifying ambiguity
- Identifying connections between ideas
- Exploring thoughts, feelings, beliefs, values
- Identifying **fallacies**

bias *n*. [singular, U]
An opinion about whether a person, group or idea is good or bad which influences how you deal with it. *It's clear that the company has a bias against women and minorities.*

contradiction *n*. [C]
A difference between two statements, beliefs, or ideas about something that means they cannot both be true. *Apparent contradictions in the defendant's testimony.*

fallacy *n*. [C, U] *formal*
A weakness in someone's argument or ideas which is caused by a mistake in their thinking.

➢ The author of Article 9 suggests that some students are used to viewing learning as primarily a matter of 'memory and repetition of the words and ideas of one's lecturers' (Thompson, 1999). Does this correspond to your own experience? Think critically about this statement and its implications. Share your ideas with another student and with your tutor.

➢ Read and annotate Article 9. Highlight words or phrases that you would like to understand better.

ARTICLE 9: CRITICAL THINKING: WHAT IS IT AND HOW DO WE TEACH IT IN ENGLISH FOR ACADEMIC PURPOSES (EAP) PROGRAMS?

Celia Thompson
Centre for Communication Skills and English as
a Second Language, University of Melbourne
HERDSA Annual International Conference,
Melbourne, 12–15 July 1999

Abstract

Until the 1990s, discussion of critical thinking has tended to focus on first language speaking contexts (e.g. Ennis, 1962; McPeck, 1981). More recently, however, especially as a result of increases in international student enrolments in the tertiary sector, what critical thinking means and how it might be taught   5 have become highly debated questions for second language learning theorists and practitioners, not only in Australia, but also in the US and in the UK (e.g. Benesch, 1993a; Gieve, 1998). This paper provides an overview of a range of theoretical approaches to critical thinking followed by discussion of the implications of these perspectives for the theory and practice of tertiary level   10 English for Academic Purposes (EAP). Finally, an example of a critical thinking classroom activity for EAP university students will be presented.

Background

Over the last ten years in particular there has been considerable growth in the number of international students enrolling in Australian universities. Some may have   15 experienced many years of education with English as the medium of instruction (for example, those from Hong Kong, India, Malaysia, Singapore and Sri Lanka) while others will be experiencing the presentation of discipline-specific subject material in English for the first time.

Differences in the amount of English language medium instruction notwith-   20 standing, for many international students studying at an Australian university at both undergraduate and postgraduate levels, this will be the first time that they will have experienced learning within a different cultural, social and economic environment. In order to successfully complete their studies, these students are required to make many educational, linguistic, cultural, social and often economic adjustments.   25 For a significant number of these students, this may include encountering the term 'critical thinking' for the first time. For such students, the shift from viewing learning primarily as the work of memory and repetition of the words and ideas of one's lecturers (see Pennycook, 1996, for example) to conceptualizing learning as a constantly evolving process of discovery, questioning and reformulating of hypotheses,   30 can be an extremely disconcerting and confusing experience.

Approaches to critical thinking

While educators in countries such as Australia, North America and the UK in particular, might place great importance on students' ability to think critically, the
35   complexities of the term need to be acknowledged and very carefully addressed. Some educationalists have referred to it as 'reflective skepticism' (McPeck, 1981) and 'reasonable, reflective thinking that is focused on deciding what to believe or do' (Ennis, 1992, p. 22). Rather than attempting to define critical thinking as an explicit concept, skill or rational response that can be easily taught, Atkinson (1997)
40   describes critical thinking as a kind of *social practice* that has its origins in culturally determined sets of behaviours that cannot easily be defined by its users (p. 72). Benesch, however, refutes the notion of critical thinking as tacit and unquestioned social practice, describing it as 'a democratic learning process examining power relations and social inequities' (1993a, p. 547).

45   ## Critical thinking in the context of English for Academic Purposes (EAP)

Once connections are made between critical thinking, social practice and political action, our understanding of the term in an EAP context and our roles as educators complexify. Viewing academic English language teaching/learning as a form of political practice is central to the work of educationalists such as Auerbach (1995),
50   Benesch (1993a; 1993b; 1996) and Pennycook (1989; 1997). According to Auerbach (1995), instructors' pedagogical approaches and choices of teaching materials both influence and are influenced by the nature of the socioeconomic and political forces that exist beyond the classroom. Denying the political nature of language education, argues Pennycook (1989), can be equated with 'articulating an
55   ideological position in favour of the status quo' (p. 591).

The ideological positioning of EAP courses is an issue that Benesch (1993b; 1996) and Pennycook (1994; 1997) explore in some depth. If EAP programs simply aim to provide students with the academic language skills and content-knowledge required to perform successfully in their chosen disciplines, then such a
60   'pragmatic' approach, claims Benesch (1993b) constitutes 'an accommodationist ideology, an endorsement of traditional academic teaching and of current power relations in academia and in society' (p. 711). Both writers stress the need to adopt an approach to learning that encourages critical questioning not only of all pedagogical approaches and materials but also of the society of which instructors and
65   students form a part.

Exploring critical thinking in the EAP classroom

In pre-university bridging programs and university level EAP courses, I have used writings by both indigenous and non-indigenous Australians on colonial and post-colonial Australian society to develop students' abilities to think critically. For

example, they may be asked to compare the kinds of values and opinions of the   70
author of the statement: 'As other peoples made the transition from barbarism
to civilization, chance protected the Aborigines from such (changes)' (Clark, 1986,
p. 9), with those of the writer who asserts that:

> Governments and institutions need to see and to find ways of working with different
> knowledges. Part of this is beginning to see European-type knowledge as just one sort of   75
> knowledge among many. (Yunupingu,1994, p. 119)

In-class discussions about such texts have resulted in students exploring the connections between what they are studying in the classroom to the broader social and
political issues facing contemporary Australian society. For instance, in more recent
times, students have been keen to find out more about the current movement   80
towards reconciliation between indigenous and non-indigenous Australians and to
reflect on the roles they themselves might play in this process.

An extended activity I have used in a number of EAP workshops with undergraduate and postgraduate students to explore the notion of critical thinking runs as
follows. After eliciting from students what they understand 'critical thinking' to mean   85
in an academic context, I give them a working definition of the term by Gieve
(1998), who states that for students to think critically at university level, they need to:

> examine the reasons for their actions, their beliefs, and their knowledge claims, requiring
> them to defend themselves and question themselves, their peers, their teachers, experts,
> and authoritative texts, both in class and in writing. (p. 126)   90

I proceed by suggesting that such critical questioning can be applied to the work of
others (as well as to our own), for instance, by carefully examining an author's
assumptions and being aware of the type of publication a work appears in. Next, I
would elicit or provide students with examples of the kinds of questions that might
be important to pursue (e.g. Who is the author? Are they male or female? What are   95
their ethnic origins, their educational or political backgrounds? What kind of information is useful and/or important to find out about the author? In what kind of
publication does the work appear? What does this reveal about the readership? What
kind of perspective is the author taking in relation to the subject matter? What kind
of language is used in the publication? When was the work published?). In addition,   100
I would mention the importance of checking that the evidence or supporting information given substantiates the main points being made. I would then suggest that
when students are researching a topic that sources are consulted that represent a
variety of perspectives on the question being explored.

On completion of the above activity, students are divided into groups of four and   105
asked to write a paragraph in response to the question: Discuss the origins of
Australia's Aborigines. Students are told they will be given four different texts as
possible resources and given the option of either attempting to synthesize the information found in the four text extracts, or focusing on the ideas presented in only
one or two of the texts.   110

Next, the groups are given time to brainstorm any ideas or information they may already have on the topic. They are then given four text extracts from very different perspectives and source types (see Appendix 1) to read 'critically'. Extract 1, by Manning Clark, has become a very controversial text with regard to its representa-
115 tion of indigenous Australians in terms akin to those used by nineteenth-century believers in social Darwinism. Extracts 2 and 4 are by indigenous Australians. The former was selected because it highlights the difficulties inherent in attempting to formulate a clear-cut response to the focus question within terms of reference that are meaningful from both indigenous and non-indigenous perspectives; the latter
120 because it does not conform to a traditional academic text type: it is a written version of a 'Dreamtime' story that would have been originally delivered in spoken form. Extract 3 comes from a reference book which has turned periods of Australia's history into a series of easy-to-define events that are described in quite simple prose.

Once students have had time to read the text extracts, they are asked to write their para-
125 graphs on overhead transparency sheets which they then present to the class. Appendix 2 shows four paragraphs written by undergraduate and postgraduate students who attended one of my pre-sessional workshops. Although these examples are few in number, they provide some insights into the kinds of issues raised by this class activity. (They also provide a rich source of material for follow-up sessions, for example, on paraphrasing,
130 synthesizing and appropriate use of in-text citation conventions).

Firstly, most students seem to rely more on the Elder text (Extract 3) as the basis for their responses. Secondly, there is a tendency to attempt a clear-cut answer to the question posed. Example 4 is notable in that it does not do this. Although, once again, Elder is the only source cited, the group acknowledges that there is disagreement about the
135 origins of the Aborigines and that more research into the topic may be required.

The next stage of the activity involves students orally evaluating the perspectives of the authors and the nature of the sources from which the extracts have been taken, followed by a discussion about their reasons for favouring the arguments found in certain extracts over those in others. Most comment that the Elder extract
140 is easier to understand and that the evidence used to support the claims made in this text is more substantial than that in the other texts. Extracts 1 and 2 (not surprisingly) seem to pose comprehension difficulties for many students, while Extract 4 tends to be dismissed as 'only a story' and 'not academic'.

Finally, I present students with a sample response to the question posed that is
145 designed to show how such disparate perspectives represented in the four text extracts might be synthesized within a single paragraph (see Appendix 3). We then discuss the importance of purpose and context in any assigned piece of academic writing, including, for example, the role played by academic discipline in influencing the selection of appropriate sources and the pursuit of certain research
150 directions. Students of Archaeology would be required to follow up on quite different resources to those studying Anthropology or Linguistics, for instance. We also discuss the implications of non-indigenous authors writing about issues concerning indigenous people and the need for the knowledge claims of the latter to be represented in forms of their own choosing.

Concluding comments   155

In this paper, I consider a number of different approaches to critical thinking in the context of teaching and learning English for academic purposes at university level. I suggest that for many international students who have studied in very different educational cultures to those found in Australia, the need to develop the ability to 'think critically' may challenge the very foundations upon which their previous   160 learning experiences have been based.

By approaching critical thinking as a form of social and political practice, I highlight the interconnections between pedagogical processes and the realities of the worlds that lie beyond the confines of the classroom walls. Finally, I present a specific writing task for EAP students about the origins of Australia's   165 indigenous people that aims to address ways in which a 'critical thinking' approach may assist students not only to complete their academic assignments effectively, but also to gain insight into some of the issues surrounding the politics of self-representation experienced by indigenous people in Australian society today.   170

References

Atkinson, D. (1997). A critical approach to critical thinking in TESOL. *TESOL Quarterly*, 31 (1), 71–94.

Auerbach, E. (1995). The politics of the ESL classroom: Issues of power in pedagogical choices. In J. W. Tollefson (Ed.), *Power and inequality in language education* (pp. 9–33). Cambridge, UK: Cambridge University Press.

Benesch, S. (1993a). Critical thinking: A learning process for democracy. *TESOL Quarterly*, 27 (3), 545–547.

Benesch, S. (1993b). Ideology, and the politics of pragmatism. *TESOL Quarterly*, 27 (4), 705–717.

Benesch, S. (1996). Needs analysis and curriculum development in EAP: An example of a critical approach. *TESOL Quarterly*, 30 (4), 723–738.

Clark, M. (1986, 6th ed.). *A short history of Australia*. Australia: Penguin.

Elder, B. (ed.) (1988). *Great events in Australia's history: From discovery to present.* Australia: Child and Associates.

Ennis, R. H. (1962). A concept of critical thinking. *Harvard Educational Review*, 32, 82–111.

Ennis, R. H. (1992). The degree to which critical thinking is subject specific: Clarification and needed research. In S. P. Norris (Ed.), *The generalizability of critical thinking* (pp. 21–37). New York: Teachers College Press.

Gieve, S. (1998). Comments on Dwight Atkinson's 'A critical approach to critical thinking in TESOL'. *TESOL Quarterly*, 32 (1), 123–129.

McPeck, F. (1981). *Critical thinking and education*. New York: St Martin's Press.

Narogin, M. (1990). *Writing from the fringe: A study of modern Aboriginal literature*. Victoria, Australia: Hyland House.

Noonuccal, O. and Noonuccal, K. (1988). *The rainbow serpent*. Australian government funded project for the Australian Pavilion World Expo.

Pennycook, A. (1989). The concept of method, interested knowledge, and the politics of language teaching. *TESOL Quarterly*, 23 (4), 589–618.

Pennycook, A. (1994). Incommensurable discourses? *Applied Linguistics*, 15 (2), 115–38.

Pennycook, A. (1996). Borrowing others' words: Text, ownership, memory, and plagiarism. *TESOL Quarterly*, 30 (2), 589–618.

Pennycook, A. (1997). Vulgar pragmatism, critical pragmatism, and EAP. *English for Specific Purposes*, 16 (4), 253–269.

Yunupingu, M. (1994). Yothu Yindi: Finding balance. *Race and Class*, 35 (4), 113–120.

▶ APPENDIX 1: SELECTION OF TEXTS

Extract 1

> So far there have been two cultures in Australia – one Aboriginal and the other European. Like the Americas, Australia was probably first colonized by Homo sapiens, ... during the last ice age ... During the passage of time between the coming of the Aborigine just about thirty thousand years ago and the coming of the white man in 1788, the changes in the appearance of Australia were caused probably more by changes in climate than by human activity. For apart from fire, the stone implements he used for hunting and food gathering, and the rock paintings on which he portrayed his vision of the world, the Aborigine handed on to posterity few other memorials of his encounter with the weird and harsh land his people had occupied since time immemorial.
>
> (Clark, 1986, p. 9).

Extract 2

> Aboriginal being and history until now, the last period, has been dominated by *Anglo-Celts. The Time of the Dreaming*, is called prehistory and a whole theoretical structure has been erected with little recourse to the Aboriginal communities ... Different scholars argue different things from the evidence they collect and often their accounts and theories seem more fantastic than the myths they seek to replace.
>
> (Narogin, 1990, p. 5).

Extract 3

It has been long accepted that Aborigines arrived in Australia some 40,000 years ago. However, recent evidence has tended to dispute this and some experts put the date of arrival as early as 55,000 before present ... For a long time archaeologists believed that the Aborigines simply walked across from the Malay Archipelago across to the Australian mainland. It is now known that this was not the case. Australia's first inhabitants arrived by sea, probably by raft or canoe. No one knows where they came from; theories about their origins range from the Indian subcontinent all the way across Asia to the islands of the Philippines.

(Elder, 1988, p. 80).

Extract 4

But here now you fullas.
You come sit down by my
Fire. Warm yourselves and I
Will tell you the story of how
This world began.

In the time of Alcheringa
The land lay flat and cold.
The world, she empty.
The Rainbow Serpent, she
Asleep under the ground
With all the animal tribes in
Her belly waiting to be born ...

Then she throw good spirit
Biami high in the sky ...
He jump high in the sky and
Smile down on the land.
The sky lit up from his smile
And we, his children, saw
Colour and shadow.
(Noonuccal and Noonuccal, 1988, pp. 20–23).

▶ APPENDIX 2: STUDENTS' PARAGRAPHS

Example 1

They came from South-East Asia because:

*   Australia is closest to South-East Asia
*   their physical appearance is much like people in Indian subcontinent
*   their population is mostly found in Northern Australia at the present time.

Example 2

In our opinion, the origins of Australia's Aborigines are probably from a part of South-East Asia as suggested in Extract 3. According to Elder (1988), there are theories stating that the early Aborigines arrived by sea from the Indian sub-continent or other parts across Asia including the islands of the Philippines.

Example 3

Our notion of the origins of Australia's Aborigines is they first came to Australia as early as 55,000 BP (acc. to Extract 3) by raft or canoe from South-East Asia and spread out throughout Australia (as mentioned by Elder, 1988).

Example 4

So far scientists are still arguing about the origins of the aborigins. One thesis stated by Elder B (ed.) (1988) is that they posibily came from South-East Asia, by raft or canoes. He showed where Aborigines came from quite specifically. However, in regards to the way they immigrated, Elder, B just mentioned seatravel, and did not give any idea about other ways such as by land bridge between Asia and Australia continent before they were seperated. Thus, this issue might require more research.

▶ APPENDIX 3: SAMPLE PARAGRAPH

There are a number of quite different versions about the origins of Australia's Aborigines. These versions reflect the particular perspectives or world-views of their authors. For example, Noonuccal and Noonuccal (1988: 20–23) describe how all people originate from the Rainbow Serpent during the 'Time of the Dreaming' (Narogin, 1990: 5). Some historians, however, refer to archaeological findings to support claims that indigenous Australians arrived here between 30,000 (Clark, 1986: 9) and 55,000 years ago from the Indian subcontinent, Asia and the Philippines (Elder, 1988: 8). In order to address this topic comprehensively, research into the oral records of different Aboriginal communities also needs to be undertaken (Narogin, 1990: 5).

▶ FOCUS A: READING

A.3 Understanding and responding

➤ Use your English–English dictionary to check the meaning of the words and phrases that you highlighted as you read Article 9. Write any that are still unclear to you on the whiteboard in your classroom, with the line number showing where they appear in the article. Ask your tutor and the other students to read the word or phrase in its context and discuss its meaning with you.

➤ Have your ideas about critical thinking and what it involves changed since you read Article 9? Discuss this with another student and then return to your definitions of 'critical thinking'. Select the one that you consider to provide the best definition. Highlight it. Copy it out and place it on the wall near where you study.

➤ Read Article 9 again and, working with another student, discuss the following quotes from the article with another student. Find out the meanings of any new words or phrases, and consider the quotes in relation to your own contexts and experiences.

1 'Over the last ten years in particular there has been considerable growth in the number of international students enrolling in Australian universities.' (lines 14–15)

2 'In order to successfully complete their studies, these students are required to make many educational, linguistic, cultural, social and often economic adjustments… (lines 24–25).

3 'The shift from viewing learning primarily as the work of memory and repetition of the words and ideas of one's lecturers (see Pennycook, 1996, for example) to conceptualizing learning as a constantly evolving process of discovery, questioning and reformulating of hypotheses, can be an extremely disconcerting and confusing experience.' (lines 27–31)

4 'Denying the political nature of language education, argues Pennycook (1989), can be equated with "articulating an ideological position in favour of the status quo" (p. 591).' (lines 53–55).

5 'Both writers stress the need to adopt an approach to learning that encourages critical questioning not only of all pedagogical approaches and materials but also of the society of which instructors and students form a part.' (lines 62–65).

6 '….critical questioning can be applied to the work of others (as well as to our own), for instance, by carefully examining an author's assumptions and being aware of the type of publication a work appears in.' (lines 91–93)

7 'I would then suggest that when students are researching a topic that sources are consulted that represent a variety of perspectives on the question being explored.' (lines 102–104)

8 'I suggest that for many international students who have studied in very different educational cultures to those found in Australia, the need to develop the ability to 'think critically' may challenge the very foundations upon which their previous learning experiences have been based.' (lines 158–161)

9 'By approaching critical thinking as a form of social and political practice, I highlight the interconnections between pedagogical processes and the realities of the worlds that lie beyond the confines of the classroom walls.' (lines 162–164)

Strategy for Success #48

Highlight ideas presented in an article for discussion later with your tutor or other students.

➢ In lines 83–154 of Article 9, the author describes an extended activity (one that lasts over two or more lessons) designed to help students develop skills of critical thinking. Below, you will find the steps that the students took when completing this activity. These steps are in the wrong order. Arrange them into the correct order, according to the description of the activity in Article 9. ANSWERS

> 'This ordering exercise is loads of fun; it examines our understanding of the article.'
>
> Mariam Tariq Ahmed Mohamed Khalil (first-year student)

The students ·········

1   .... orally evaluate the perspectives of the four authors and the nature of the sources from which the extracts have been taken.

2   .... read a sample response to the question.

3   .... discuss why they preferred the arguments found in certain extracts over those in others.

4   .... discuss the importance of purpose and context in academic writing.

5   .... read and consider a working definition of the term 'critical thinking'.

6   .... brainstorm the topic.

7   .... get into groups of four, and are assigned a topic.

8   .... think of some examples of the kinds of questions that might be important to pursue, and discuss others provided by their tutor.

9   .... write their paragraphs on overhead transparency sheets and present them to their class.

10   .... describe what they understand by 'critical thinking' in an academic context.

11   .... read 'critically' four text extracts about the topic that represent different perspectives and source types.

➢ When you have rearranged the steps of the lesson, first work with another student and discuss the purpose for each step, that is, consider the aims of the tutor who designed the activity and its steps. Then, ask your tutor to follow the steps with you. Help him or her first by getting yourselves into groups of three or four and:

• agreeing upon a topic
• finding four articles about the topic that represent different perspectives and source types. Consider the questions supplied in lines 95–100 of Article 9 to help you here.

➤ When you have completed the activity, think critically about the activity as a whole, in terms of its aims, which were to help students develop skills of critical thinking. To help you do this, consider the questions below with another student. Make a note of your responses. You may use them later.

1 What contribution did the various steps make?
2 How did you benefit from the lesson?
3 How did others benefit?
4 Which was the most useful part?
5 Which was the least useful part?
6 What would you recommend doing differently next time, and why?

A.4 Text structure

➤ Read again the section entitled 'Exploring critical thinking in the EAP classroom'. How might the addition of subheadings help the reader? What subheadings would you add?

➤ Read the section in Article 9 entitled 'Concluding comments' (lines 155–170). The author uses this section to summarize and highlight the key points she has made. She writes:

1 'I consider a number of different approaches to critical thinking in the context of teaching and learning English for academic purposes at university level.'
2 'I suggest that for many international students who have studied in very different educational cultures to those found in Australia, the need to develop the ability to "think critically" may challenge the very foundations upon which their previous learning experiences have been based.'
3 'By approaching critical thinking as a form of social and political practice, I highlight the interconnections between pedagogical processes and the realities of the worlds that lie beyond the confines of the classroom walls.'
4 'I present a specific writing task for EAP students about the origins of Australia's indigenous people that aims to address ways in which a 'critical thinking' approach may assist students not only to complete their academic assignments effectively, but also to gain insight into some of the issues surrounding the politics of self-representation experienced by indigenous people in Australian society today.'

Read Article 9 and identify the lines where the author makes, in greater detail, the four points above. Check your ideas with another student and with your tutor.

▶ FOCUS B: LEARNING LANGUAGE

B.1 Language of evaluation

➤ When writing and thinking critically, language helps us to express, identify or describe:

qualify *v.*
To add to something that has already been said, in order to limit its effect or meaning. *Could I just qualify that last statement?*

refute *v.* T *formal*
To prove that a statement or idea is not correct. *An attempt to refute Darwin's theories.*

insight *n.* [C]
A sudden clear understanding of something, especially a complicated situation or idea. *The research provides new insights into the way we process language.*

contentious *adj.*
Causing a lot of argument and disagreement between people. *Animal welfare did not become a contentious issue until the late 1970s.*

implicit *adj.*
Suggested or understood without being stated directly. *His statement is being seen as implicit criticism of the work of research laboratories.*

1   agreement or disagreement
2   certainty, doubt or **qualification**
3   assumptions
4   evaluations.

The phrases below are all taken from academic writing. Organize them according to the four categories above. You will find four examples for each category above. ANSWERS

(a)   The study had a number of limitations, however.

(b)   This is in accord with Smith (1999), who observes that …

(c)   Benesch however, **refutes** the notion of…

(d)   These conclusions must be qualified by the understanding that …

(e)   This investigation successfully highlights the need for …

(f)   The research was successful to the extent that it has enabled us to gain **insight** into …

(g)   The author appears to assume that …

(h)   These results need to be understood in light of the fact that …

(i)   A cautious interpretation of these results might lead us to conclude that …

(j)   The implications of these results are unambiguous.

(k)   This idea is **contentious**, however …

(l)   The assumption appears to be that …

(m)   This interpretation is based upon the unfounded belief that …

(n)   However, the experiment failed to show that …

(o)   **Implicit** in this article is the view that …

(p)   This observation is consistent with that of Kirby, who stated that …

B.2 Key words for thinking critically

➢   The 'Academic Word List' (Coxhead, 2000) referred to in Chapter 3 contains a number of words that are particularly useful in critical thinking. Examples include:

- assess
- accurate
- benefit
- challenge
- justify.

Choose one of the following activities:

1   Study the 'Headwords of the Academic Word List', available by following the instructions in Chapter 3, page 68. Select 10 more words from this list that you think would be particularly useful when evaluating ideas. Add them to your related words record. Complete the information required in the table, using your English–English learner's dictionary to help you.

OR

2   Study the list of skills for critical thinking provided in section A.2 above. Select 10 verbs from this list that you would like to find out more about. Add them to your vocabulary record or to your list of collocations. Complete the information required in the record, using your English–English learner's dictionary to help you.

▶ FOCUS C: WRITING

C.1 Writing critically

➤   Using the words that you identified in section B.2, write a reflective critique *either* of the extended activity that your tutor prepared for you at the end of section A.2 above, *or* critique another lesson that you have recently experienced. If you choose to do the former, refer to the notes you made when you reflected critically on the lesson.

In your writing, include all of the following:

- a description of what took place
- an explanation of why the various stages were included in the lesson
- a description of the criteria for material selection
- an evaluation of what was useful, and why; what was less useful, and why
- an outline of anything you would like to change about the lesson, and how you would do this.

Before you write, remember to agree with your tutor upon a subset of annotations from the companion website which you would like him or her to use when marking your work.

C.2 Critiquing peer writing

➤ Work with another student. Exchange the writing that you prepared as part of the 'lesson' described in section A.2. Give each other constructive feedback on the writing. Then improve your writing accordingly.

▌ FOCUS D: RESEARCHING

D.1 Asking good questions

➤ An important skill for critical thinking is the ability to ask good questions. Here are some good questions to ask:

1 What are the issues and conclusions?
2 What are the reasons?
3 Which words or phrases are ambiguous?
4 What are the value conflicts and assumptions?
5 What are the descriptive assumptions?
6 Are there any fallacies in the reasoning?
7 How good is the evidence?
8 Are there rival causes?
9 Are the statistics deceptive?
10 What significant information is omitted?
11 What reasonable conclusions are possible?
    (Browne and Keeley, 2004: 13)

Extend this list by adding four more questions to it. To help you, refer to the list of skills in section A.2 above. Base your questions upon these skills. For example, the skill of 'avoiding overgeneralization' could give us:

12 Are there any examples of overgeneralization?

➤ Make a copy of your 15 questions and place them on the wall near where you study. Keep these questions in mind as you study.

D.2 Evaluating internet sources

➤ In Chapters 1 and 4, the idea of thinking critically about an article was introduced and explored. Can you remember what the acronym ACAREAS stands for?
➤ Why is ACAREAS particularly important in relation to information that is available on the internet? Discuss this question with a team of students and make notes of the key points that you identify. Share these with another team. Use their ideas to extend your own.
➤ Choose one of the following activities:

1   Find an example of information on the internet that is likely to be reliable according to ACAREAS. Share this with another student and explain why you have judged the information reliable.

OR

2   Find an example of information on the internet that may not be reliable according to ACAREAS. Share this with another student and explain why you have judged the information unreliable.

▌ FOCUS E: STUDYING

E.1 Analysing term papers and examination questions

When writing an essay, or answering an examination essay question, a key skill is the ability to understand and analyse the question. Questions may begin with a question word such as 'why' or 'how', or 'is' or 'are', for example, but it is very likely that you will be asked to do something more specific.

For example, you may be asked to:

Analyse	Demonstrate	Illustrate	Review
Appraise	Describe	Indicate	Select
Argue	Develop	Interpret	Show
Arrange	Differentiate	Justify	Solve
Assess	Discuss	Label	Specify
Categorize	Distinguish	List	State
Clarify	Enumerate	Locate	Suggest
Classify	Evaluate	Match	Summarize
Comment on	Examine	Name	Support
Compare	Exemplify	Order	
Consider	Explain	Outline	
Construct	Formulate	Predict	
Contrast	Define	Propose	
Critique	Identify	Relate	

Benjamin Bloom, an American educational psychologist (1913–1999) developed a **taxonomy** for classifying educational objectives (Bloom, 1965) in relation to three overlapping areas: knowledge, skills and attitude (or cognitive, psychomotor and affective areas respectively). Within the area of knowledge, or cognitive, objectives, he distinguished six levels which are organized from the most concrete or simplest (knowledge of facts), to the most abstract (evaluation). They may be illustrated as follows:

> **taxonomy** *n.* [C, U]
> The process or a system of organizing things into different groups to show their natural relationships, especially plants or animals.

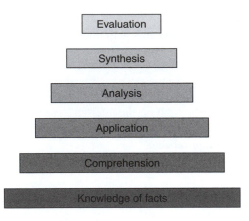

> Find out more about Bloom's Taxonomy. In particular, find out which of the six levels above may be considered 'critical thinking' or 'higher order thinking skills'. Use reliable sources on the internet to help you. Describe what you have found out to another student.

> Check the meaning of any of the verbs in the list above in an English–English dictionary if you need to. Then, working with another student, find four verbs in the list that describe something that would happen at each level. For example, if you *label* a diagram, you would be demonstrating your *knowledge of facts*; but if you *assess* something, this would fall under the category of *evaluation*. It may be possible for a verb to fall into more than one category. When you have finished, compare your ideas with another pair of students. ANSWERS

Strategy for Success #49

Don't restrict your reading to your own subject area. Read about education and learning too, because as long as you are a student, these are also your subjects.

> Before you begin to answer an essay or examination question, first, underline the question word or verb. Then use your highlighter to mark up topic words.

Here are three examples, two from the field of EAP and the third from Political Science:

Why is there a need for 'EAP'? Illustrate your answer with examples from your own experience.

Choose two different teaching methods and discuss their similarities and differences.

What is globalization? Is it good or bad and for whom?

Use the underlining and highlighting to guide your outline. Follow the strategy you learned in Chapter 5, and prepare an outline for a 1500-word essay in response to one of the two questions above. If you choose to answer the third question, the student's work below may give you some ideas.

Strategy for Success #50

Think critically about essay and examination questions before you begin to plan your answer.

E.2 Responding to tutor feedback on the content of written work

Feedback from your tutor on the content of your written work is likely to reflect his or her critical thinking. Below, you can read the introduction to a student's essay on the subject of globalization, with the feedback she received from her tutor. The student, Tuka Waddah Talib Ali Al Hanai, was taking a course in Political Science.

What is Globalization? Is it Good or Bad and for Whom?

Introduction

With the advent of the internet and other communication technologies it is inevitable that countries will have larger and more instantaneous access to resources that were not previously available to them. No more has it become a question of 'how should we obtain this mineral or service?', but more of a question of, 'how should it be utilized?'. We have become a more global world. This raises the issue of globalization.

Comment[MW1]: This is good but I think you need to add something more here. Globalisation is mostly technology driven but it has various dimensions which we can categorise as the movement of people, capital (money) and ideas (and their affect uponculture).

The word 'globalization' is a broad term which invites many interpretations, and is often a source of heated debate. For the purpose of this essay the term will relate to the large scale integration of countries throughout the world. More specifically, I will use the term to refer to the integration of economies through trade, finance, workers, information and technology [1]. This essay will look at what globalization includes, whether it is harmful or beneficial, and whom it affects. Below, I will consider these issues under three broad themes: multinationals, free versus regulated economies, and international bodies.

Comment[MW2]: Why these three?

There are equally convincing arguments on both sides of the globalization debate. Looking back at recent history within the last few decades, there are

Comment [MW3]: Not sure what you mean by 'environment'. Also you should give examples of the countries that have benefited and suffered

Comment [MW5]: Give examples of these factors.

Comment [MW4]: Right, so it's their fault. These are important issues. Do you plan to develop them later in the essay?

many countries that have greatly benefited from being exposed to competition on an international scale while other countries have suffered from being in that same environment. [1] and [2] state that the main reason certain countries have failed to benefit from globalization is due to the policies they adopted. However, there are also factors which are beyond the control of countries that affect their performance [1, 2].

➢ Work with another student. Discuss and note down the steps you would take in response to the feedback that the student who wrote the introduction above received. Then compare your ideas with the revised work, below.

What is Globalization? Is it Good or Bad and for Whom?

Introduction

With the advent of the internet and other communication technologies it is inevitable that countries will have larger and more instantaneous access to resources that were not previously available to them. No more has it become a question of 'how should we obtain this mineral or service?', but more of a question of, 'how should it be utilized?'. We have become a more global world. This raises the issue of globalization.

The word 'globalization' is a broad term which invites many interpretations, and is often a source of heated debate. For the purpose of this essay the term will relate to the large scale integration of countries throughout the world. More specifically, I will use the term to refer to the integration of economies through trade, finance, workers, information and technology. In other words, it can be considered as the movement of capital, people and technology or ideas [1]. This essay will look at what globalization includes, whether it is harmful or beneficial, and whom it affects. Due to the depth and complexity of the subject, I will explore the topic under what I consider to be the most influential aspects of globalization: multinationals and free versus regulated economies.

There are equally convincing arguments on both sides of the globalization debate. Looking back at recent history within the last few decades, there are many countries that have greatly benefited from being exposed to competition on an international scale such as the USA, South Korea and China [2,3]. While other countries such as Argentina and several African countries have suffered from being in that same environment of fierce competition [1,3]. [1] and [2] state that the main reason certain countries have failed to benefit from globalization is due to the policies they adopted which concerns the way economies are regulated and will be addressed later on in the essay.

➤ Work with another student. Highlight the parts of the introduction where the student took steps to address her tutor's comments. How successfully has she done this? Evaluate her efforts and share your ideas with your tutor.

▶ FOCUS F: APPLYING TO YOUR OWN SUBJECT

F.1 Thinking critically about a subject-related article

➤ Find a subject-related article or book chapter that you are interested in or that you need to read, and:

- annotate it
- answer five or more of your 15 questions (see section D.1 above). Make notes
- describe your article or chapter to another student. Focus in particular on the answers you found to your five questions.

F.2 Thinking critically about subject-related term papers and examination questions

➤ Find past examination papers or essay questions related to your subject. Ask your tutor for his or her help here. Analyse the language used. Describe how you would answer the question.
➤ Write your own subject-related essay examination questions. Share these with your subject tutor. Answer one of them.

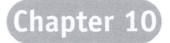

Chapter 10

Finding Your Voice

In this chapter, you can read an extract from a **book chapter** about the academic argument and how to present it in your writing.

You can develop your skills in these areas:

Focus A: Reading

A.1   Looking ahead
A.2   Understanding and responding

Focus B: Learning language

B.1   Language of logic
B.2   Transitions

Focus C: Writing

C.1   Writing logically
C.2   Logical fallacies to avoid
C.3   Redrafting peer writing
C.4   Fifteen steps to writing a good academic argument

Focus D: Researching

D.1   Developing, supporting and presenting an argument

Focus E: Studying

E.1   Reflecting upon the effectiveness of learning

Focus F: Applying to your own subject

F.1   Identifying and summarizing a subject-related argument

▶ FOCUS A: READING

A.1 Looking ahead

In this chapter, you can read about the academic 'argument'.

➤   How do you think an 'academic argument' might differ from the kind of 'argument' that we can have with our family, friends, or complete strangers? Discuss this point with another student, then share your ideas with your class. Gather enough information to help you to prepare a definition of the phrase 'academic argument'. Make a note of this in your portfolio.

➤   Work with another student to answer the following questions:

1   Why is an academic argument useful? What does it help us to do?
2   Can you think of some topics that would lend themselves to academic argument?
3   How many different forms of academic argument can you think of?
4   What skills or strategies do you think you would need to make a good written academic argument?
5   What is the relationship between the ideas in your own writing and those of others? What does 'finding your voice' mean to you? Ask your tutor about his or her experience of this in relation to his or her own writing.

> 'I like the way that this chapter doesn't give you the meaning of 'academic argument' directly; you have to guess first then deduce it from the article. This is critical thinking!'
>
> Mariam Tariq Ahmed Mohamed Khalil (first-year student)

➤   Read Article 10. Take notes and annotate it. Highlight words or phrases that you would like to understand better.

▶ ARTICLE 10: THE ARGUMENT ESSAY DEFINED

Extract from Cioffi, F. L. (2005) *The Imaginative Argument*.
Princeton, USA: Princeton University Press.

In a way it is unfortunate that we need to use the term 'argument' to describe a kind of writing, for 'argument' most typically means a heated dispute, an altercation, a verbal fight. Actual fights may indeed follow the verbal fight of an 'argument' too – an argument is a serious, emotional, and confrontational experience. It's worse than
5   a spat, more angry than a discussion, more heated than a mere debate.

But forget all that. None, or little, of it really applies here. Instead, here (and in other textbooks about argumentation), 'argument' refers to a kind of discourse, an organized verbal attempt to persuade an audience through the use of logic and reason. Obviously there are other ways to persuade people – ranging from torture and
10   coercion, on one hand, to cajolery, satire, burlesque, or advertisement, on the other. But logical argument – if you will permit a value judgment – is the most civilized, the most high-minded mode. It's the mode suggested here, anyway, and logical argument has its own system of rules and prohibitions, its own structure, and its own ontology, much of which I will attempt to delineate in the following pages.
15   Written argument may take many forms. For example, a description might strive to show a new way of looking at something, such as a poem, a system of government, or a tax loophole; a classification would place something in a large, organizational matrix or system; an evaluation makes a judgment about something based on comparison of that thing with a stipulated ideal type; a proposal might
20   suggest a future course of action or a present problem that needs to be addressed; a comparison-contrast might compare two different things, issues, ideas, or texts in an effort to illuminate something about one or both of them; a cause-effect paper might show how a situation or state of affairs could lead to or cause another; a definition might argue for a new way of characterizing something. In his *Rhetoric*,
25   Aristotle gives twenty-eight valid 'topics' for argument, but these can for the most part be distilled into the seven modes I have suggested above.

These modes – description, classification, evaluation, proposal, comparison-contrast, cause–effect, and definition – give you the structure or subgenre of your whole paper, but they don't tell you in any detail what you actually have to do.
30   Basically, working within these modes, your paper needs to *explain something*. Usually a paper will attempt to explain something relatively difficult – something in need of explanation – but sometimes the simplest things only *seem* simple. On closer inspection, they reveal themselves as not quite so simple and hence really do need to be explained.

Let me be more specific and offer some strategies that you might use when you
35   attempt to explain. While these strategies are not mutually exclusive – indeed, many overlap – I nonetheless offer them as examples of what an argumentative paper can usefully do by way of explaining. Your paper can do one or more of the following:

1   *Interpret.* An interpreter usually renders one language into another, and in some sense that is what an interpretation paper does as well. It argues meaning or elucidation of something difficult and perhaps obscure. It translates one version of English into a more accessible version. You might focus on some aspect of language, in such an analysis, or you might look at what various 'keywords' mean. This involves more than merely defining them – indeed, you might conceive of what special meanings the words have in the context of the work. For example, when the philosopher John Rawls writes about 'the veil of ignorance,' you need to know what kinds of things he has in mind with respect to creating a fair system of organizing a society. You also need to know dictionary definitions of words. On one exam I took, I was given a poem, 'The Chambered Nautilus,' and asked to explicate it. My task was made far easier by the fact that I for some reason knew the nautilus to be a type of seashell. Make sure that you look at all aspects of a work, including the title! For example, the short poem 'Little children you all may go/But the one you are hiding will fly' makes some sense on its own, but its title, 'Song of Primitive Man Chipping Out an Arrowhead,' gives it a different meaning altogether. When Marshall McLuhan chose his famous book title, *The Medium Is the Massage,* what did he mean?

2   *Uncover assumptions.* Often there are assumptions that need to be unpacked or unmasked. Whether an essay examines a speech, a paleontological theory, a novel, or a yacht, there are underlying assumptions and elements inherent in the makeup of each of these genres (speech, theory, novel, yacht), as well as individual variations from novel to novel, or yacht to yacht, for example. This kind of paper would argue not just that certain underlying assumptions exist, but that they function in some interesting, elaborate, or perhaps sinister way. Sometimes an author's words themselves embody preexisting theoretical commitments. In fact, even the author might not know these implicit assumptions or they are so deeply rooted in the psyche that all of us might be unaware of them. But looking for these is often a useful, even sobering task.

3   *Reveal significant patterns.* A paper might argue both for the existence of patterns of some kind (giving examples to support its assertions) and for the idea that such patterns are meaningful, important ones. These patterns can be linguistic (repetition of certain words, sentence structures, or images), thematic, generic, or even stylistic. You might, for instance, discover some pattern that could explain how a building works – say, the use of curves or of the number six in the Chrysler Building. Or you could find something interesting about word-pattern in a novel. For example, Martin Amis, while reading *Crash* by J. G. Ballard, notes that the author uses certain keywords many times: 'perverse' sixteen times, 'geometry' twenty-one times, 'stylized' twenty-six times. These curious repetitions seem to suggest something about the author's sensibility, as does the fact that, for example, in Ben Franklin's autobiography, the word 'ingenious,' or some variation thereof, appears more than thirty times. But pattern finding need not be limited to word counting. Georg Simmel points out

that in Shakespeare's plays the minor characters tend to be killed by outside forces, while the major characters seem to die as a result of internal problems. An interesting pattern – what does it mean? You might ask yourself, too, whether there is a pattern evident in the way that the author handles certain
85 kinds of characters or situations. Is there a pattern of action that seems to predominate with reference to the way a plot unfolds? Does it remind you of other patterns of action? Sometimes such a paper can compare the patterns of the subject with overarching pattern-generating schemes, such as those provided by history, sociology, psychoanalysis, feminism, myth.
90 4 *Reveal pattern breaks.* This kind of paper would have to incorporate elements of (3) above, but it takes the revelation of patterns a step further, showing how the apparent patterns are not always followed and are either purposely or inadvertently violated. It might then speculate why the patterns break down.
95 5 *Recontextualize.* Such a paper shows how, when looked at in another context – one provided by current events, other works, a new idea or explanatory scheme – a work, idea, or artifact takes on a wholly new meaning. Simply, it views the work – poem, story, whatever – as part of a larger structure. For example, all movies, novels, poems, plays, or books about terrorism must be seen in a new
100 light since the events of September 11, 2001. On a less political note, you might look at a painting or sculpture, for example, in light of its initial reception, or in light of what was going on in the artist's life (or the life of his/her social class, or the life of the artist's nation) at the time it appeared.
6 *Generalize.* Such a paper argues that the system, text, artifact, or thing under
105 scrutiny represents a larger, more expansive universal. For example, the new security measures at airports represent how we as citizens have lost the War on Terror. The proliferation of prescription drug commercials on television suggests a larger reliance on drug use as a way of life. Fiction can be generalized this way too: a story might be about a woman, but this story could
110 perhaps be explained as being about the plight of every woman – or every person. A story about looking for a parking space might be seen as being about something as general as the nature of quests. A story about a boy's disappointment with his visit to a mall Santa Claus might be seen as a story about growing up and coming to terms with the alloyed quality of anticipated pleas-
115 ure. Another way to think about this would be to see certain elements of a piece of writing or a situation as being metaphorical, as representing something else. (The extreme version of such a tactic is the allegorization of experience that many cultures adopt. And allegory is 'one story that is really another, very different story,' to use Henry James's definition. Almost all of
120 *Aesop's Fables* are allegories, for example.)
7 *Argue for effect.* This paper might argue for how something has an impact on a reader, viewer, participant. It tries to show how the elements of whatever is under analysis have a direct (or not-so-direct) connection to the way people respond to that subject.

8   *Extrapolate*. A paper might take the argument of an essay or the general 'mes-   125
sage' of a work and show its silliness, ridiculousness, or nonsensicality by
extending it to its logical next or last step. Your paper would demonstrate and
explain the work's weakness, shallowness, or incoherence. (Usually people
employ this strategy, 'reductio ad absurdum,' to attack other arguments or philosophical propositions.)   130

Overall, you need to remember, though, that whatever strategy you employ – and
some things seem to be more amenable to certain strategies than others – your
paper needs to argue for something not obvious, not taken for granted, not super-
ficial, not readily conceded. You want to reveal something that you have in some
genuine sense *discovered*. Your paper will prove why what you have discovered has   135
resonance and importance. At the same time, you don't want to 'explain away' the
text or subject matter: your essay will not replace or supplant what it is that you
are writing about. Remember that if you feel that you've explained everything,
then probably something is wrong with the angle you have taken. As the critic and
writer Murray Sperber often warns, avoid creating a critical machine that grinds   140
to hamburger everything in its path!

Keep in Mind That ...

Your own writing is not intended to be a reiteration of the class's or the instructor's
ideas. Rather, the papers being written here should be an elaboration, an extension,
and an expression of your own ideas. Your own voice – your own insights – should   145
predominate. It is, however, necessary to understand and build on the ideas of the
texts, class, and instructor; to ignore these or to present them as your own (or as
silly and jejune) would be a mistake. But overall, most instructors appreciate
creativity and originality of insight rather than mere recasting or parroting of previously expressed ideas. External sources, too, should not usurp or displace your own   150
voice in the course of an essay; rather, they should be used to bolster, to contextual-
ize, to delineate, and to sharpen your own position. This of course may vary from
class to class – probably some classes do require both acceptance and reiteration of
the ideas of the instructor and texts: they want you to demonstrate that you 'got it,'
to quote my erstwhile colleague. Yet finally it's up to you to figure out to what extent   155
you are expected to be entirely original and to what extent you just need to demonstrate that you have understood and can reproduce the various concepts (reading
materials, ideas from lectures) in a class.

▶ FOCUS A: READING

A.2 Understanding and responding

➤ Study the words or phrases below in their contexts in Article 10, and add them
to your vocabulary record or your collocation record. They are all taken from
the section of Article 10 which relates to 'finding your voice'.

1	taken for granted (line 133)	7	recasting (line 149)
2	superficial (lines 133–134)	8	parroting (line 149)
3	conceded (line 134)	9	usurp (line 150)
4	resonance (line 136)	10	bolster (line 151)
5	supplant (line 137)	11	contextualize (lines 151–152)
6	reiteration (line 143)	12	delineate (line 152)

➤ Having read Article 10 and studied the words and phrases above, revise your answers to the questions in section A.1 above. Check your work with another student or your class.

➤ Read Article 10, lines 27–158 again, and, working with another student, together select 10 quotes or extracts from the article that you would like to consider in relation to your own context and experience. Here are two examples that you might choose:

'…sometimes the simplest things only *seem* simple. On closer inspection, they reveal themselves as not quite so simple and hence really do need to be explained.' (lines 32–33)

'Often there are assumptions that need to be unpacked or unmasked.' (lines 56–57)

➤ Exchange two or three of your quotes or extracts with those of another student and discuss the new ones you have been given.

➤ Answer the question posed in lines 54–55, and find out what you can about McLuhan's choice of title. It relies upon a play on words, or 'pun'.

➤ Describe to your tutor or another student what you now understand by the need to 'find your voice' in academic writing. Use some of the 12 words that you studied above in your description.

Strategy for Success #51

Consciously try to develop your own 'voice'. One way to do this is by taking control of your material; don't let it control you.

▶ FOCUS B: LEARNING LANGUAGE

B.1 Language of **logic**

logic *n.* [singular, U]
A way of thinking about something that seems correct and reasonable, or a set of sensible reasons for doing something.
What's the logic of your argument?

➤ Work with another student. The following words and phrases are useful when considering how logical conclusions are. Add them to your vocabulary record. Complete the information required, using your English–English learner's dictionary to help you.

proposition	paradox
mutually exclusive	to beg the question
induction	analogy
deduction	validity
conclusion	dichotomy

B.2 Transitions

➤ In Chapter 3, you identified discourse markers organized according to their function. Using discourse markers appropriately can help your reader to follow your argument. Seven functions were identified. These were to:

(1) focus attention on what follows
(2) add supporting information
(3) provide an example
(4) clarify
(5) show that ideas contrast, but do not contradict, each other
(6) show that ideas contrast each other
(7) indicate cause and effect.

Discourse markers can perform other useful functions. They can:

(8) emphasize
(9) show similarity
(10) describe place or position
(11) indicate a sequence of events
(12) indicate events over time
(13) summarize or conclude.

Work with another student. Match the following discourse markers to functions 8–13 above. You will find three for each function. ANSWERS

nearby	in conclusion	in brief
subsequently	beyond	adjacent
likewise	finally	recently
in fact	currently	next
then	just as	of course
on the whole	similarly	indeed

➤ Work with another student. Discuss the difference between the four words or phrases below. Think in terms of their meaning and style.

* Finally
* Lastly
* At last
* In the end.

➤ Check your ideas with another pair of students and your tutor. Which are you most likely to use in academic writing?

Strategy for Success #52

Use transitions to help you to signpost the logic of your argument, not to replace it.

▶ FOCUS C: WRITING

C.1 Writing logically

Good writing depends upon expressing your ideas logically. Your writing should help your reader to trace the argument you are presenting.

---

coherence *n.* [U]
When something such as a piece of writing is easy to understand because its parts are connected in a clear and reasonable way. *An overall theme will help to give your essay coherence.*

---

train of thought *noun phrase*
A related series of thoughts that are developing in your mind. *The phone interrupted my train of thought.*

➤ The following paragraphs are extracts from the first draft of a research report prepared by a group of students who were investigating the benefits of sending a group of students from their institution to Australia to study English. Read them, and identify problems for the reader caused by a lack of logic or **coherence**. Work with another student and discuss what you would do to improve this work. Think in particular about:

- expressing ideas logically and coherently so that you can follow the writer's '**train of thought**':
- transitions between paragraphs
- transitions within paragraphs
- one topic sentence per paragraph, with supporting ideas.

Extract 1: Introduction

English is the most popular language in the world so it is useful to be able to speak English fluently. Nowadays English language is used everywhere, English is the major language of news and information in the world, it is the language of business, and people all over the world communicate with each other in English. Since all of that, people need to learn English in order to communicate with all the developments in the whole world. So we think that our research topic is important, since all of the students need to learn English because their study is in English and their future careers will be in English. They will communicate with others in English and they will do their research in English. So obviously, the language is the most common language in the whole world.

Extract 2: Method

Each team member transcribed an interview assigned to her; therefore, the transcriptions were done individually to save time and to divide the work among team members. We wrote down the significant points that helped us with our topic. We compared the answers and noted the differences, similarities and the connections between them in order to write our research recommendations. Moreover, we identified three different overseas English language schools and their features. Then we compared them against our criteria and to help us here we designed an evaluation matrix. At last we chose the most suitable school which meets our client's requirements and the students' preferences.

Extract 3: Discussion

The students face some difficulties because of the level of English they learned in secondary school. They should like English and they should find it interesting to learn. A good way of learning is that the teacher should encourage students to ask more questions, explain and share their ideas with each other. Teachers can help students learn quickly by giving them homework to practice what they are learning. Before the end of lessons teachers should make sure that what they have explained is understood and clear to all students and the best way for students to keep the new words and things they learn in mind is practicing it outside classrooms away from teachers. Additionally, they should watch and listen to some English faculty in order to improve their pronunciation.

Smaller classes are seen to be more helpful for students as the teacher can spend time with students who need help, and it is easier for them to communicate with each other. Being in classes with both genders could possibly be a problem as some parents from this culture would not like their daughters to be in a mixed gender class but this might help the students share their information.

Strategy for Success #53

Thinking well will help you to write well.

C.2 Logical fallacies to avoid

premise [C] also premiss BrE
A statement or idea that you accept as true and use as a base for developing other ideas. *The idea that there is life on other planets is the central premise of the novel.*

➢ When you make an academic argument, the conclusions you draw need to be supported with evidence. This evidence is sometimes known as the **premises** upon which your argument is built. A fallacy is an error in your reasoning, that is, in the connections you have made between your conclusion and your evidence, and there are several common ones that you can avoid if you know about them. Below, you can read some fallacies that have occurred in students' work. First, ask your tutor to explain the fallacies to you. Working with another student or students, match the examples to the fallacy, below. If you find this difficult, work it out together with your tutor. `ANSWERS`

Strategy for Success #54

Avoid common logical fallacies such as the assumption that if B occurred before A, then B must have caused A.

Example

1 University X introduced interactive whiteboards. The next cohort of students achieved better results in their English courses. Therefore, interactive whiteboards can help students to learn more effectively.

2 Compared to students at our institution, students at University X graduate with higher GPAs. University X gives its students laptops when they register. We should do this too at our institution.

3 If we don't stop using up our supply of oil and gas, we'll destroy the planet.

4 We have only met her once but we can tell that she will be difficult to work with as part of a team.

5 Our director supports teamwork. Therefore, because she is a highly qualified and respected academic, all our courses should involve teamwork.

6 Final examinations should be abolished. Performance should be assessed by course work alone. 70% of students agree.

7 Writer X has written several articles about how first-year students need to improve their communication skills. But no one likes her, so we shouldn't pay any attention to what she says.

8 If you don't believe in God, then you must believe in evolution.

9 We concluded that Washington University library was the best, because it had better facilities and resources than the other two we evaluated.

Fallacy

(a) False dichotomy

(b) Slippery slope

(c) False cause

(d) Appeal to authority

(e) Using the poor character of the person offering the evidence to discredit the evidence

(f) Red herring

(g) Drawing a hasty conclusion

(h) Begging the question (that is, the conclusion contains its own evidence)

(i) Because everyone else does.

➢ As a class, discuss ways to avoid such fallacies in your own writing.

C.3 Redrafting peer writing

➢ Improve the students' work in section C.1 above. Write your new draft onto an OHT, or use a word processor if your classroom has a computer and projector.

To help you to improve the work, take the following steps:

- Ensure that ideas are presented logically and that you can identify a train of thought – use the discourse markers that you have studied above and avoid making a logical fallacy.
- Make sure that each paragraph has one topic sentence and a few supporting ideas.
- Check transitions between and within paragraphs.

➢ Display your work for your class to see and explain the steps you have taken to improve it.

C.4 Fifteen Steps to Writing a Good Academic Argument

➢ Work with another student. Turn to the map of this book on pages 8–11. Read column C, 'writing'. Make a note of key points to include in a checklist called 'Fifteen Steps to Writing a Good Academic Argument'. For example, the first one might be 'Know your audience'.

➢ Compare your list with that of another pair of students. Use their ideas to complement your own.

➢ Compare your list with the one on the next page. Tick the ones you have included. Their order is not so important. Discuss any you missed with another student.

➢ You can photocopy this list and place it in a prominent position, near where you do most of your writing.

▶ FIFTEEN STEPS TO WRITING A GOOD ACADEMIC ARGUMENT

1 **Do what you are asked to do in the task.**
   - ○ Supply *evidence* (which can be proved), *assumption* (which can reasonably be inferred from evidence), and *opinion* (which is how you understand the evidence) according to the task requirements. If you are asked for one, do not give the other.

2 **Read critically about your topic.**
   - ○ Do not assume that because it is in print that it is accurate or true.

3 **Write for an identified audience.**
   - ○ The writing you produce for your tutor, a professor in your discipline, a student newsletter or a journal should differ in a number of respects, such as length, style and content.

4 **Provide a thesis statement.**
   - ○ Your introduction should include a clear, identifiable thesis statement.

5 **Include a topic sentence in each paragraph.**
   - ○ Each paragraph should include a clear, identifiable topic sentence.

6 **Add supporting details to each paragraph.**
   - ○ Each paragraph should include a number of details that support or develop your topic sentence.

7 **Present your ideas logically.**
   - ○ Let one idea lead into another and ensure a logical progression and development. State your premises clearly and make the connection to your conclusion as clear as possible.

8 **Write with an appropriate degree of caution.**
   - ○ Avoid overstating your assertions.

9 **Provide transitions that guide the reader from the ideas presented within and between paragraphs.**
   - ○ But avoid overusing these words and phrases. If the ideas you are presenting develop logically, you will need to use transition words and phrases only occasionally.

10 **Use discipline-related terms and concepts appropriately.**
   - ○ Understanding them is the first step to using them appropriately. Depending on your audience, you may wish to define key terms near the beginning of your writing.

11 **Write according to the standards of your institution or tutor.**
   - ○ You may be expected to provide a cover page, or write in Times New Roman 12, for example. Find out what these standards are and apply them.

12 **Quote and paraphrase appropriately and correctly, and provide a list of references according to the standards you have been given.**
   - ○ Make sure that all quotes and paraphrases contribute to and strengthen your argument.

13 **Use headings and subheadings to guide the reader.**
   - ○ As a minimum, always include a title, introduction, conclusion, a main body heading of your choice and references.

14 **Write in a style expected of your discipline.**
   - ○ Avoid overuse of first person and second person. Focus on actors and actions instead (who did what).

15 **Proofread.**
   - ○ Check for mechanical errors (grammar, spelling, punctuation).

▶ FOCUS D: RESEARCHING

D.1 Developing, supporting and presenting an argument

➤ Choose one of the topics below, or consult your tutor if you would like to research another topic.

- The benefits of studying English in an English-medium environment
- The status of English in your own country
- The effect of class size on learning
- How English is taught in school
- The best way to learn a language
- The best way to teach language
- Different learning styles.

Use your topic to prepare a question that you would like to answer. Check this with your tutor before you begin work. Then identify three or four key sources. Follow the fifteen steps above to writing a good academic argument.

➤ Give your first draft to your tutor. Take account of his or her feedback when preparing a second draft.
➤ Give your second draft to another student to read. Take account of his or her feedback in preparing a third draft.
➤ Make a copy of your final draft for everyone in your class. Read any or all of the other students' work.

▶ FOCUS E: STUDYING

E.1 Reflecting upon the effectiveness of learning

➤ Look back through this book and the notes you made in your portfolio. What activities and tasks helped you learn effectively? What worked less well? Make two lists.
➤ Compare your list with that of another student. Discuss your choices. Find out why some activities and tasks helped him or her but not you. Consider adapting your approach to the activities and tasks that worked less well for you.

Strategy for Success #55

Think critically about the effectiveness of your own learning.

▶ FOCUS F: APPLYING TO YOUR OWN SUBJECT

F.1 Identifying and summarizing a subject-related argument

➢ Review the definition of an 'academic argument' that you prepared in section A.1 above. Rewrite it in the light of the work that you have completed as part of this chapter.

➢ Find a subject-related article that presents an argument that you are interested in. Identify the following:

- the thesis statement
- the premises
- the conclusions drawn.

➢ Write a summary of the argument which a non-specialist could follow. Exchange your work with another student and read his or her summary.

➢ In all your future **reading**, **researching** and **writing** always look for the thesis statement, the premises, and the conclusions drawn. Reflect critically upon the logic of the arguments presented.

END WORD

Throughout, I want to stress that the very writing of the essay itself – the process of writing – has just as much value as the finished product. And while that finished product may well form the basis for a published article or essay, the thought, the writing, the doing, the slaving-away-at-the-keyboard effort that the finished essay required emerges as the more valuable result. Ultimately, too, you need to realize that this effort of writing a paper is even more rewarding and meaningful than the grade or than what the professor has to say about the finished product. In a variation on the old saw 'The spoils is the game, not the victory', I want to offer 'Writing finds its rewards in the I'm-writing, not the I've-written'. Now getting you to believe this – that will be the difficult part. (Cioffi, 2005)

References

American Academy of Family Physicians, Policy and Advocacy (2007). AAFP Definitions for Policy Statement, Position Paper and Discussion Paper. Retrieved February 2 2007 from www.aafp.org/online/en/home/policy/policies/a/aafpdefinitions

Amritavalli, R. (1999). Dictionaries are unpredictable. *ELT Journal*, 53(4), pp. 262–9.

Beder, S. (1997). Addressing the issues of social and academic integration for first year students: a discussion paper. First published by Ultibase: ultibase.rmit.edu.au. Retrieved December 15 2006 from ultibase.rmit.edu.au/Articles/dec97/beder1.htm

Bloom, B., (1965). *The taxonomy of educational objectives (Handbook 1)*. Harlow, UK: Longman.

Brandt, C. (2008) Material matters: the case for EAP as subject matter of EAP courses. *Learning and Teaching in Higher Education: Gulf Perspectives*, Vol. 5, No. 1, January.

British National Corpus. Available April 20 2008 at http://www.natcorp.ox.ac.uk/.

Browne, M. N. & Keeley, S. M. (2004). *Asking the Right Questions: A Guide to Critical Thinking*. New Jersey: Pearson Education Inc.

Cioffi, F. L. (2005) *The Imaginative Argument*. Princeton, USA: Princeton University Press. Retrieved December 15 2006 from press.princeton.edu/chapters/s7936.html

Coxhead, A. (2000). A New Academic Word List. *TESOL Quarterly*, 34(2): 213–38.

Coxhead, A. (2005). Reviewed work: Upton, T. A. 'Reading Skills for Success: A Guide to Academic Texts' (2004) in *Reading in a Foreign Language*, Vol. 17, No. 1, April. Retrieved December 15 2006 from nflrc.hawaii.edu/rfl/April2005/reviews/coxhead.pdf

Findarticles. Available September 20 2007 at findarticles.com/

Gillett, A. (1996, updated 2007 by personal communication). What is EAP? *IATEFL ESP SIG Newsletter*, 6, 17–23. Retrieved December 15 2006 from www.uefap.com/articles/eap.htm

Hill, J. (1999). Collocational competence. *English Teaching Professional*, Issue 11, April.

Holmes, M. (2007). Markin version 3.1. (A shareware Windows program for marking student essays). *Creative Technology*. Retrieved June 20 2007 from www.cict.co.uk/software/markin/download.htm

Hyland, K. (2002). Options of identify in academic writing. *ELT Journal*, Volume 56/4, October.

Just the word. (2007). Available June 27 2007 at 193.133.140.102/JustTheWord/

Kuo, C. H. (1999). The use of personal pronouns: role relationships in scientific journal articles. *English for Specific Purposes*, 18(2): 121–38.

Laufer, B. (1989). What percentage of lexis is necessary for comprehension? In C. Lauren & M. Norman (Eds), *From Humans to Thinking Machines*, pp. 316–23. Clevedon: Multilingual Matters.

Longman Dictionary of Contemporary English (2003). UK: Pearson Education Ltd.

'Markin' software. Available August 21 2007 at www.cict.co.uk/software/markin/features.htm

Massey University, 'Headwords of the Academic Word Lists' Retrieved November 24 2007 from language.massey.ac.nz/staff/awl/headwords.html

Neil's Toolbox (2007). Referencing a web page or electronic report. Retrieved June 25 2007 from www.neilstoolbox.com/bibliography-creator/index.htm

Nishina, Y. (2007). A corpus-driven approach to genre analysis: The reinvestigation of academic, newspaper and literary texts. *Empirical Language Research Journal*, 1(2).

Scholfield, P. (2005). Why shouldn't monolingual dictionaries be as easy to use as bilingual or semi-bilingual ones? Retrieved June 28 2007 from longman.com/dictionaries/pdfs/Mono-Bilingual.pdf

Spack, R. (1998). Initiating ESL students into the Academic Discourse Community: How far should we go? In R. Spack & V. Zamel (Eds), *Negotiating Academic Literacies: Teaching and Learning Across Languages and Cultures*. US: Lawrence Erlbaum Associates, Inc.

Sutherland-Smith, W. (2005). Pandora's box: academic perceptions of student plagiarism in writing. *Journal of English for Academic Purposes* 4: 83–95.

Thompson, C. (1999) Critical thinking: what is it and how do we teach it in English for Academic Purposes (EAP) programs? *Proceedings of the HERDSA Annual International Conference*, Melbourne, 12–15 July 1999, University of Melbourne, Australia: Centre for Communication Skills and English as a Second Language.

Upton, T. A. (2004). *Reading Skills for Success: A Guide to Academic Texts*. Ann Arbor, MI: University of Michigan Press.

Vrbinc, A. & Vrbinc, M. (2004) Language learners and their use of dictionaries: the case of Slovenia. *EESE 3/2004*. Retrieved June 28 2007 from www.uni-erfurt.de/eestudies/eese/artic24/marjeta/3_2004.html

Webb, C. (1992). The use of the first person in academic writing: objectivity, language and gatekeeping. *Journal of Advanced Nursing*, 17(6): 747–752.

Winkler, B. (1998). *Electronic Dictionaries for Learners of English*. Research Students' Conference Proceedings. The Centre for English Language Teacher Education, UK: University of Warwick.

Index